By Faith and Reason

By Faith and Reason
The Essential Keith Ward

Edited by
Wm. Curtis Holtzen and Roberto Sirvent

DARTON · LONGMAN + TODD

Wipf and Stock Publishers
199 W 8th Ave, Suite 3
Eugene, OR 97401

By Faith and Reason
The Essential Keith Ward
By Ward, Keith and
Holtzen, Wm. Curtis

ISBN 13: 978-1-62032-856-9
Publication date
12/17/2012
Previously published by
Darton, Longman and
Todd Ltd, 2012

A catalogue record for this book is available from the British Library.

Phototypeset by Kerrypress Ltd, Luton, Bedfordshire
Printed and bound in Great Britain by Bell & Bain, Glasgow

Part III
Science and Religion

Part IV
The Bible and its Interpretation

Part V
Inter-Faith Dialogue and Disagreement

Contents

Acknowledgements

Throughout the process of this work, from its conception to completion there have many people who have invested, affirmed, and encouraged us along the way.

Special thanks first to *Keith Ward*, not simply for his body of work, but for his kindness in opening up his home to two American strangers, patience for our seemingly endless e-mail questions, graciousness in speaking to publishers on our behalf, and his generosity for granting us use of several of these essays. He is the epitome of a gentleman and a scholar. Thank you to our editor *Virginia Hearn* for her guidance in the production of this work as well as her infectious enthusiasm throughout the process. Thanks to *Tom Oord* for his expertise, advice, and encouragement in the production of this reader. Thanks must be extended to *Tyler Patterson* who put in countless hours formatting the book's chapters. To *Carl Toney* who was kind enough to scan all of these documents so they would only need to be formatted and not retyped. To *Nicole McDermott* for helping us track down dozens of Ward's articles and books. Thanks to *Paul Rogers* for both his urging us to make this book happen and for his financial support. Thanks to *Michael Burdett* and *Kate Kirkpatrick* for sharing their connections at Oxford University. Special thanks to our friend *Joe Grana*: you may never know how much you mean to us. And of course, we offer thanks to our families, for without their love and affection none of this would have been possible. Roberto would like to thank his parents *Beatriz* and *Humberto*, his brother *David*, and his niece *Alaina Marie*. Curtis would like to thank his wife *Wende* and their daughter *Roman*.

In addition to those mentioned above we wish to thank the many people who were kind enough to listen to us as we talked on and on about this project. Paul Alexander, Heidi Cohn, Adrian Coxhead, Kelly Dagley, Steve Edgington, Butch Ellis, Robin Hartman, Nathalie Hewitt, Elliott Lawless, Erik Maiershoffer, David Matson, K.C. Richardson, Steve Richardson, Frank Scotti, Hal Shrader, Karen Swaney, Brityn Thackham, Phil Towne, Blair Wilgus, Jim Woest. Thanks to all the administration, staff, and faculty of Hope International University. Lastly, thanks to our students for demonstrating intellectual courage in the classroom.

We, along with Darton, Longman & Todd, are grateful to the various publishers for allowing us to reproduce the following copyrighted material:

9. 'Christianity and Evolution: A Case Study.' Sarot, Marcel, and Gijsbert van den Brink. *Identity and Change in the Christian Tradition*. Frankfurt am Main: P. Lang, 1999. Copyright © 1999. Reprinted by permission of Marcel Sarot and Gijsbert van den Brink.
10. 'The Soul and the Brain.' *In Defence of the Soul*. Oxford: Oneworld, 1998. Copyright © 1998. Reprinted by permission of Oneworld Publications.
11. 'Open Future.' *Pascal's Fire: Scientific Faith and Religious Understanding*. Oxford: Oneworld, 2006. Copyright © 2006. Reprinted by permission of Oneworld Publications.
12. 'The Nature of Biblical Inspiration.' *The Word of God?: The Bible After Modern Scholarship*. London: SPCK, 2010. Copyright © 2010. Reprinted by permission of SPCK – Society for Promoting Christian Knowledge.
13. 'Breaking out of Literalism.' *God, Faith & the New Millennium: Christian Belief in an Age of Science*. Oxford: Oneworld, 1998. Copyright © 1998. Reprinted by permission of Oneworld Publications.
14. 'Morality and the Bible.' *Is Religion Dangerous?* Oxford: Lion, 2006. Copyright © 2006. Reprinted by permission of Lion Hudson.
15. 'By Faith Alone.' *Re-Thinking Christianity*. Oxford: Oneworld, 2007. Copyright © 2007. Reprinted by permission of Oneworld Publications.
16. 'The Study of Truth and Dialogue in Religion.' Parrinder, Edward Geoffrey, and Ursula King. *Turning Points in Religious Studies: Essays in Honour of Geoffrey Parrinder*. Edinburgh: T. & T. Clark, 1990. Copyright © 1990. Reprinted by permission of The Continuum International Publishing Group Ltd.
17. 'Truth and the Diversity of Religions.' *Readings in Modern Theology: Britain and America*. London: SPCK, 1995. Copyright © 1995. Reprinted by permission of SPCK – Society for Promoting Christian Knowledge.
18. 'Theology as a Comparative Discipline.' *Religion and Revelation: A Theology of Revelation in the World's Religions*. Oxford: Clarendon Press, 1994. Copyright © 1994. Reprinted by permission of Keith Ward.
19. 'Religion and the Possibility of a Global Ethics.' Runzo, Joseph, and Nancy M. Martin. *Ethics, in the World Religions*. Oxford: Oneworld, 2001. Copyright © 2001. Reprinted by permission of Oneworld Publications.

Introduction

'Philosophy has no equations, predictions, or conclusive confirmations – that is precisely why some of us become philosophers in the first place.'

– Keith Ward

It has been said that 'all labels are libels' but philosopher-theologian Keith Ward has successfully eschewed the libel that comes with labels. He has done this not by avoiding labels but embracing them – many of them. Ward is orthodox and radical, constructive and critical, academic and popular, philosophical and theological, evangelical and ecumenical, liberal and born-again, serious and witty, reasonable and faithful. But perhaps the label that fits best is 'scholar'.

This project has grown out of years studying, teaching, and reflecting on life's big questions. Because we teach at a university aimed to simultaneously challenge and affirm our students' faith, we often leave class wondering if we have failed at both. Challenge the students *too much* (whatever that means) and they leave anxious. Affirm their faith too much and *we* leave anxious, questioning our integrity as educators. Yet the students are not alone. We, too, the professors, need affirmation. We, too, need to have our assumptions, presuppositions, and biases challenged. We, too, need that voice in our life, even when – or *especially* when – it is uncomfortable. We, as persons of faith and reason, need and crave that teacher just much as everyone else.

For us, Keith Ward is that teacher. And whether you are a scholar or student, pastor or skeptic, this book is sure to inspire and challenge you. Especially if you share our story.

Keith Ward is one of the most prolific scholars alive, possessing the seamless ability to articulate creative, nuanced, and profound positions on today's most heated philosophical and theological debates. In fact, it is not uncommon to hear his name mentioned alongside heavyweights like Moltmann, Pannenberg, and Hick. Ward has held posts at several prominent universities, including Cambridge and Oxford, and was honoured to deliver the prestigious Gifford Lectures in 1993–94. Even after his retirement in 2003, through both writings and lectures, Ward has continued to play a prominent role in advancing discussions about faith, science, religion, and comparative theology.

This collection of essays is arranged into five sections. The first includes a piece written exclusively for this project. In it, Ward offers an insightful personal reflection on how he learned – first-hand – that a 'philosopher can turn into a theologian.' The second essay is drawn from his book *Is Religion Irrational?* and sets out the general assumptions underlying a serious, sympathetic, and critical study of religion. In both of these selections, Ward attempts to show that faith and reason are *not*, as some would suggest, incompatible.

The second section contains works addressing Ward's conception of God. For every theologian the existence and nature of God serves as the crux of his study. It is the hub from which all Christian theology is worked out. Ward's theological writings reflect a faithful engagement with Christian tradition while remaining mindful of modern scholarship. In this section, Ward explores the idea of God as principle, person, and the ground of being. Issues of the triune nature and self-emptying love of God are also included.

In the third section, the reader is invited to rethink the relationship between science and religion. Modern science has posed a number of challenges to religion, and the Christian faith is no exception. Many philosophers, scientists, and theologians have made the claim that science and religion are incompatible. By addressing issues such as the possibility of miracles, the role of evolution, brain science, and the nature of the cosmos, Ward challenges that notion, arguing – rather passionately – that science does not nullify faith. Rather, each informs and illuminates the other.

The fourth section addresses the prominent fundamentalist (and often evangelical) view that the Bible is the inerrant last word on all matters moral and theological. Ward argues that such an assumption is mistaken. Any proper reading of the Bible, he claims, reveals various internal inconsistencies that disarm fundamentalist claims of absolute authorial unanimity. But this diversity of thought within scripture should not be seen as a threat to faith. Rather, he urges us to take the Bible seriously, not literally; inspired, but not inerrant. The writings in this section include works on the nature of biblical inspiration as well as the use of scripture in moral reasoning.

In the final section, issues pertaining to religious diversity and pluralism are addressed. Although many argue that all religions are the same, and others insist that their truth claims, while different, are not incompatible, Ward rejects such notions, arguing that certain truth claims are necessarily exclusive. By engaging in comparative theology, Ward offers a critical approach where such truth claims are neither exempt from challenge nor placed beyond the realm of inter-faith debate. This section brings the reader to a greater understanding of – and appreciation for – the world's great faiths and the possibility of a shared global ethic.

By Faith and Reason: The Essential Keith Ward is aimed to introduce you to a masterful teacher – *our* teacher. Although we had never met Ward (that is, until, he and his wife graciously invited us into their home to discuss this project), he fulfilled a need few other professors or mentors could: he addressed the big questions, the same questions we were afraid to voice. These questions include: Why have Christian fundamentalists and the New Atheists held our faith hostage? What does it look like to explore a Christianity unafraid of science? What do we do with biblical texts that portray God as morally troubling? What is the core truth of the gospel? What is the point of prayer? How do we know what matters and what *really* matters? How can we restore beauty, awe, and wonder to our faith?

It is not just that he entertains these questions; he also reminds us that these questions are worth asking. It is good to ask them, and we are right to ask them. Keith Ward, then, is more than a teacher, for despite his decades of study and lifetime of reflection, he *still* has questions – questions he does not answer for us, but asks *with* us. Yes, he still has his convictions which he defends passionately. But his work affirms a faith we yearn for, a faith that embraces mystery as an insight into truth, rather than an obstacle. And perhaps that is the best kind of affirmation we can hope for; that when plagued with questions about God, life, and everything in between, we know we are in pretty good company. As a result, it would be wise to see Keith Ward as more than a teacher … he is a champion of faith and reason.

Wm. Curtis Holtzen and Roberto Sirvent, Spring 2012

I

Faith and Reason

1

Friend or Foe? Reflections on the Relationship Between Faith and Reason

I have always loved philosophy, even before I knew there was such a subject. I wondered about the ultimate origins of things, and the real nature of things, perhaps hidden from ordinary sight, and about what was truly good, and what goodness was, and about how anyone could really know anything about such things. I was, no doubt, a very odd little boy, asking questions to which no one knew the answer, and which were generally regarded as distinctly peculiar.

When I found out that there really was such a subject as philosophy, and that people like Plato, Aristotle, Aquinas, Hume, and Kant were great writers who had discussed such questions in detail, and apparently respectably, the outwardly rather dull but inwardly exciting and adventurous course of my future life was set.

For me philosophy was always about the big questions. And it was not a merely theoretical study. It was about how you should live, what you should aim at, what the important things in human life were, and how you might attain them. It was, in short, an intellectual quest for truth and goodness, and to undertake such a quest, arrogant and over-ambitious as it might seem for any human being, meant beginning to find out what the greatest writers of the past had said, and what conclusions they had come to. I have spent my life doing that, and have ended up as (successively) both a Professor of Philosophy and of Theology.

I have found that some people find that surprising. Is philosophy not very different from theology, they ask? Is philosophy not about always asking questions and letting reason go where it will, meeting all authorities with a skeptical smile, while theology is a matter of faith and accepting beliefs on authority or revelation?

I think such questions misunderstand the place of reasoning in human life. Reason is not some sort of faculty which always comes up with correct answers. When philosophers reason as hard as they can, they almost always disagree with each other. The first lesson you learn from a study of the history of ideas is that reasoning leads to disagreement. Different starting points or axioms seem reasonable to different people, and reasons that seem strong to some people seem weak to others. There is no such thing as completely impartial and universal reason.

Think, for example, of the age-old dispute about whether humans are determined to do whatever they do, either by God or by scientific laws, or whether they can sometimes make free choices that are not so determined. Some people think that scientific laws are so well-established that they must determine everything. But other people think that moral responsibility is so important that humans cannot be completely determined by forces outside their own choice. These differing starting points will be evaluated differently, and very sophisticated arguments can be developed to defend them against objections. Reason alone does not decide the issue.

Nevertheless, beliefs can be held reasonably or unreasonably. What will a reasonably held belief be? It will be one that can state its starting point clearly, see what its implications are, avoid inconsistencies and confusions, be aware of alternative views held by others, consider those views carefully and sympathetically, and be ready to respond to criticisms. By contrast, an unreasonably held belief will be one which is confused about what is meant by terms like 'determination' or 'freedom', which fails to see the implications of the belief, which is inconsistent or confused, which pays no attention to the views of others or fails to state them in a way that would be acceptable to their defenders, which ignores critical objections, and which refuses to try to defend itself by argument, but merely repeats the belief more loudly. An unreasonable belief may also get its facts wrong, or be unaware of them, or it may be unaware of the interpretations of the facts given by fully informed analysts (in this case, various interpretations of Benjamin Libet's experiments, for example).

Reasonably held beliefs will often have to appeal to authorities. A reasonable person in disputes about freedom and determinism will need to learn the relevant concepts, the main arguments and their historical development, and the general practice of good argumentation – all of which are taught by good practitioners. Then the relevant facts must be gleaned from reputable sources, and also the general interpretations of those facts which are accepted by fully informed critics. Most of this information will have to be accepted on authority by most people, and the authority will be of two main sorts – conceptual and factual. You must learn about the concepts, arguments, and interpretations that are relevant; and you must learn about the facts from those in the best position to have discovered them.

I hope it goes without saying that accepting authority does not mean blind or unquestioning acceptance. Nevertheless, there is quite a lot of trust involved. You have to trust that scientists have made careful observations and have reported them honestly, and that philosophers are aware of all relevant arguments and have considered them fully and sympathetically. Where disagreements exist, it is fair (and reasonable) to say that most people will not consider that they can on their own dispute the relevant factual or conceptual claims (I could not, for example, reasonably dispute the Theory of Relativity, whether I like it or not. I am simply not competent to do so). However there are cases where experts disagree, and cases where that might matter a lot to how you live. Experts disagree on freedom and determinism, and that might make a big difference to how you treat criminals. In such cases it is reasonable to adopt a belief on practical grounds, after having done your best to see what arguments there are on either side, and having accepted that no possibility of universal agreement is in sight.

Once you see that, you will no longer be tempted to think that all reasonable people will agree with each other, or that reason is incompatible with accepting many things on authority. You will see that reasonable disagreement must be based on full knowledge of the various relevant options, and that reasonable authority must be based on either conceptual knowledge and insight, or access to specialised factual knowledge, or preferably on both. But you can choose your authority in the light of your own limited experience and commitments, as long as the issue does not, after full investigation, seem to you to be decisively closed.

I have taken the issue of freedom and determinism as an example of informed and apparently unresolvable disagreement, but there are many other examples. Are mental events different in kind from physical events? Is life after bodily death possible? Are moral truths objective or subjective?

Is the universe basically mind-like or completely impersonal? Is experimental science the only means of discovering truth? In the history of human thought, these are all highly disputed and unresolved issues. Most people have some opinion on all these issues, but it is not the case that all informed and intelligent people agree on any of them. I am persuaded of the truth of some beliefs in these areas – most importantly, that there is a mind-like basis (God) to the physical universe, so that materialism is false.

Like all these issues, reason cannot decide this issue. But it is possible to believe reasonably – being aware of criticisms, seeing implications, and giving relevant if non-conclusive arguments in favour. In the history of philosophy, the vast majority of philosophers have agreed with me about the reasonableness of belief in God. Indeed, the philosophers generally called Rationalists, like Descartes, Leibniz, and Spinoza, all believed that the universe was rational, that there was a reason why everything was as it was, that this reason must ultimately be founded in a conscious or mind-like reality which provides a reason for everything, and that the reason, formed in the mind of this ultimate reality, must ultimately be that the existence of this cosmos (including the mind-like reality itself) is of great intrinsic value, being worthwhile just for its own sake.

It is odd that people who call themselves Rationalists today usually reject this belief. Interestingly, they tend to use the word 'rational' in quite a different sense, to mean that you should not believe anything unless you have observational, public, testable, sensory evidence for it. I am not sure that this is a rational belief at all. Even in physics, surely a science if anything is, it is considered reasonable to believe in Higgs' Boson, or Superstrings, or the Multiverse, without sufficient evidence for these things having been found. You can believe in them because they are parts of an elegant explanatory theory, or they follow from such a theory. Of course in physics you hope you will find evidence to confirm your belief, because you are, after all, thinking of physical processes which can in principle be tested by experiment. But hoping for evidence is not the same as having evidence, and if you fail to find the evidence it is not considered unreasonable to continue to maintain the theory (think of Einstein's refusal to accept Heisenberg's Indeterminacy Principle as a final result in physics. In face of all the evidence, Einstein was not considered unreasonable for maintaining that there must be 'hidden variables' because his theory required it).

There are many factual claims that are not testable in any way we can think of. These range from simple everyday claims like my claim that last night I dreamed that I was in Bermuda, to more complex claims like the claim that every event is completely determined by its physical antecedent causes or the claim that there is a conscious reality (God) which brings the cosmos into being. It is obvious that there can be no direct public physical test of any belief about a non-physical reality. The best we could do would be to devise a conceptual thought-experiment: is the cosmos such that it could be brought about by a conscious reality for the sake of its intrinsic goodness? Some empirical claims will be relevant to such a thought-experiment but it is unlikely that any will be decisive.

Can we be aware of non-physical realities? My philosophical opinion is that we certainly are. We are aware of our own thoughts, feelings, and sensations. We are aware of mathematical and moral truths (if there are such truths, they are not about physical states of affairs). If there is an ultimate non-physical reality (God) we might expect to be aware of it sometimes, and many apparently sane people think they are. There is, then, I would say, as a strictly philosophical opinion, good experiential (though not repeatable or publicly testable) evidence of non-sensory, non-physical realities. The move to the idea of God is a move to an elegant and integrative hypothesis (rather like those posited in science) which gives a coherent account of how non-physical and physical realities relate to one another in a wider explanatory scheme.

All this is meant to make clear that a philosopher can turn into a theologian, someone who studies the idea of God, quite easily. It is also an autobiographical account of how I, beginning as a conventionally atheistic philosopher, came to believe that the idea of God, as a supreme spiritual (non-physical) reality, provides a much more reasonable account of the world we experience than does the alternative theory that physical realities (whatever exactly they are in our weird quantum world) are the only ultimately real things that exist.

This is only the beginning of the exciting intellectual adventure of exploring what a supreme spiritual reality (God) who creates the universe for the sake of intrinsic goodness is likely to do in that universe, or how much of the divine nature and purpose God is likely to reveal, and in what way, and how humans might be involved in realising goodness. That cannot be a matter simply of abstract speculation, for if God has done anything, there will be traces of divine action and recorded experiences of divine reality throughout human history. And, decisively, there will be the personal impact of divine reality upon the life of those who seek to be receptive to it.

My personal journey has led from reason to faith. Philosophy led me to think that belief in God is reasonable, in fact the most reasonable hypothesis about what the world and what goodness truly is. That led me to ask what traces or alleged apprehensions of God could be found in human experience and history. That led me seriously to consider belief in Jesus Christ as a decisive revelation of God's nature and purpose. And that led to faith – firm commitment to a vision of goodness and love in the person of Jesus and to the hope of final deliverance from moral failure and evil, despite all the moral and intellectual vacillations that characterise human life and thought. As Thomas Aquinas put it, 'Faith is that habit of mind whereby eternal life begins in us' (*Summa Theologiae* 2a, 2ae, quest. 4, art.1).

Christian theology can be seen as the attempt to work out how God has revealed the divine purpose in and through Jesus, and how deliverance from evil might be achieved through him. But no one works these things out from scratch. Christian churches have thought about these issues for centuries. To do theology is to learn what they have said, why they have said it, why they have often differed from one another, how their thinking has developed, and how their thoughts relate to the wider historical contexts in which they lived. In the contemporary world, the vast increase in knowledge of the world disclosed by the natural sciences, and the greater understanding of other cultures and belief-systems made possible by better communications and travel, provide new opportunities for seeing the revealing and saving work of God in a wider and deeper context. For this reason, much of my work has been concerned to see how Christian ideas of God have developed and changed over the centuries, how Christian faith is best expressed in a scientific age, how we can best read and interpret the Bible in a very different culture from those cultures in which its various 'Books' were written, and how Christian faith relates to other great religious traditions in the world.

These are the topics covered by the readings collected in this book by Roberto Sirvent and William Curtis Holtzen. I am grateful to them for taking the time and trouble to read and select from my published work in such a sensitive and careful way. Taken as a whole, the readings constitute an argument that it is possible to make a firm commitment to Christian revelation while defending to the full the free use of philosophical and critical reasoning. Not only is it possible. It is entirely proper, for reason is, or should be, the friend of faith. Faith in the Christian God is after all, among other things, faith that the world itself, created through the *Logos* (Reason or Wisdom) of God, is rational, and as such it can be rationally understood by those who are created in the image of God.

2

Are Faith and Reason Incompatible?

'What has Athens to do with Jerusalem?' With this question the early Christian writer Tertullian tried to distance philosophy from Christian faith. He is also the author of the infamous statement, 'It is definitely to be believed, because it is absurd.' One religious attitude is that human reason has nothing to say about religious faith. Faith comes directly by revelation from God, and it may contradict human reason, which may be incapable of thinking properly about God at all.

Many modern atheists agree with this, but assume that it makes religious belief irrational and indefensible. This is one way of thinking about religion, though it may apply in a special way to the Christian faith, which asserts the strange-sounding claims that the eternal God died, and that a dead man rose to life again. Such things, Tertullian thought, could never be thought up by philosophers. If they seem to conflict with philosophy, so much the worse for philosophy.

Some modern atheists agree that the very idea of God is philosophically absurd. But they see this as a reason against religious belief, not in favour of it. How can there be a mind with no brain, that does not exist in any place, and that is able to do anything yet allows gross suffering to exist? Or how could there be a revelation from such a mind when there are a thousand competing revelations in the world, all of them claiming absolute certainty yet none of them having enough evidence to convince all rational observers? The believer may say, 'Just have faith.' But when there are a thousand faiths to choose from, which one should we choose? If there are no reasons for our choice, it seems arbitrary. If we say, 'God will tell us which is true', then why does God apparently tell different people – Muslims, Jews, Christians, and Hindus, very different things?

Clearly there is a problem. But before I examine it further, I need to stress that Tertullian's view is not the only one, or even the main one, among Christian theologians. Most early Christian writers thought that Athens had a great deal to do with Jerusalem, and the early Christian creeds are full of Greek philosophical terms such as 'substance', 'person', and 'nature'. Medieval theologians such as Anselm and Thomas Aquinas believed that Christian faith could be almost wholly justified by reason. They thought they could show that belief in God is reasonable; then that it is reasonable to think God has revealed the divine nature and purpose; and that, given these beliefs, the specific content of Christian faith, while it goes beyond what reason can establish, is deeply consistent with reason.

I have obviously sided more with writers such as Aquinas. I have tried to show that it is reasonable to believe in a self-existent eternal mind as creator of the universe. If you accept that, it is very reasonable to think that such a mind would communicate something of its nature and purpose to human persons. Indeed it would be unreasonable to think that a God who wanted humans to co-operate in achieving a divine purpose for the cosmos had never told them what that purpose was, or how to achieve it. So it is reasonable to look for a revelation or communication from God that says what the divine purpose is, and to take it as a genuine source of new information.

It is very important to see that, when we begin to look for a revelation, none of us starts from a position of complete neutrality, looking around at all alleged revelations and coolly deciding between them. We are born and brought up in a specific culture and at a specific point in history, and we are taught the values and beliefs that are characteristic of that culture and history. This book, for example, is aiming to be as reasonable and impartial as possible. But it is written in English in the twenty-first century and from a Christian, though partly secularised, cultural background. Even in the first chapter[1] when I defended the possibility of a natural knowledge of a personal God, as a matter of autobiographical fact, as I tried to make clear, I knew about that possibility because of my own early education.

Most people will have a story to tell of their own experiences of religion and of their own intellectual approach to the big questions about God, the

1 Chapter 1, 'Why Does Belief in God Matter', in *Is Religion Irrational?*

soul, human freedom, and morality. We cannot escape our upbringing, and we should not pretend that our own beliefs are just obviously true and ought to be obvious to all rational people. We can also see how our beliefs change as we come across new knowledge from science, history or philosophy, or from meeting with people of very different cultures and backgrounds. We hope that this change is a development to a wider and deeper understanding, and not just some sort of arbitrary fluctuation in belief. So we can see the importance of deepening the beliefs we start from by gaining as wide a knowledge as possible of the world.

This leads me to two conclusions. To put them in a slightly grandiose way, the first might be called the principle of historical particularity. We all begin from a background of beliefs and values that we have learned from others, and have either found helpful or reacted against. They shape the way we think and our most basic attitudes to experience – such as whether we find it natural to see our experience as a continuing encounter with a personal God, or whether that does not resonate with us at all, so that we have no feeling for religion. Moreover, we realise that the beliefs and values that were taught to us themselves have a history which is particular, not universal. The beliefs I was taught go back, even though the people who taught me those beliefs did not always realise it, through a number of German Christian scholars such as Harnack and Hegel, to the Protestant Reformation, and before that to great medieval theologians such as Aquinas, then to the early Church Fathers, and to the first disciples of Jesus. You can trace the line further back, through the traditions recorded in the Hebrew Bible, until the origins are lost in prehistory, but probably can be found in the largely unrecorded traditions of an early Middle Eastern group of nomadic tribes.

This leads to the second conclusion, which I will call the principle of historical development. All human beliefs have a history. From their point of origin in history they have developed as they have incorporated, or sometimes reacted against, new knowledge, new moral beliefs, new experiences, and new critical arguments. We can ask of any human belief at a specific point in history, what did it develop from? Against what did it react? What problems was it seeking to resolve? What are its weaknesses? And what new insights does it embody? So the early beliefs of a Semitic tribal people developed into the sophisticated moral theism of second Isaiah in the fifth century BC, partly under the pressure of encountering new and powerful competing cultures, and having to deal with the problems of defeat by and exile in the Babylonian empire.

If we take Christianity as an example of a religion whose history has been well documented, we can very clearly see how it has developed in many ways over the centuries. Indeed, the history of Christianity could be seen as a series of revolutions in thought, as it has developed from its original Jewish background into the astounding set of different Christian churches in the world today – from very ritualistic Eastern Orthodox liturgies to charismatic mega-churches and silent Quaker meetings.

The first great Christian revolution was its almost complete reinterpretation of the Hebrew scriptures, and of the hope for a coming messiah, an anointed leader who would liberate Israel from its enemies and establish the rule of justice and peace in the world. Of course, as Jews rightly point out, Israel was not liberated by Jesus from Roman occupation, and Jerusalem is still, tragically, one of the most violent places on earth. Justice and peace do not rule in the world. But followers of Jesus insist that he was the messiah, and they do so by reinterpreting the idea of messiah so that it no longer refers to a political reformer. Jesus is, for Christians, a spiritual king and his rule is in the hearts of men and women throughout the world. That is a remarkable revolution in thought, but once it has been made, Christians can plausibly argue, from their point of view, that the Hebrew Bible – what they call the Old Testament – does point toward such a spiritual king who will inaugurate, not a political kingdom, but a new spiritual covenant with God.

A second revolution followed hard on the heels of this one, as Christianity became a predominantly Gentile faith, and actually gave up the Jewish Law, the Torah. Virtually all the first Christians were observant Jews. But within a generation the church had become a largely Gentile organisation, even, disgracefully, becoming anti-Jewish in some ways. More positively, the church took belief in one loving redeemer God to the whole Gentile world. That was a dramatic revolution too.

Then, between the fourth and eighth centuries, Christians took on the vocabulary and thought-forms of Greek philosophy, and developed the orthodox creeds, an intellectually impressive worldview at the cutting edge of the thought of those times. Jesus was seen as the eternal wisdom of God, who became incarnate to reunite humanity and the whole of creation with God. It is not hard to see this as a natural and proper development of what was always implicit in the Gospels. But it is certainly a revolution in thought, transforming Christianity from a small messianic sect into a sophisticated philosophical worldview.

Developments in the understanding of life after death, and doctrines such as transubstantiation followed in the Latin or Roman Catholic Church, but a major revolution occurred at the Reformation, when some of these doctrines, and the church itself, became subject to criticism. This licensed new waves of critical thought and enquiry in Christian thinking, questioned hierarchical authority in matters of faith, and eventually established the essentially liberal idea of freedom of personal belief as central to Christian faith, in both Catholic and Protestant traditions.

Today another revolution is in progress, as new discoveries in science force Christians to reflect very hard about what they think about evolution, about the destiny of the universe, and about the place of human life in this vast universe. Many of these questions are still disputed or unresolved, but there is no doubt that there have been major developments in Christian thinking through the centuries, as the original faith has come into contact with wider social and intellectual forces.

I am not trying to give a mini-history of Christianity as such. My purpose is to show how one tradition of religious thought has developed historically by its response to a succession of political, social, and cultural changes. The same general principle is true of every long-lasting religious tradition. There is no such thing as one unchanging interpretation of the Christian, or of any other, religion. There is instead a story of continual development which divides into a number of diverse streams as differing responses to new situations arise.

Sometimes people think that they would like to return to the original pure Christian faith. But this is much harder to identify than we might think. In all likelihood there were always a number of different responses to Jesus in the early church. In the earliest church there was no New Testament; there were no creeds; and there were no agreed doctrines, such as those of the Trinity and the incarnation, which, three or four hundred years later, were to become tests of orthodoxy. So the earliest form of Christian discipleship might well have been very different from anything we can come up with today, with our long history of scriptures, commentaries, creeds, and interpretations by many different churches from which we select the one that seems best to us – but not, it is clear, to everyone.

It might be easy to misinterpret what I am saying: I am not trying to say anything controversial. In particular, I am not denying that there are some truths of Christian faith, some things which are true whether groups of Christians believe them or not. What I am saying is that human understanding of these truths has, as a matter of demonstrable historical record, varied enormously at different times, and shows a sort of development of understanding (and sometimes, regrettably, a refusal to develop) in the light of new knowledge and experience.

But that simple fact carries an important implication for our own thinking about religion, whether we are generally in favour of religion or against it. Whatever our initial view is, it is important to extend our experience as much as possible, so that our knowledge of the world will be both wide and deep, well-informed and fully aware of the history, diversity, and fragility of human thought. Armed with an awareness of one's own historical situation, and with a desire to place ourselves in the widest and best-informed context of human understanding, we can then begin to consider our own beliefs both sympathetically and critically, knowing that our understanding of them is unlikely to be absolutely correct just as it stands, even if it contains fundamental insights that should be preserved. So we must move as well as we can toward greater understanding.

An important distinction to make here is the distinction between truth and human understanding of that truth. For instance, it is either true or false that there is a creator God. That truth (whatever it is) is absolute, and not dependent on any human belief. But our knowledge of that truth is far from absolute. It is relative, because it depends on what we have been taught, the experiences we have had, and how we have reacted to those experiences – all of which things are very personal and particular. And our specific interpretation of that truth (what we think God is) is even more relative, because our interpretations fall under the two principles of historical particularity and historical development.

A good example of this is precisely the view of God that I am offering here. I have said that God is eternal in being, but is also changing and temporal in relationship to the world of space-time. I believe that is true. But I am well aware that many traditional believers in God deny that God changes in any respect. Others reject the doctrine of changelessness as a sort of Aristotelian intrusion into theology. So I realise that my view is just one among others, and that I have developed it by meeting and responding to the arguments of many previous thinkers who have wrestled with these problems. It would be wrong to give up and say that, since there are so many disagreements, it is not worth having any opinion. And it would be equally wrong to say that my view is so obviously correct that all who reject it are stupid or wicked. I think my view is the most adequate known to me because I think it resolves some problems that other views do not, and it manages to include both God's eternity and God's real relationship to creatures in what I think is an adequate and coherent way.

In other words, we can believe there is an absolute truth, and that we ought to pursue it. But there are many cases (and they include almost all religious doctrines) when we cannot be sure that our interpretation of that truth (our particular interpretation of God, for example) is absolutely and finally correct. In fact I would say that it would be much more reasonable to think that, while our own interpretation seems to us to be an improvement on what went before, it should not ever seem even to us to be wholly adequate to its object.

Where does this leave us with the question of the relationship between faith and reason, and with the problem of the many competing revelations of religious truth? I think it rules out Tertullian's extreme view that we should just believe something because it is absurd. There are too many absurd doctrines to choose from, and there is little to choose between them. But we need to put Tertullian's view in historical context. When he thought of philosophers, he was thinking of the many competing and often radically skeptical views of the Greek and Roman philosophers of his day. They were rarely religious and tended to be skeptical about the claims to revelation made by various religious groups. They did often believe in a supreme mind of the universe, as Plato and Aristotle had done. But they tended to see this mind as unchanging or inactive, and in particular they tended to ridicule Christian claims that God had been incarnate in Jesus and that Jesus had risen from the dead. So Tertullian saw the philosophers as idle speculators with no religious commitment who opposed alleged revelations as irrational.

When he spoke of believing absurdities, he obviously did not mean that he believed in stupidities. He meant that he believed in divine revelation in Jesus of things that could not be inferred by rational speculation alone. Moreover, these revealed things were 'absurd' or 'impossible' in a very special way. They were impossible only if there was no God who could act decisively in history, who might express the divine being in the life of a human being, and who might raise a finite human life to the life of eternity.

If there is a God, we might actually expect that there would be extraordinary events that might show a deeper spiritual reality underlying the ordinary material processes of the physical world. Miracles are only absurd to people who think that there are universal laws of nature which cannot be broken, and that there is no spiritual mind that may, for very good reason, produce real and extraordinary effects in the physical world. For Tertullian, God does what is impossible for nature alone to do – and that shows that it is God who is acting. God unites the natural to the supernatural. That is impossible only for those who think there is no supernatural, or that it cannot affect the natural world of events in space and time in any way.

Tertullian's faith was founded on the testimony of the apostles to the life, death, and resurrection of Jesus, testimony to a set of historical events that are impossible without God, and cannot be demonstrated by reasoning alone. But, he thinks, those events occurred, the testimony is believable, and so reasoning cannot disprove them.

When it is put like that, Thomas Aquinas's view that divine revelation in Jesus is deeply reasonable is not so different from Tertullian's after all. For Aquinas means that the resurrection of Jesus is reasonable if there is a God who wills resurrection to eternal life for all, and who raises Jesus from death as a vindication of Jesus' divine authority and as an anticipation of the destiny that God wills for all humanity. When you have those background beliefs, the resurrection becomes far from absurd. It becomes a window into the eternal purpose of God.

Faith and reason are not two totally distinct faculties, with completely different modes of operation. Reasoning does not tell us what the world is really like, without any reference to God. Faith does not tell us that God exists and acts, without any appeal to reasoning. Reason has to take all relevant facts into account. These facts might include the existence of God who, as creator, may make specific differences to what happens in the world of our experience. Because human reason is so weak, it leaves many weighty questions unresolved – including questions about human free will, about materialism and idealism, about the nature of time, about ultimate moral principles, and about the existence of God, a self-existent and eternal consciousness. Faith in God therefore cannot rely on reasoning alone, or it would be perpetually in a state of indecision. Yet we can see that it is possible to have a reasonable belief in a creator God, and I have tried to show that.

A sort of faith, and often a very historically specific sort of faith (whether for or against God), is already present for many people before they even begin to start reasoning. In a sense, we all start from a faith position. We take on trust – and rightly so – what we are taught as children. But it is devoutly to be hoped that we will not stay there forever.

I have heard it argued that we should not teach children religious views when they are young, so that they can make up their own minds later. That seems a very odd statement, which we would not dream of making about scientific or moral views. If children have no knowledge of religion, or no sense that it is important to many people, or of what it means to them, how can they ever make a rational decision about it? We must tell our children what is important in our lives, and that will include giving them a very positive account of religion, if we hold such an account to be important, even though we should also invite them to think about it for themselves as they grow older.

Positive religious faith is not based on abstract speculation about the nature of the universe. It is based on a personal decision to participate consciously in a spiritual reality that is disclosed or revealed to us in our experience. This decision is partly based upon an analysis of our experience as somehow radically imperfect or corrupted. This analysis is common to the great world faiths, and it is the root of the impulse to religious practice. Buddhists take as their first great holy truth that 'all is suffering'. Hindus claim that humans are ignorant of their true spiritual natures. Christians speak of 'sin' (the Greek word is *hamartia,* which means 'missing the mark') as a radical inability to do what is right. Somehow, millions of people feel, humans are locked into a world of futility, despair, anxiety and fear of others. They are alienated from the world, from their work, from their family and colleagues, and even from themselves.

This sense of alienation is captured perfectly by Jean-Paul Sartre in his 1944 play *Huis Clos,* sometimes translated as 'No Exit', the most famous quotation from which is, 'Hell is other people.' Three characters, sitting locked in a room, are in a claustrophobic relationship, each one trying to seduce, destroy, or judge the others and in turn afraid of their judgment and 'objectifying gaze', in a circle of unending hatred, contempt, and fear. They feel themselves to be trapped in the room, and yet the doors open when they want to leave. They are nevertheless unable to leave, but are psychologically compelled to go on torturing and being tortured by one another forever. This, Sartre suggests, is the real hell, being locked into the gaze of others, an inescapable gaze which judges, condemns, and seduces but never forgives.

As an atheist, Sartre offers no escape from this prison, at least within the play itself. But he reveals its nature very starkly. The major world religions offer means of release from this self-created alienation. But they do not offer some *deus ex machina,* a god descending from on high who can magically free us from this world, from the little room of our self-deception and self-centeredness. There is in fact no 'machine' but the one constructed by our own fears and hatreds. But there is a deeper underlying reality beyond the self and the life of egoistic desire, knowledge of which reveals the illusion for what it is. The disclosure of that reality is 'revelation', the intimation of a real presence of love and power, compassion and creativity, which can lead us to see our world differently and to overcome the crippling sense of alienation. Genuine faith begins when people realise their alienation and commit their lives in trust to such a transforming experience of revelation or disclosure.

If such experiences are among the facts upon which reasoning operates, this will be a powerful motivation for developing a rationally and morally acceptable idea of what we believe that spiritual reality to be. In my case that disclosure was mediated through a particular Christian tradition which I learned as a child. But it is reasonable to suppose that similar disclosures occur in many different traditions. It is also reasonable to suppose that where children are taught that religion is silly or irrational such disclosures will not occur, or will not be interpreted as disclosures of a higher spiritual reality. Sartre was unable to accept any religious solution to the human problem that he saw so clearly, largely because he took God to be a prying judgmental tyrant. It hardly needs saying that religious believers do not see God that way. They see God as a compassionate source of wisdom and creativity, who gives purpose to human striving without taking away the authentic freedom and autonomy that meant so much to Sartre.

If we apply the principles of historical particularity and historical development what we expect is that there will be many different historical origins for disclosures of spiritual reality. There will be, especially in very different cultures, many different developing reflective interpretations of those originative disclosures. And there will be many people who do not have such disclosures, or do not recognise them as having any objective reality. So it is not surprising that there are many different 'revelations'.

The religious situation is not like having a lot of conflicting books set alongside each other that all claim to be full of true propositions, while we, from a position of strict neutrality, are asked to choose which one is really true. It is rather that each of us has already received some religious or non-religious formation, in a particular historical and cultural position. As we develop in reflection and experience we may adapt this formation in various ways, and those ways will be a blend of cultural influence and personal creativity, to a greater or lesser degree. We all have an inadequate grasp of the fundamental beliefs from which we begin, and we all need to grow by widening and deepening our understanding as we adapt or reject those initial beliefs. This is how human beliefs develop, in religion as in morality, philosophy, the arts, history, and science.

What I have tried to do in this chapter is to set out the general assumptions with which we might undertake a serious, sympathetic yet critical, study of religion. We will be looking at a very diverse, continually changing, and historically particular set of alleged disclosures of spiritual reality and human responses to those disclosures, and we are bound to be engaged in this study in a deeply personal and committed way. It seems right to approach the subject in an initially sympathetic way, trying to understand what religious belief means to those who accept it. But of course we must use our critical faculties to the full, and so we will find that some beliefs (and possibly all religious beliefs, in the end) are inadequate to our understanding of the world. One of my complaints against many modern atheists is that they do not adopt such an initially sympathetic yet critical approach. They are thus unable to study religion seriously or in a properly scholarly way, turning discussion of religion into a mere exercise in rhetoric and bombast. To the extent that this is so, much modern atheism is deeply irrational and subversive of scholarship.

Bearing that in mind, in the next chapter I will examine the idea of divine revelation and defend the belief that the self-existent and eternal God of the philosophers does reveal the divine nature and purpose, in rather different ways, in a number of the religious traditions of humanity.

II

Concept of God

3

The Personal Ground of Being

In which the reader will find that God is not a person without a body, and may wonder if God can ride a bicycle or *whether God knows if humans will ever land on Mars. The reader will discover why nineteenth-century Germans became more and more depressed, and that the Trinity, though it is indeed three persons in one substance, is not three people sitting in a bowl of soup. Finally the reader will find that evolution need not be the desperate struggle for existence that some pessimistic souls suggest, but may be seen as a striving for higher life and consciousness. God may not ride a bicycle, but God knows plenty of people who can, and will ensure that in the end they will do so exceedingly well.*

God as Omnipotent Person

This guide to God may not have delivered what was expected. Not only have I not set forth the doctrine of a supernatural person who can do absolutely anything, who knows absolutely everything, and who would never cause harm to anyone, but I have castigated that doctrine as a travesty of what the best-known philosophers of all ages have written about God.

There are certainly plenty of people who do think God is pretty straightforwardly a supernatural person. They no doubt existed in ancient Greece, and thought that Pallas Athene really would fly down to help when they were in trouble. On the other hand, the fact that she never did was not apparently of great concern to them – which may make you suspect that they were not really concerned about the literal reference of their language, whatever they might have said when asked. There are plenty of people who think God is like that today – but again, they do not seem to be seriously concerned when God never appears, or when God says 'No' to most of their prayers.

Nevertheless, is it really plausible to say that God is not to be conceived of as a person in any sense at all? The great classical writers certainly cause us to qualify the idea of 'person' to an enormous extent, but is there no place in their thought for the personhood of God? And can the idea of God as person not be defended in a sophisticated way?

Of course it can. In America there is a justly renowned school of personalist philosophers, such as Edgar Brightman and Peter Bertocci. And one of the most widely quoted definitions of God in recent philosophy is given by the Oxford philosopher Richard Swinburne. God, he writes, is something like 'a person without a body (i.e. a spirit) who is eternal, free, able to do anything, knows everything, is perfectly good, is the proper object of human worship and obedience, the creator and sustainer of the universe.' (This is the second sentence of the introduction to *The Coherence of Theism*). His books provide the best exposition and defense available of his own definition, so it would be a total waste of time for me to make up what would only be a less elegant and scholarly version of it here.

It needs to be noted, however, that the idea of 'person' that is being used might be quite different from whatever applies to human persons. For Swinburne, God is eternal, perfectly free and omnipotent, which human persons certainly are not. Swinburne gives these terms a meaning which is more obviously personalistic than the classical tradition, but God still turns out to be very different from human persons.

In Swinburne's interpretation, 'eternal' does not mean, as it does for classical theologians, 'timeless'. It means without beginning or end. 'Free' does not mean that God might do any logically possible thing. On the contrary, it means God will always do something if God knows that doing it would be better than not doing it. God is totally and purely rational, and if we were just as rational, we could predict almost everything that God would or would not do. 'Omnipotent' does not mean that God can bring about any logically possible state. For instance God must do good and avoid evil. So God is not a moral agent, in the sense that God is capable of doing wrong, and is under obligation to do what is right. Put more generally, on this understanding, an omnipotent being is one who can do anything that falls within the realm of the undetermined or non-necessitated actions of that being which is the source of all actual and possible powers. As Swinburne himself puts it, 'A being who is perfectly free and omnipotent in my sense has as much control over things as it is logically possible that a being could have' – and we might not know exactly what the bounds of that 'logical possibility' are.

This is a very qualified notion of omnipotence, but (I think) is a perfectly coherent one. We simply do not know how much control over things a perfectly good and rational being would have, what undetermined things there are to be done, or what would necessarily follow from its nature. It is very easy to invent a phrase such as, 'a universe just like this, but without any suffering in it'. But how can we possibly know whether such a universe is really possible? Well, we might say, with God all things must be possible. But it is not so easy. Even if God is the source of everything other than God, and the source of all powers, so that nothing can be more powerful than God, we have not the slightest idea what powers God actually has. 'All powers, of course,' you say. But has God got the power to ride a bicycle or to run a mile in three minutes? If you are tempted to say 'Yes, of course,' remember that God does not have a bicycle, and has no legs either.

'But God can make legs.' This is not totally absurd. Some Christians believe that God did make some divine legs, namely, the legs of Jesus of Nazareth – though Jesus did not have a bicycle. Some people think that God in fact has everybody's legs, if they believe that everything is part of God. It might even be held that a good reason for creating a universe with people and bicycles in it is precisely so that God could experience what it is like to run and ride bicycles.

The real problem, however, comes from our thinking that God must be able to do anything we can think of or imagine. Because we, ignorant as we are, can imagine lots of things which are really quite impossible. For example, we can imagine going back in time to kill our grandparents before they had any children – you can even see films in which such things happen. Yet we can see that such a thing is obviously impossible, since without our grandparents we would not exist, so we could not kill them. We think we can imagine finding a square equal in area to a given circle – but mathematicians can prove that is logically impossible. We think we can imagine the force of gravity being just a little stronger than it actually is – but physicists can tell us that, if it were, then electrons would collapse into the nuclei of atoms, there would be no atoms, and so there would be no organised universe at all.

The truth is that we are just not very good at imagining things properly and in enough detail to see whether they are possible. It does not follow that because we think we can imagine something, it must be possible. In chapter 4,[1] we found that some people thought they could imagine a God who exists in every possible world. But other people were equally certain they could imagine a possible world without a God in it. Obviously they cannot both be right. One of them must be imagining the impossible, but there is no agreed way of telling which.

Our imaginations are a poor guide to what is really possible, because we have absolutely no idea of what sorts of things can really exist, or of what might be necessary or optional for God. So I think we just have to say that God is powerful enough to create the universe, and that no other being could be more powerful, and that is as much as we have a right to expect from omnipotence.

Discussions about the omnipotence of God usually run into abstruse discussions of whether God can make a stone that is too heavy for God to lift, or whether God could commit suicide, or make a being more powerful than God is. If God cannot make such a stone, God is not omnipotent. But if God cannot lift it, God is not omnipotent either. All these puzzles end by saying that there are some things even God cannot do, but they do not undermine his omnipotence, since omnipotence has to mean simply that no being could possibly be more powerful than God.

The Problem of Evil

It should be pointed out that this at once resolves the so-called problem of evil (though of course only in an intellectual sense; the existential problem of facing up to evil remains as hard as ever). The intellectual problem of evil is the problem of how an omnipotent and good God could create a universe with evil in it. All we have to say is that no universe with rational beings roughly like us in it could exist without evil, and that God, who is the most powerful being there could possibly be, has to create some such universe. Moreover, this God is good, because God is of supreme value, intends that the universe should produce good things, helps it to do so, and will ensure that it does so.

As you would expect, Plato saw this long ago, when he held that God's shaping of the universe is limited by necessity. Fully fledged theists place necessity in the divine being, instead of regarding it as something external, limiting God. And they regard God as the creator, not just the shaper, of

1 Chapter 4, 'The God of the Philosophers', from *God: a Guide for the Perplexed*.

the universe. This enables them to say that God positively wills the universe to exist, and wills it for the sake of the goods it contains and makes possible. Nevertheless, what God wills must be an expression of the divine being and the possibilities it contains. Though God affirms the divine being, and its actualised nature is perfectly good, God does not choose it; it is necessarily what it is. Many of the unactualised possibilities in it are evil, or undesirable and not rationally choosable for their own sake. God will not therefore actualise them for their own sake; God will not positively intend them to be actualised.

God does intend to actualise a universe (at least one, and maybe many). God does so because it is good to do so, and because it is in the divine nature to do so. But such actualisation may involve the actualisation of some actual evil and much possible evil (evil that can be unpreventably realised by free finite agents). Even the most powerful possible being cannot prevent that, though it can share in and sublate (or redeem) such evils, making them integral parts of a whole that is good in a unique way, and that can be recognised as such by all sentient beings which are capable of such recognition.

Of course we do not know whether all this is true or not. But it makes sense. It resolves the problem of evil. And once you admit that you cannot imagine or comprehend the nature of God, you cannot rule such a proposal out by appealing to some shaky definition of omnipotence such as 'the ability to do absolutely anything I can imagine, or that I can state without apparent contradiction'. It follows that God does not positively intend everything that exists, but only the good things. God does not intend the bad things. God has to accept them, since they (or many of them, anyway, such as the deaths of animals) are necessarily there, or they are produced by good things that have somehow gone wrong (like human beings). If you say that is not omnipotence, it may be the best you can get. Anyway, it is a perfectly good definition of omnipotence, because it says that God contains all the potentialities there are, and that all possible power comes from God. If you want more, you may be letting your imagination get out of control.

Fichte, Schelling, Schopenhauer and Nietzsche: Beyond Good and Evil

It may be felt that making some evil necessary is a dangerous move which threatens the goodness of God. A whole line of German philosophers after

Kant, who regarded themselves as either post-Christian or anti-Christian, began to reject the view that God is good. **Johann Gottlieb Fichte** (1762–1814) claimed to be completing the thought of Immanuel Kant. Kant held that all our basic concepts of thought, and even space and time, are contributed to knowledge by the knowing self, and are not features of the objective world. Fichte concluded that the whole universe is the product of a vast cosmic self, the Absolute Ego. This Ego is not personal, but realises itself gradually in history, until it results in a human society in which everyone 'joyously does what is right', and there will be no further need for religion. In this sense, Fichte's God could still be called good, despite having no personal relation with the universe. Kant, however, did not like this, complaining that Fichte's Absolute Ego was bigger than his (Kant's) Absolute Ego, and suspecting that Fichte really thought he (Fichte, not Kant) was the Absolute Ego.

But the idea of the universe realizing itself through a process of self-development caught on. **Friedrich Wilhelm Joseph von Schelling** (1775–1854) decided that the Absolute Ego was largely unconscious. Out of a primordial blind necessity, which is a non-rational and unconscious Will, nature and spirit both evolve. Whereas in the thought of Hegel, Reason is ultimately in control, for Schelling the Will, the non-rational and heroic striving that transcends morality and accepts the necessity of evil as part of its development, becomes primary. Now the universe or Nature takes over from God as cause of itself, and a stress on necessity leads to advocacy of a trans-moral power of the will and of heroic striving, the 'struggle for life' which was so much to influence Charles Darwin. This is probably as near to pantheism as philosophers get.

German philosophers now became gloomier and gloomier, and the goodness of the supreme being began to disappear altogether. **Arthur Schopenhauer** (1788–1860), usually regarded as the greatest pessimist of all time, saw the whole universe as the tragic appearance of a blind striving of the will, a striving which leads inevitably to conflict, unhappiness and suffering. So the course of eighteenth-century German philosophy flows from the happy necessity of Leibniz, which accepts the universe as rational, and as the best of all possible worlds, even if it is usually unpleasant, to the unhappy necessity of Schopenhauer, which does not accept the universe but cannot get out of it. But the worst was yet to come.

Friedrich Wilhelm Nietzsche (1844–1900) looked forward to the advent of the superman, who would completely reject Christian values such as mercy and submissiveness, and incarnate in himself the pure will to power, in a life serene and pitiless, strong and free. The God who intends good but cannot avoid creating some evil has been transformed (sublated, but in the wrong direction) into the universal Will which is beyond good and evil, and for which ceaseless striving without a moral goal is the only reality.

That is what happens when the vision of transcendent Goodness is lost, and one sees only the struggle and suffering and the will to power of the universe itself as the final reality. The fact is that evil plainly exists in the universe, so if you identify the universe with God you are going to have to include actual evil in God. For all the main revealed traditions, however, God is supremely good, and so must transcend the universe in the primordial divine nature. It might just be worth repeating that most Indian traditions, which have sometimes been called 'monist' or 'pantheist', do accept the goodness of God, so even if the universe manifests God in some way, God remains beyond the universe in goodness.

The problem for the theist who accepts, perhaps on grounds of prophetic revelation, that God is good, is to account for the evil in the universe. This can be done, I have suggested, by supposing that even a good God creating a good universe for a good reason may have to create some evil, though God can never positively intend that evil either directly or as a means to some independently existing end. This in turn requires that God is in an important way transcendent to and distinct from the universe, and that God does not directly intend everything that happens in the universe, though God is the cause of everything in the universe.

Omniscience and Creative Freedom

Swinburne might not go as far as I have gone in ascribing internal necessities to the divine being. But he does qualify 'omnipotence' so that it has to mean 'compatibility with the necessary nature of God', so I do not think I have strayed too far from his basic insight.

He qualifies 'omniscience' in a similar way. 'God knows everything,' Swinburne says, which does not mean, as in the classical tradition, 'God knows of every possible true or false proposition that it is true or false.' It means, 'God knows everything that it is possible for any temporal being to know' – and God is a temporal being. So, for example, undetermined events in the future are not now knowable by any temporal being. The future might be open, and even God has to wait to find out what happens – unless God decides to determine the future unilaterally.

This may seem very restricting. If God does not know exactly what I am going to do next, this may have huge unforeseen consequences for the future. I may write a letter which causes a physicist to leave his job, which means that the American Space Program grinds to a halt, which means that no one ever lands on Mars. Or I may not. So God does not know whether humans will ever get to Mars. Presumably, for similar reasons God does not know whether or not the world will end with a nuclear explosion, having no idea of what will be going on a few years from now. That sounds like an odd definition of omniscience.

Of course it is not true that God has no idea of what might happen. God knows, and indeed makes possible, all the possible things that might happen in the future. God controls the alternatives between which people choose. Furthermore, God can determine choices if God so wishes, so God can control the future completely. But normally, for the libertarian anyway, God refuses to exercise such control. God permits people to be free, within limits that God lays down. God can step in to eliminate evil or help efforts to achieve goodness, but God lets agents largely decide their own exact future. In other words, if God wants people to get to Mars, God will find some way of getting them there. But God might prefer to wait and see what ideas people come up with.

There can be a real element of creative freedom in the universe, and the existence of such creative freedom might be of great value. But the universe never gets out of control. God knows and will ensure that in the end evil will destroy itself and good will be realised and conserved. God knows that finite agents will never pass beyond God's power to forgive and help them. And God knows that the divine purpose for creation, that new values should be created and enjoyed, will be realised. God is as omniscient as any being can be that wills that a universe of creative freedom should exist. And that is what omniscience is.

God: Person or Personal?

So it is possible to give eternity, freedom, power and knowledge an interpretation rather more restricted than that of the classical theologians, and, I think, rather more appropriate to a fully personal being. Even so, if this God is called an 'unembodied person', that does not mean, as it might ordinarily mean, a continuing spiritual substance who infers, feels, deduces, and learns to act and react to other persons. It is used in an 'analogical sense', which Swinburne defines as meaning that God is more like such persons than like other things which are not persons. God is more like a thinking thing than like a rock or a vegetable. But God might still be very different indeed from the persons we know about in ordinary experience.

In this sense, we might say that a human being is more like a frog than a star – they share DNA and, possibly, consciousness. I myself would still find it odd to say that I was a frog, even an analogical frog. But perhaps that is because I am more like other things – chimpanzees, for example – than I am like a frog. If I was the last human being in the world, I might say, by analogy, that I was a chimpanzee. I would be more like a chimpanzee than anything else around.

All the same, this might be very misleading for other non-analogical chimpanzees, were they to understand me. They might very well say, 'You don't look much like a chimpanzee to me.' 'That may be so,' I could reply, 'I admit I have loosened some of the syntactical connections of the word – so, for instance, being a chimpanzee no longer entails being hairy all over. But I assure you that I am a genuine, if analogical, chimpanzee.'

This conveys very well why many theologians have been wary of saying that God is, even analogically, a person. God might be more like persons than like anything else in the created universe. But it might still be quite misleading to say that God 'is' something which only really exists in the created universe. Why not stay with the thought that God is, in some respects, more like persons than like sub-personal entities? That is, there is something in God that resembles awareness and purpose more than it resembles unconsciousness and accident. We can truly say that God is aware of the universe, and intends it to exist.

If we did not use some terms drawn from the finite world that we know about, then we could say nothing about God at all. Even those who speak of 'the Good', and of 'the darkness between stars' are using terms drawn from the finite world. There is no escape from analogy – from speaking of God in terms of finite things. It is a question of how far you are prepared to go. Speaking personally, saying that 'God is a person' is a step too far for me. It does seem to make God too much like a finite entity. Swinburne, however, does suggest an alternative phrase (which in fact comes from Paul Tillich), that God is 'the personal ground of being'. I confess to feeling much happier about that, since it makes the point that the ground of being, the ultimate source of all that is, possesses something more like consciousness than like a permanent state of unconsciousness, and something more like intention than like complete accident or oversight.

It might still be true that, in some ways, God is more like non-personal things than like personal things. If you ask, 'Is God more like darkness than like persons?' the correct answer might be, 'God is a bit like both, in different respects.' Maybe we need more than one set of analogies to speak least inadequately about God.

How is God like darkness? Remember this has to be a special sort of darkness. Not sheer nullity, but, in R.S. Thomas' words, 'the place where we go seeking'. It is like an infinite depth, into which we are willingly, though often fearfully, drawn, which elicits awe and abandonment of intellectual analysis. It is the thought of the incomprehensible abyss of infinity that relativises any talk of persons – who are, after all, finite things. If you look at the Michelangelo painting on the Sistine Chapel roof, or at Blake's much reproduced picture of the *Ancient of Days*, then you may want to say, 'That is not God. God is the unpicturable, the unbounded, and by contrast with all the limited spaces we imagine, using colour to delimit their boundaries, God is the darkness, the beyond, the inexpressible.'

But there is not much you can do with the inexpressible. Religions have usually needed pictures to evoke devotion, submission, love and desire. Even Islam has pictures, not visual but verbal, of God on the throne of glory, with all-seeing eyes and all-encompassing hands. Infinity appears, for the sake of devotees, in a multitude of names and forms. And these are usually personal names and forms.

It is hard, after all, to love the Good, when it cannot even be envisaged. To be existent goodness, more than a mere possibility, the Good must be subsistent. It must consist of an actuality of supreme value, of something supremely worthwhile. And nothing can actually be supremely worthwhile unless it involves consciousness and positive valuation of that worth. Thus the Good has to be thought of as in some sense self-conscious feeling, aware of itself and satisfied in the contemplation of its perfection. If we are to know the Good, we are called to share in the self-contemplation of perfection, in that non-dual consciousness of an object non-different from itself, and of its unchangeable perfection.

Because it involves consciousness and bliss, and just for that reason, the Good may be thought of as in some remote sense personal, if not 'a person'. Yet a good reason for not calling it a person is that it has, as such, no relationship to others, no duality, no mutuality of give and take.

Persons as Relational

The darkness and the Good are different ways of envisaging God, as the final object of human contemplation and adoration. But those ways are still too abstract to catch the imagination and evoke the passion of more than a few intellectuals and mystics. What hope is there for human beings who contain passion that needs to be redirected, enmeshed in material well-being, that needs to be untangled? For them (and that is, for nearly all of us at some level), God needs to take a more personal form, a form which can be embraced and loved, pictured in words or images. It is now that God takes form as, in a sense, a person, an Other which encounters us as stern or kind, judging or forgiving, severe or compassionate.

To see God as a person is to see God as an Other who encounters us in a personal way, who has a relationship with us which is one of father (or mother) to child, or lover to beloved. This view is associated particularly with the Boston 'personalists', such as Peter Bertocci, and with a group of British theologians at the beginning of the twentieth century, including H.H. Farmer, John Oman and John and Donald Baillie. They were particularly concerned to stress the way in which God is not an impersonal force, but one who relates to us in encounter as a person, as a 'Thou' to an 'I', and evokes respect and love from us. However, they also stressed that to speak of God as person should not be taken as the only word about God. It draws attention to a condescension of the infinite God who is perfect goodness, a *kenosis* or self-emptying, a limitation of infinity to encounter the finite on its own ground. This would be what Kierkegaard called the absolute paradox, the absurd – that the infinite should be finite, and the perfect should be involved in our joys and sorrows. But the paradox is dissolved when we remember that the infinite is only so for us and for our sake.

It is not that the infinite is really a person, who thinks and feels, wonders whether to create a universe, makes moral decisions, feels lonely and would like to have some friends, and wonders whether we will love God or not. It is rather that the infinite relates to us in a personal way, contracting infinity to finite form in order to bring us and all creatures capable of it to moral and intellectual maturity and lead our finite lives into fulfilling relationship with their infinite source and goal.

Thinking of God in this way as a relational being, a personal being in relation to a universe of finite spirits, can be strengthened by taking insights from both Hegel and Whitehead, and supposing that the Supreme Spirit realises the most creative potentialities of its own being precisely by generating and relating to beings who are genuinely other than it is, who stand over against Spirit, and who have their own proper autonomy. God can create genuinely free agents, and so the process of history will not be the artistic product of a lonely genius. It will be a product of the interaction of many finite agents and the one unlimited creator of all things, who restrains the divine power so that such relational freedom can exist.

In such a universe, evil will be the product of wills that choose selfish goods, not part of the divine self-expression (this is the Whiteheadian bit), but evil will be eliminated when the historical process has run its course (this is the Hegelian bit). Its elimination will end the historical process, or at least all that process in which egoistic choice remains a possibility, so we should be careful about asking for its total elimination too soon.

History becomes an arena of real moral choice for each rational individual. Within it, God may indeed seek to persuade or encourage rather than single-handedly determine. But in the end God will ensure the triumph of goodness and the elimination of evil.

This happens already for both Hegel and Whitehead in the consequential nature of God, in the divine experience and memory. It is not clear that either philosopher believed in any personal existence after death. But there is no reason, so far as we can see, why a creator God should not be able to ensure that all agents may be given an opportunity to discern the meaning of their own lives within the completed divine pattern. That would be heaven, life fulfilled in God, and maybe that is the destined completion of the cosmic process. The completion could not exist without the process, but the process is one that has its completion outside itself.

In this grand cosmic scheme, God is the one who creates an intelligible universe containing finite agents, and who restrains divine power to give them freedom. God is the one who shapes them by love to realise new and distinctive values in time. God is the one who ensures that evil is self-destroying in the end, and who redeems suffering by sharing it and sublating it in a wider experience in which it is not forgotten. Its pain is dulled, and it is given a positive role in building up the final vision of the universe in which all contradictions are unified and reconciled. God is the one who draws all the goods of creation into a completed divine experience, in which creatures might be able to share in a way suited to their capacities.

Some religious traditions, or parts of them, take the personal form as the final form of Godhead. For them, God really is in some sense a person, an individual who encounters humans in an accessible, even recognizable way. But most traditions regard the personal form as just one part of a much richer divine reality. Thus Sankara, in the Indian tradition, takes the Supreme omnipotent Lord to be a manifestation of *nirguna Brahman*, the Absolute without qualities. And in Christianity, the person of Jesus is usually taken to be the earthly form of just one of the three aspects of the divine being that together make up the Trinity.

The Idea of the Trinity

The Christian idea of the Trinity is beyond the scope of this book, which is just about the idea of God in general (I have written about it in *Christianity: A Short Introduction*). But we cannot ignore the fact that most of the writers I have mentioned have been Christians, and the largest theistic faith does think that God is, in the words of the Athanasian creed, 'three persons in one substance'. (As you might expect by now, this creed is not by the fourth-century St Athanasius. It is a Latin creed of somewhat later date, and is usually not now said in churches. One reason for this is suggested by my experience the last, and only, time I tried to get an Anglican congregation to recite it aloud in church. When they got to the phrase, 'the Father incomprehensible, the Son incomprehensible, and the Holy Ghost incomprehensible ... and yet there are not three incomprehensibles', they all burst out laughing. The whole thing was just too incomprehensible, and so the Trinity still seems to many people.)

It might seem bad enough to say that God is a person. But to say that God is three persons sounds much worse. Muslims often just think that this is polytheism, believing in three gods. Christians might be confused, but they are not polytheists. It is just unfortunate that the traditional phrase, 'three persons in one substance', tends to evoke a picture of three people sitting in a bowl of soup. Things get worse if you go on to think of these three persons having discussions with one another about how things are going. 'I think one of us should become incarnate,' says one. 'I'll go,' says another. 'What am I going to do while you are away?' says the third.

This impression could be dispelled by the additional doctrine that each of the persons is omnipotent and omniscient. This does get rid of arguments and interminable discussions over strategy, since each person already knows exactly what the others have decided or will decide, and each knows exactly what the others know. The price, however, is that life in the heavenly soup threatens to become rather boring. 'I thought I would create a universe,' says one. 'I knew you were going to say that,' says the second. 'I think I will create one as well,' says the third. 'Well it had better be the same as mine,' says number one. 'You already know that it is,' says number two. 'I knew you were going to say that,' says number three. None of these persons can ever surprise the others, or tell them anything they did not already know. 'Let me tell you what I did today,' says one. And the others reply in unison, 'Don't bother. We already know.' How frustrating! None of them can do anything that the others do not know all about, and they can never be in conflict with one another (or they would not be omnipotent). What, in short, is the point of having three persons, if they all agree completely about everything, and all know and do exactly the same as the others?

The *only* thing to do is give up this picture of three distinct individuals altogether. There is *only* one individual (that is what 'substance' means), God. But there are three 'persons' (the early Greek word was *hypostases*, which is probably better, precisely because nobody knows exactly what it means) within the being of God. One way of putting this today would be to say that there are three different aspects of the one divine being, that none of them can be collapsed without remainder into the others, and that all of them together are necessary to an adequate idea of God.

One aspect is that God is the utterly transcendent creative ground of all being, beyond human comprehension, the unlimited ocean of infinity, the abyss beyond duality from which all things issue, the ultimate cause of all.

A second aspect is that God is the supreme intelligence in which all possibilities exist as thoughts exist in the mind. Here all the archetypes of being are rooted, and ordered with perfect wisdom. Infinity takes form as mind and self-luminous awareness, and exists as the uncreated light of wisdom which gives form and intelligibility to all things.

A third aspect is that God is the dynamic energy which gives actuality to the forms conceived by the divine wisdom, which values and affirms them, and which delights in their particularity.

God as transcendent abyss, God as particular yet unbounded intelligence, and God as the immanent creative energy of being – these, it might be said, are three distinct ways of being God, all of them necessary to the divine nature, and all bound together in a uniquely perfect reality which is at once deeply personal and yet infinitely more than either one rational individual or three such individuals of the same sort. God as threefold, as Trinity, remains forever a mystery, but it is not an absurdity. The reality of God remains beyond human comprehension, but the idea of a threefold God can be seen to be deeply rational, and to be unequivocally a form of monotheism, of belief in one God.

Of course, to most Christians all this may seem rather abstract. The Christian God is not, after all, known as threefold because of some abstruse philosophical argument. God is said to be threefold because Jesus is in some way seen as the incarnation or embodied image of God, because he referred to God as 'Father', and because the Holy Spirit is experienced as a present life-changing reality. But Christian reflection can deepen these primary beliefs by showing how they express a particular understanding of a God who relates to humans as personal, but who is infinitely more than 'a person'.

So in the Christian faith, the first aspect of the divine being is the transcendent cause of ground of being, which Christians call, in a metaphor, the 'Father' of beings. The second aspect is the wisdom or intelligence which finite things to a greater or lesser degree image or express. Christians see Jesus of Nazareth as 'the Christ', the one who is the human embodiment of divine wisdom, who expresses the divine love and is a freely obedient vehicle of that love in his own person, and who is for humans the 'image of the invisible God' (Colossians 1:15). The third aspect is the immanent creative power within the cosmos, which is felt in human lives, inspiring them to courage, heroism, insight and the creation of works of beauty and power. This is 'God within', the Spirit who works inwardly to shape all things towards their own unique fulfillment as manifold images and vehicles of the divine.

A Trinitarian idea of God means that God cannot be called a 'person', in any straightforward way. God can for some religious traditions, including the Christian, be truly expressed for us in the form of a person, but the full reality of God is far beyond anything we can think of as a person. Jews and Muslims, and other believers in God who reject the idea of the Trinity, could, in my experience, be quite sympathetic to this interpretation of the Trinity, if the qualifications required by the acceptance of analogy were kept firmly in mind – though they might still reject the idea that Jesus is the unique personal form of God. There is never going to be complete agreement about God and the way in which God relates to us. But it should be obvious by now that theists do not all agree with one another anyway, whether they belong to the same 'religion' or not. We have learned something, however, when we see that the disagreements are not simple contradictions, as if everybody knew exactly what they were talking about, and could draw up a clear list of what they agreed with and what they disagreed with. One of the lessons of a study of ideas about God is how very feeble the human mind is, and how very little it can understand of a reality that is supposed to be supreme in value and power.

The Revelatory Roots of Religion

I have been talking about reflective, philosophical thought about God. But, as I have tried repeatedly to stress, most religions, if not all, depend not only on reflection, but also, and indeed primarily, on revelation. That is, they look to some person or persons for authoritative guidance to spiritual insight. It is very natural to think that if there is a God, God will give some revelation of the divine nature and purpose, and any such revelation will necessarily have to be given at a particular time and place, and through some specific individuals. There are many claims to revelation, and it is only too obvious that they do not all agree in detail. Yet there is one important consideration which should take the sting out of many of the differences that exist.

Revelations are not, despite what some people might hope for, clear and precise sets of doctrines and commands. Taken at their deepest level, revelations are tremendously mysterious, and they are revelations of a being who remains ultimately mysterious. All genuine revelations are revelations of mystery. Like the ancient oracles of Greece, they do not give definite and unambiguous answers to our direct questions. They seem to give cryptic and very ambiguous utterances, which we have to tease out through meditation, prayer and often through a liberal use of imagination. They speak in terms of metaphor and symbol, and different religious traditions diverge partly because of their different ways of interpreting these symbols.

The root of Semitic ideas about God lies in the experience of the ancient Hebrew prophets, who discerned God primarily as ethical demand and historical purpose, giving the descendants of Abraham a special part to play in working out this purpose. This still leaves open many variant understandings of just what the demand and purpose is. How is the Torah to be kept, to the letter or in the spirit? What does God want of the Jews, should they try to make converts or not? There are many varieties of religious Judaism, all of them seeking to be responsive to the primary prophetic experience in a way that feels right for them.

One of these varieties was that of a small group of Jews who saw the nature and purpose of God disclosed in a new and vital way in the life, death and (they believed) resurrection of Jesus of Nazareth. Their new movement was soon flooded with Gentiles, and the Christian Church split off from Judaism as a movement with distinctive views about a God who could become incarnate. Still, there were always many varieties of Christianity. Some of them made the claim to be 'orthodox'– that is, holding correct beliefs as defined by some authority. But they did not agree on what that authority should be, some (Roman Catholics) preferring the Bishop of Rome, others (Eastern Orthodox) insisting on full councils of all the Bishops, and yet others (Protestants) denying that there was any human authority with the right to define correct belief for everybody else.

Islam might be seen as a faith that seeks to return to a more prophetic tradition, not being sympathetic to the idea of an incarnate God, and wishing to open the Law (*Shari'a*) to the whole world, not just the Jews. Traditions within Islam range from sorts of Sufism which almost seem to identify the world with God to forms of Sunni Islam which see God as wholly other than creation. When the thought of Aristotle was used to expound an idea of God, Muslim philosophers were the first to apply it, and established very independent schools of philosophical thought which, unfortunately, have not on the whole endured. Thus the Semitic traditions of religion have much in common, though they differ both among themselves and with one another about the precise interpretation to be given to their revelatory origin. Revelation, it is very clear, must be very unclear, if so much genuine and conscientious diversity can exist among those who seek to adhere to it.

There is another main set of traditions in which revelation from God is claimed, that of India. There the Vedas and Upanishads are traditionally said to have been revealed to ancient sages by the gods. They form the basis of traditions that tend to see the personal God (or the gods) as manifestations of *Brahman*, Absolute Reality, and the universe as in some sophisticated sense one with the Absolute. The variety of traditions ranges from an intensely personal theism, in Vaishnava schools, to the non-dualistic philosophy of Sankara.

In all these traditions, there are prophets or religious teachers who are taken to be the primary source of revelation, and then there are many different schools of interpreting or developing that revelation. Since cultures and peoples are so different, it is not surprising that there are many different ideas of God, and many different paths towards knowledge of God. Yet the situation is not that the main religious traditions are simply in total conflict and opposition. There is in all this variety of tradition and interpretation a great amount of convergence in thinking about God, as writers puzzle out what is meant by a being of supreme power and value. It can fairly be said that the differing strands of thoughts are all found, in some form, in each major religious tradition.

It is important to remember, and I have tried to stress, that thinking about God is not just an intellectual exercise. It is thinking about the best way to live as a human being, and about the deepest understanding of the world in which we live. For some people, God does not help at all, and is even an obstacle to an honest understanding of the universe and the adoption of a free and mature way of life. For other people, thinking about God remains at an oversimplified level, the level of a supernatural person in the sky. But in a world where we can all cope, more or less, with computers and air travel, it is not hard to be more aware of the centuries of reflection that have gone into thinking about God, and also of new possibilities of thinking about God in our really quite recent scientific understanding of nature.

When we start to think about God, we will all start from some particular viewpoint. What we have learned as children, what we have read and experienced, what our own society teaches us about natural ways of feeling and acting, all these things will provide us with a viewpoint from which to start. It is then possible, in our world, to come to a fuller knowledge of the viewpoints of others, and thereby to broaden and deepen our own perspective. It will never be possible, or desirable, to see from every point of view at once. But it is possible to expand our knowledge and experience so as to have the widest view that is available to us. Reflecting on the history of ideas about God, seeing how such ideas have developed and interacted, noticing how they have emphasised different aspects of human experience and expressed different fundamental human commitments, our own initial ideas are bound to change. Such change is not to be feared, for it can hardly fail to be a growth in knowledge and understanding.

Conclusion: Seven Ways of Thinking About God

It is time to take stock of the ground that has been covered. It might be tempting to think that, after looking at all these views of God, we can at last come up with the truth. The temptation should, however, be resisted. What we can realistically hope for is to avoid the crudest misunderstandings of the beliefs of others, and to see the uncertainties and unclarities of many of our own beliefs. We might also hope to obtain more clarity about the beliefs to which we are most fundamentally committed. While any reflective human belief must be to some extent exploratory and provisional, there will nevertheless be some beliefs we cannot renounce without renouncing our own integrity. To discover what these are, and to formulate them more sensitively and judiciously, is one goal of philosophical reflection.

With this in mind, if you ask what the most fundamental thing is about believing in God, I would say that it is believing that there is a personal ground of being, that the universe is in some sense grounded in a personal reality. The universe is not the product of blind unconscious will, law or accident. It is the product of a reality which we may rightly call conscious, purposive, wise and good. Moreover, a form of relationship is possible to that transcendent personal reality which leads towards an overcoming of ego and a life of compassion, wisdom and bliss. It becomes appropriate to approach all our experiences as encounters with that personal reality, embedded in and mediated through the extremely complex network of physical laws and finite free acts that go to form the world in which we exist.

4

God as a Principle of Cosmological Explanation

The purpose of this paper is to explore the way in which the formulation of a Christian doctrine of creation is helped by modern cosmology, and the sense in which the doctrine of creation adds an important explanatory element to the form of explanation given by quantum cosmologists. The paper falls into six sections. After a discussion of the classical Christian view of creation by a timeless God, I maintain that the concept of a temporal God provides a more adequate analysis of the notions of omnipotence and of creation. I then develop a model of creative temporal freedom which is meant to steer a middle way between determinism and sheer randomness, and suggest that there are two important ways of explaining the nature of the universe – the nomological and the axiological. The first of these, often taken as an ideal in physics, leaves one with an ultimately blind necessity; the second leaves one with an apparently fortuitous contingency. Taking both together, the most adequate explanatory concept seems to be that of a being which is necessarily existent, and which brings events into being by a process of creative emergence for the sake of the values they realise or make possible. I conclude by suggesting that this is in fact a concept of God which both modern cosmology and modern Christian doctrine help to shape, which shows the contribution a doctrine of creation by God can make to the explanatory theses of quantum cosmology.

Creation and Timelessness in Classical Christian Thought

Christians assert that this cosmos is created by one self-existent being of supreme perfection. To say that the universe is created is to say that it is brought about intentionally, that its existence is the expression of a consciously formed purpose. It is not to say, nor does it imply, that the universe has a beginning in time. Theologians have usually stressed that the universe is not brought about in time, in the sense that there exists an uncreated time within which the physical universe comes to exist at a particular point. Augustine makes the point with particular clarity; and although I will be critical of his view in this paper, his discussion forms a classic statement of the Christian position. When Augustine asked the question, 'What made God create heaven and earth then, and not sooner?'[1] his reply was that 'no time passed before the world, because no creature was made by whose course it might pass.'[2] That is, as he understood it, time is a certain sort of relation between objects, and where no objects exist which are related by that relation, then the relation does not exist either. The temporal series extends back, as a relation, T, between objects, to an object which simply has no relation T to anything preceding it. Since 'beforeness' is a relation between two objects, the first object is not related by 'beforeness' to anything. There is nothing 'before' the temporal universe; neither any objects nor any time. For Augustine, God brought about time and space as well as all the things that are in them. Just as God did not create space at a certain place, but non-spatially caused all places to exist, so God did not create time at a certain time, but non-temporally caused all times to exist. Whatever reservations one may have about a doctrine of non-temporal causation, it does not seem self-contradictory to say that A wholly depends for its existence upon B, though there is no temporal relation between A and B. At any rate, this is a view Augustine is committed to. As far as this doctrine goes, there might or might not have been a first moment of time; both possibilities are consistent with the dependence of all times, however many there are, upon God. Augustine did accept, like most classical theologians, on grounds of revelation, that this universe had a beginning in time; though he also suggested that there might have been an infinite number of universes before this one, in which case, of course, time would have no beginning.[3]

If this is the case, it follows from the doctrine of creation that God, the creator, is a non-spatio-temporal being. As the creator of the whole of

1 Augustine, *City of God*, bk. 11, ch. 4 (New York: E. P. Dutton, 1957), 314.
2 Ibid., bk. 11, Chap. 6; 317.
3 Ibid., 359.

space-time, God is beyond space-time. This is an important part of the traditional belief that God is transcendent. This statement, however, like most statements in theology, immediately needs to be qualified. God is not, for any standard theistic view, outside spacetime in the sense that God is excluded from every space and time. On the contrary, God is omnipresent.[4] That is to say, every object or event standing in spacetime relations only exists by the originating and sustaining power of God. Without such a Divine activity of bringing into being and sustaining in being (these being simply different aspects of the same act in God), nothing could exist even for the smallest moment. That relation of *holding in being* is the most intimate one that can be conceived; it is a relation of immediate and total origination, and is between God and every created object, whenever it exists.

Thus it is wholly inadequate to think of God having created universe at some remote point in time – say, at the Big Bang – so that now universe goes on existing by its own power. This popular misconception, 'the creation' is the first moment of the spacetime universe, and that universe continues by its own inherent power, wholly misconstrues classical theistic tradition. It is irrelevant to a doctrine of creation *ex nihilo* whether the universe began or not; that the universe began was usually accepted because of a particular reading of Genesis 1.[5] The doctrine of creation *ex nihilo* simply maintains that there is nothing other than God from which the universe is made, and that the universe is other than God and wholly dependent upon God for its existence. Creation is, properly speaking, the relation which holds between every point of spacetime and the creator, such that each moment exists in total dependence upon the sustaining being and will of the creator. God is not nearer to the beginning of time than to any other point of time. On the contrary, God is present and active, in the most intimate and fundamental way, at every point of spacetime. God is not excluded from any space or time. Though God, as creator, infinitely transcends spacetime, precisely because God is creator, God is present and active at every point of spacetime.

The classical form of theism which is found in most of the Church Fathers and which is especially clearly formulated by the thirteenth-

4 Cf. Aquinas, *Summa Theologiae*, I a, 8, 2: 'As the soul exists wholly in the body, so God exists wholly in each and every thing.' (New York: Hill), vol. 2, 117.

5 Ibid., Ia, 46, 2: 'That the world has not always existed cannot be demonstratively proved but is held by faith alone,' vol. 8, 79.

century theologian Thomas Aquinas, asserted that God is eternal, in the sense that God is timeless.'[6] That is, God contains no *internal* temporal relations – no 'before' and 'after,' no past to be remembered or forgotten, and no future which is as yet undecided – and God has no *external* temporal relations – does not exist before, after or at the same time as any other thing whatsoever.

The creation of the universe can then be represented as the total dependence of spacetime, in all its parts from beginning to end (if time has a first and last moment), upon a timeless being, in whom there is no change, coming into being, or passing away whatsoever. As Augustine put it, 'all that ever God created was in (God's) unchanged fixed will eternally one and the same.'[7] One must not think of God wondering whether to create a universe, deciding it would be a good idea, choosing which one to create from a selection of possibilities, and then bringing it into being. Since God is in the strictest sense immutable, being wholly timeless, there is never a time when God has not yet decided to bring about a universe, or has not yet decided which one to bring about, or has not yet brought it about. God timelessly brings the universe into being. There is, in the Divine being, an immutable intention to bring precisely this universe into being, an intention which is actualised by the very same act by which it is formed. As Aquinas puts it, 'As the divine existing is essentially necessary, so also is the divine knowing and the divine willing.'[8] God's willing the universe is not something that God came to a new decision about; it is part of the immutable Divine being from all eternity.

God, Temporality and Omnipotence

This classical view seems to match rather well the 'block view' of space-time which some physicists hold – the view that every point of space-time is in some sense existent, and that the sense of passage through time which is characteristic of humans does not point to a fundamental and irreducible characteristic of unobserved physical reality.[9] For the classical view clearly entails that God knows every moment in time, from first to last, in one timeless act of knowing. God does not need to *foreknow*

6 Ibid., Ia. 10. 2: vol.2, 139.
7 Augustine, *City of God*, bk. 12, ch. 17, 361.
8 Aquinas, *Summa Theologiae*, Ia. 19, 3; vol. 5, 17.
9 Cf. the article by C. J. Isham and John Polkinghorne in this volume.

anything, since God knows it directly, in a timeless manner. God stands in need of no inferences or predictions, but knows all spatio-temporal events, from first to last, in one unchanging intuition.

Despite this pleasing congruence, however, there are deep theological difficulties with the idea of a wholly timeless God, and it may be doubted whether the idea is really entailed by a doctrine of creation. What the doctrine of creation requires is that God should transcend spacetime, as its intentional cause. That does entail that God cannot be limited in spacetime. But it does not entail that God cannot be in time at all, in any sense; and it does not entail that the Divine being contains no analogates of past, present and future. In fact, both the doctrine of omnipresence, which makes God present to every time, and the Christian doctrine of incarnation, which identifies God, in some sense, with a human being who lives in time, seem to imply a form of Divine temporality. If God is present at every time, the clearest thing to say is that, in creating spacetime, God creates new temporal relations in the Divine being itself. That is, by the same act by which God creates events in spatio-temporal relations, so God thereby creates the relation of being co-present with many times. Thus one is able correctly to say, at each time, 'God *now* exists' – which, strangely, is not true on the classical view, since for that view.

God, properly speaking, has no temporal properties.

The classical view also has to invent complex logical epicycles to explain how it is true that God lives, suffers and dies in Jesus Christ, and yet the Divine nature itself has no temporal relation to Jesus at all. A more straightforward reading might be that God is the subject of temporal properties, and is co-temporal with Jesus in an additional way to that in which God is co-temporal with everything: namely, by being active in the life of Jesus in a way in which God is not directly active at other times.[10]

There is an even greater advantage in ascribing to God a certain sort of temporality, which is not that of our spacetime. That is, only if some form of open future exists in God can it be possible for God to do new things, to be genuinely and radically creative and to come to new decisions. The classical idea of omnipotence involves the thought that God can do anything possible that is compatible with God's own existence and prior decisions. But it would be an odd definition of 'omnipotence' which denies

10 Such a revision of the classical immutabilist view is expounded in Thomas Moms, *The Logic of God Incarnate* (Cornell University Press, 1986).

to God the possibility of ever doing anything new. This would seem to deny the applicability of the concept of 'power' to God at all.[11] If God is, as the classical tradition has asserted, 'purely actual without any potentiality at all,' then it follows that God can never do anything other than God does (there is no potentiality in God for doing anything else). There may well seem to be a restricted notion of power, and a richer concept of omnipotence may be the idea of a God who can bring into being an infinite number of new things throughout endless time. One may even argue that the assertion of omnipotence entails that any necessarily omnipotent being must necessarily possess contingent properties. For if it is possible to create some contingent worlds, then the creation of any such world must itself be contingent (i.e. some other contingent world could have been created). So any being which can create contingent worlds must logically be capable of contingent acts. So it must necessarily be contingent in some respects. Far from necessity and contingency contradicting one another in God, certain necessary properties entail certain contingent ones – as the necessarily possessed Divine property of being able to create any world compossible with God entails the necessary possession of contingent properties by God. Thus only a God who is necessary in the possession of some properties (including existence, omnipotence, goodness and omniscience) and contingent in the possession of others (the capacity freely to create some of many possible universes) can be maximally great.

Asserting a form of temporal passage of God in this way obviously requires the logical possibility of speaking of time without space. But if a non-spatial being like God can exist at *all,* then there seems no good reason why God should not change; and that in itself entails a sort of time without space. If one admits the real possibility of a being which has no spatial extension – and I do not find it plausible to assert as a necessary truth that the existence of anything that should be extended in space – then it is a separate question whether such a being can be in two contradictory states, one causally related to the other. If that is possible, and again there is no good a priori argument why it should not be possible, then one has a close analogue of time, as that which allows contradictory states of the same being, standing in causal relation to one another, to exist. Thus there is no good a priori argument against the possibility of change in

11 Aquinas, *Summa Theologiae,* I a. 3. 1: 'In the first existent thing everything must be actual; there can be no potentiality whatsoever'; vol. 2, 21.

a non-spatial being, and therefore of temporality in such a being. Though the time with which physics deals in a relation between physical objects or events, there is another form of temporal relation of which we are aware, which is the relation between different states of some consciousness. One need not deny that all human states of consciousness are related in some way to neurological changes, to see that relations between successive conscious states are not analytically or necessarily related to relations between successive physical states. Most philosophical materialists would accept that such physical/mental state identity as there may be is contingent. So it is logically possible, so far as one can see, that temporal relations can exist in conditions of non-physical change. Given this bare and apparent logical possibility, one can feel as confident as one can about anything in this area in suggesting that, if God is creatively free, then God is temporal, though God transcends the physical spacetime system of this universe. This seems to many contemporary theologians a more adequate account of Biblical talk of God than does the classical view that God cannot ever do what God has not changelessly willed.[12]

The assertion of a temporal God is compatible with the assertion of omnipotence, and it is not necessary to follow the many process thinkers who deny that a temporal God is omnipotent.[13] Their case is that, if creatures are to share in the creative freedom of God, then God cannot determine all their actions. A truly open future permits the existence of creaturely freedom in a strong sense – that 'if a person is free ... no antecedent conditions and/or causal laws determine that he will perform the action, or that he won't.'[14] Moreover, the agent can actualise any one of a number of possible future states, even while its character at a given time remains precisely the same. So there will be many states – the results of free creaturely acts – not determined by God. That, however, need not cause one to deny that God is omnipotent. All one needs to say is that God *could* determine all things, but decides to let creatures determine some things themselves for a good reason – perhaps so that a community of creative love can exist between creatures and God, as the Judeo-Christian revelation asserts. God retains total power, but is not compelled

12 Cf. Keith Ward, *Rational Theology and the Creativity of God* (Oxford: Basil Blackwell, 1982), ch. 7.

13 Cf. A. N. Whitehead, *Process and Reality* (New York: The Free Press, 1978), 346: 'He does not create the world, he saves it . . . leading it by his vision of truth, beauty, and goodness.'

14 A. Plantinga, *God, Freedom and Evil* (London: Allen and Unwin, 1975), 29.

to exercise it at all times. It is relevant that God can ensure that the Divine purposes are realised at some stage; God is not doomed to be perpetually frustrated by creaturely choices. Yet it may be an important fact, which classical theologians were not fully able to take account of, that creatures are free in this creative sense and that God is free to respond to them in creative freedom too.

A Model of Creative Freedom

The best analogy for such creative freedom is something like the writing of a piece of music. This is an analogy which has been deployed effectively by A. R. Peacocke,[15] and the point of it is to suggest a form of causality which is neither wholly deterministic nor completely arbitrary. At any given point in composition, the note that is to come next is not *entailed* by any past or present note or any combination of them. A number of possible notes might exist but there is literally nothing which determines that one of them should. One the other hand, the note that will next exist is not arbitrarily assigned, as if a computerised random generator could do as well as Mozart. So what governs the choice of the immediately successive note? Simply the creative, directing activity of the composer, who generates musical patterns because of their beauty. It is important that there is an intentional activity at work; that is what prevents the process from being arbitrary. It is mind-directed or intentional. It is important that there is an intentional activity at work; that is what prevents the process from being arbitrary. It is equally important that the intention is to create a unique and original form of beauty. It is concerned with the generation of order and sensory and affective appeal. So one has a mind concerned with the production of beauty, working to continue an unfinished pattern. Central elements of this situation are (1) the pattern itself, (2) the active concentration of a mind with certain skills and capacities, (3) canons of beauty and taste which can be modified but which provide models of creative activity and (4) human pleasure in certain sorts of sensory pattern which form the basis of selected goals (i.e. realised states of value).

Deterministic models of causality work with a basically deductive scheme, for which the future can only unfold what is already contained in the past (one cannot have more in the conclusion of a deductive argument

15 A. R. Peacocke, *Creation and the World of Science* (Oxford: Clarendon Press, 1979), 105.

than there is in the premises). In cases of creativity one has what might be called a teleological model of causality. For such a model, the future builds on the past, by adding to it in a way which seeks to realise certain goals in the process of creation. At any moment of the temporal process, one has an incomplete pattern, a creative agency and a general goal (itself emerging from the recognition of desires of certain sorts) setting the direction of creativity. It is consciousness which recognises certain states as desirable, which accordingly sets certain goals of activity and which realises these goals through continuing an apprehended process. At each moment its successor moment is generated by a directive agency informed by its apprehension of the past, endowed with characteristic skills and dispositions and oriented by its conception of values.[16]

What this means is that one cannot consider time as a series of quite discrete events, each complete in itself, one succeeding another either by some form of quasi-entailment or quite arbitrarily. At least as far as conscious and free agents are concerned, and as far as they are conscious and acting rationally, each temporal moment is filled with an awareness of the past and oriented towards a possible future, as part of a dynamic process in which future events are emergent – genuinely new and yet continuous with and to some extent developmental of what has gone before. And this flow towards the future is essentially directed to the realisation of values, which are what give the temporal process intelligibility.

Whitehead has, in my view, very helpfully emphasised the value of creative emergence and therefore of temporality, a value which gives a much more positive reason for the creation of a spacetime universe than the traditional account provided. He has given creaturely freedom and creativity a much more important place in the explanation of how things have come to be as they are; and he has suggested a form of causality which fits the facts of human experience quite well. It is a consequence of a Whiteheadian view that, where there are many developing sentient beings with limited knowledge, their aims will often conflict and from such conflict suffering and destructive processes will flow. Natural and moral evil are inevitable in a world with general structure. However helpful that may be with the problem of evil, many theists feel that a process view

16 A. N. Whitehead has deployed these notions effectively in *Process and Reality* (New York: The Free Press, 1978) though I am restricting their range to conscious agents, as he does not.

nevertheless undesirably limits the power and sovereignty of God. Whitehead was basically an atomist, believing that the real causal impulses of the world derive from its atomic constituents, the 'actual occasions.' He did give God a place as the 'poet of the world,' or the lure towards greater harmony and beauty.[17] But he was not able to give a convincing account of how such conflict as there is could ever be overcome and the Divine purposes ever be wholly fulfilled.

On the account I am suggesting, human freedom and creativity remain basic constituents of the universe, but God has a much more active and positive role to play, as Christian revelation claims. God is the master creator, laying down the pattern, influencing creaturely choices towards a goal whose general nature is given by God but whose specific character is, in many respects, determined by creatures. God creates our capacities; he influences them towards good. But we express them in specific ways; we can and should do so by free reliance on God, who will ensure that their potential for good is realised, though in a uniquely creative way that only we can specifically determine. To use another analogy, that of the master chess player, used by Geach and Polkinghorne,[18] God enters into the game to ensure that it is concluded in the way that he desires. In this way, he ensures that all the evil caused by the misuse of creaturely freedom will be ordered to good, though the tragedy of its occurrence cannot be simply obliterated by anything God does.

Nomological and Axiological Explanation

In the light of this discussion, one might suggest that there are two complementary models of intelligibility by means of which one can understand a world containing free actions. They might be termed the nomological – a model familiar to physicists – and the axiological – often found in the social sciences. For the first model one understands the genesis of the new by appeal to general principles or laws of regular succession. That there are simple, elegant and mathematically stateable laws which describe the structures of the universe is a surprising and remarkable

17 A. N. Whitehead, *Process and Reality*, 346.
18 P. T. Geach, *Providence and Evil* (New York: Cambridge University Press, 1977), 59. John Polkinghorne, *Science and Providence* (London: SPCK, 1989), 98.

fact,[19] and their formulation enables scientists to understand and predict many of the processes of nature. For the second model one understands the genesis of the new by appeal to values which are to be realised by beings of certain distinctive capacities and modes of awareness. This model does not provide general laws which facilitate prediction. It provides an idea of the values which are appropriate to beings of a certain nature and enables one to understand why such beings act as they do. The first model ends with the postulation of ultimate brute facts; the second with the postulation of ultimate values or desirable and worthwhile states.

The two models are not wholly disconnected, however. For the first model is strongly evaluative, in seeking the simplest, most elegant and mathematically fruitful postulates. This is in fact an aesthetic criterion, answering the question about why ultimate brute facts are as they are, by suggesting that they are the most beautiful (elegant or simple) set of facts which give rise to the interestingly complex universe we apprehend. One can either say that it just happens that such a value – of ultimate mathematical beauty – is instantiated in our universe; or one can turn to the second model for intelligibility and say that such beauty exists because it realises a state of great intrinsic value.

On the other hand, if one asks why the values that are realised in this universe should be just as they are – why these values are realised and not any others, which perhaps we cannot fully imagine – then one has to refer to the natural capacities and desires of beings within the universe. The values of sensitivity, creativity and freedom, wisdom and justice which form the objective good of this universe and comprehensible as fulfillments of the natures of the sort of sentient social animals which have evolved in a physical universe of a particular structure. The values which this universe realises are those states which unfold the potential implicit in its ultimate natural constitution. Thus to see what values this universe expresses one needs to discern the natural tendencies and capacities of beings in the universe, which in turn refer back to the ultimate brute facts of the universe. This insight is enshrined in the Christian tradition that true human good is to be found in appropriate fulfillment of natural human

19 'The physical universe is put together with an ingenuity so astonishing that I cannot accept it merely as a brute fact,' Paul Davies, *The Mind of God* (New York: Simon and Schuster, 1992), 4.

inclinations; that goodness is rooted in the nature of things, and is not some sort of arbitrary decision or purely subjective expression of feeling.[20]

Ultimate brute facts and ultimate values are not disconnected. Using the first model of intelligibility alone leaves one with ultimate brute facts which are just there for no reason at all. Clearly many physicists are unhappy with this ultimate non-rationality, and have sought some sense of quasi-logical necessity which will dissolve away the last recess of arbitrariness.[21] But they are thereby resorting to the Principle of Sufficient Reason, which would make all things necessary implications of some initial state which is itself necessarily existent. For some quantum cosmologists, one can speak, albeit controversially, of an initial state (of quantum fluctuations in a vacuum) which is necessary, in that it instantiates the only set of states compatible with quantum theory.[22] But of course one still has to ask in what sense such a theory could be necessarily existent, or give rise to a physical instantiation of itself. Traditional theism comes surprisingly near to such a hypothesis, in holding that there is a being, God, which contains the basis of all possible universes, which exists necessarily and which generates this universe as one contingent realisation of the exhaustive set of possibles in its own being. The theistic model suggests how a mathematical theory could be existent (as conceived in the Divine mind) and how a universe could be generated from it (by an intentional act); but it might be seen as simply a more pictorial way of putting the quantum cosmologists' proposal that this universe originates from a necessarily existent being, or is itself necessarily existent in its deep structure. However, although this model of intelligibility does eliminate arbitrariness from the universe, which is very satisfying for a physicist, it also seems to reduce the phenomena of freedom and creativity, of value-realisation, to relative insignificance. One main advantage of introducing the concept of God is that it enables the aspects of necessity and creativity to be held together in one coherent, non-arbitrary and non-deterministic form of explanation.

20 'Reason of its nature apprehends the things towards which man has a natural tendency . . . and therefore to be actively pursued,' Aquinas, *Summa Theologiae,* Ia 2ae, 94, 2; vol,' 28, 81.

21 'We would prefer a greater sense of logical inevitability in the theory,' Steven Weinberg, *The First Three Minutes* (London: 1977), 17.

22 Cf. the article by C. J. Isham, 'Quantum theories of the creation of the universe', in *Quantum Cosmology and the Laws of Nature: Scientific Perspectives on Divine Action.* Vatican City State: Vatican Observatory, 1993.

The Idea of Divine Necessity

The possibility of God as a necessary being could, of course, be denied. One clear form of denial is given by Richard Gale. He argues that, if a necessary being exists, it excludes the possibility of a world without a God, or of a world with unjustifiable evil in it, or of a world which is evil overall. For a necessary being is a being which exists in every possible world, by definition. Yet these other conceivable states, says Gale, are intuitively logically possible; therefore God cannot be a necessary being – there are possible worlds in which God does not exist.[23] Indeed, Gale holds that 'if God is so conceived (as having necessary existence), it follows that he does not and cannot exist.[24] This is certainly false and a careless slip on Gale's part. If God is conceived as existent in every possible world, what follows is merely that no world is possible without God. Now to this Gale simply retorts that he can imagine a world without God; therefore at least one world is possible without God, therefore God cannot be a necessary being. But this is only so if it follows from the fact that Gale can imagine X that X is possible, and I see no reason to accept that one can imagine an infinite number of worlds without God; all one has to do is think of all possible worlds and subtract God from them, leaving them otherwise the same. But does it follow from this that such imagined worlds are existentially possible? This would require the axiom: 'Whatever I can imagine is possible.' Far from being true, this seems false in many cases. Mathematicians imagined squaring the circle for centuries; but it is not possible. I can imagine that there is an even number which is not the sum of two primes; but such a thing is probably not possible. The plain fact is that what one can imagine is not a reliable guide to logical possibility in complex cases. And if logical possibility means lack of contradiction, it is almost certainly untrue that any state at all which is not self-contradictory might actually exist. We simply have no idea of the conditions of the possibility of real existence. The Humean Ontological Argument, that what one can conceive is actually possible, is no better than the Anselmian Ontological Argument, that since we can conceive a necessary being, it must exist. If a necessary being exist, then unjustifiable evil is not existentially possible in any world; and we would see this if and only if we could clearly conceive

23 Richard Gale, *On the Nature and Existence of God* (New York: Cambridge University Press, 1991), 224–37.
24 Ibid., 202.

the conditions of real existence and possibility. So Gale should have said, if God is conceived as having necessary existence, it follows that many things we think we can imagine are in fact so sketchily, incompletely or confusedly conceived that they cannot even possibly exist. Is that very surprising? I should have thought it was a fairly familiar philosophical experience, as anyone should agree who has met a range of Absolute Idealist, sense-datum theorists, central-state materialists and phenomenologists. At least some of them are talking about things that are not even possible – Gale even thinks theists are, or might be, such people. I conclude that, for all we know, there is a possible being which, if it is possible, is actual. The argument to it mentioned here is not an argument from concepts alone, an ontological argument, but from the postulate of the absolute intelligibility of the cosmos, the completion of that search for understanding which is such a natural and valued trait of the human mind. That requires, if taken to its fullest conclusion, the grounding of all actual states in a reality which necessarily exists and thus uniquely and fully answers the question, 'Why is there anything at all?'

There have been those, such as Spinoza, who have held that the universe emanates from the necessarily existent being, God, by the Principle of Sufficient Reason, by some internal necessity. As I have mentioned, that seems to be a position espoused by Weinberg, though without explicit use of the idea of God. Such a move, however, is in conflict with the existence of real creativity and freedom either in God or in the universe. So the alternative, and traditional Christian, view is to give the reason for the ultimate brute physical facts of this universe being the way they are as the realisation of those ultimate values which are implicit in the physical structure. This appeal to the second model of intelligibility does explain why the ultimate brute facts are as they are; but it leaves unanswered the question of how values can have causal power. The ideal intellectual resolution of the quest for universal intelligibility would therefore, it seems, be found in a being which exists by necessity as the ground of all possibility, and therefore of all necessary values, and with the power to bring any compossible states about. Since it brings states about for their value, it can be properly termed good. It is thus omnipotent, being able to actualise any state; omniscient, knowing what states can be actualised; and benevolently good, actualizing states for their value. Further, insofar as it can choose its own states, it will choose maximally good states for itself; so that it will itself be of supreme intrinsic value, a Maximally Valuable Being.

Can the necessary being choose its own states? If it is necessarily existent, then it must possess its essential nature in every possible world; so it cannot choose its essential properties to be other than they are. Those essential properties will include omnipotence and omniscience and unlimited benevolence, and thus meet the standard definition of the minimal essential properties of a maximally valuable being. Now I have argued that an omnipotent being will necessarily possess some contingent (therefore non-essential) properties. These are possible states of God which may or may not be actualised. It is these states which any omnipotent being will maximise to become a maximally valuable being. There probably is not one maximal state of the greatest degree of the greatest number of the greatest kinds of value; but a number of incommensurable valuable states. In that case the values of maximally valuable being will be maximal in the sense that they will comprise a set of compossible values which are always greater in degree and extent than any others in fact and which are endlessly realizable in new combinations. God may not be a being of one statically supreme state of intrinsic goodness, but a dynamic reality of the endless realisation of intrinsic values, which are underivatively rooted in the Divine creativity itself. As necessarily existent, and having both necessary and contingent properties, the general nature and existence of the contingent properties being necessarily rooted in the necessary properties, and their specific actualization being subject to the necessary property of being freely creative, God is not an arbitrary or random brute fact. As the foundation of value, God can provide a reason for actualizing a set of possibilities as expressive of some set of ultimate values. And as free and creative in its particular actions, God can avoid both the morally dubious determinism of sufficient reason and the rationally dubious randomness of brute factuality.

The Idea of Creative Emergence

Thus the best possible intelligible explanation of the universe, its maximal explanation, is to be found, not in a set of physical brute facts and not in a form of 'personal explanation' which is rooted in the merely given nature of some personal being but in a necessarily existent source of all possible and actual beings which creatively brings to be a universe in which creatures can cooperate in realizing a distinctive set of values. This source, this self-existent, supremely perfect and freely creative being is God. In this sense, theism is the completion of that search for intelligibility which characterises the scientific enterprise. The universe can be seen as intentionally brought into being to realise a distinctive set of values, and the laws of nature are the general principles which set the conditions for the unfolding of natural tendencies which bring those values about through a temporal process of emergence. The discovery of the remarkable amount of 'fine-tuning' in the physical structure of the universe greatly enhances our view of the universe as one elegant and closely interconnected whole.[25] The universe is both rational and contingent; for necessity and freedom are both key characteristics of it, and require precisely that sense of creative but non-arbitrary emergence which is the mark of the Divine creative act itself.

This model of causality is different from the classical philosophical model of Sufficient Causality – the entailment model, which fails completely to account for the fact that the universe, as we know it, contains qualities which did not exist in its primordial constitution. And it is different from the Humean regularity model, which sees laws of science simply as statements of observed regularities between events. It is a model of *creative emergence,* accounting for the existence of things by seeing them as creative realisations of envisaged intrinsic values (states valued for their own intrinsic qualities, not their consequences or effects).

The Christian doctrine of creation cannot be construed properly either by the sufficient causality model or by the regularity model. At least for orthodox belief, the universe does not flow from God as a deductive entailment of the Divine being. And there is certainly no regular observable succession between Gods and the production of universes. But it could be construed by a creative emergence model, according to which this universe is a novel imaginative expression of specific intrinsic values. The particular values chosen are a subset of the many values which exist eternally in God, and they are chosen precisely by the sort of creative spontaneity in God which is itself a very great value to possess. This universe exists for the sake of the values it can realise and it is a realisation of those values in ways which have not previously existed, which might

25 John Polkinghorne, *Science and Creation* (London: SPCK, 1988), 22–23.

have taken a different particular form, but which partly because of their novelty and individuality are of inherent worth.

If this is true, there is a teleological explanation for the universe; it exists as a dynamic patterned process, realizing distinctive values through emergent creativity. Rational creatures may reasonably be seen on this model as cooperating in this creative emergence of the natural order. They are sub-creators with specific roles in the general creative pattern which issues from God. We would understand this explanation fully if we could see what values were to be realised, the condition of their realisation, the nature of the God who brings them about and the way in which God is able to structure events to ensure their final realisation. But since we understand none of these things very well, the explanation remains a very general one, postulating simply that this universe does exist in order to realise specific values, and probably appealing to revelation to say in more detail what those values are. It still has great explanatory force to say, if it is indeed true, that the universe has a goal of value, which is realised in the process of its temporal existence.

The sort of explanation which cosmologists typically seek is in terms of some fundamental set of initial conditions and laws of behaviour which will give rise to a universe like this. It is clearly possible that such a set of conditions and laws could simply happen to exist, as one improbable set among an indefinitely large number of other equally improbable sets. Richard Swinburne defines an 'ultimate explanation' as one in which some set of conditions and laws exists which entails all states of affairs in our actual universe, but which is not itself explainable at any time.[26] They are 'ultimate brute facts.' He hypothesises that there is a prior probability that the set of ultimate brute facts will be simple rather than complex. However, this seems counter-intuitive, since, in the array of all possible universes, there seems no reason why there should be more simple universes than complex ones. On the contrary, since complex universes may be built in various ways out of simple ones, if probability applies at all in such an area, it would seem more probable that a complex set of brute facts would exist, since there are more complex than simple possible universes.

Swinburne's 'weak' argument for the probability of God – that the probability of a simple God is low, but not as low as the probability of a complex universe – thus fails to get off the ground. It is not more probable,

26 Richard Swinburne, *The Existence of God* (Oxford: Clarendon Press, 1979), 75.

a priori, that a God exists and would create a universe like this than that this universe just exists. Indeed, bringing in God just seems to complicate things unnecessarily, since any particular state of affairs is hugely improbable anyway. It is true that the existence of some ultimate brute facts would explain the nature of this universe, making clear why things should be as they are, given certain initial conditions. But those brute facts remain inexplicable (in principle, since Swinburne dismisses the idea of a self-explanatory cause as incoherent). And it is possible, as some quantum creationists maintain, that an adequate ultimate explanation is available in purely mathematical terms, without bringing in God.

Yet what such explanations omit is any consideration of emergence in the universe, particularly of the emergence of value, consciousness, freedom and creativity. Since these things do exist, a maximal explanation must combine both the element of necessity which is found in sufficient reason explanations and the element of free creativity found in value-realisation explanations. That is precisely the sort of explanation the doctrine of creation postulates. What modern cosmology does is to show the elegant structure and the parameters of natural necessity, the unity and necessity of nature. It sets the notion of Divine action in its broadest and most all-embracing context. Christian revelation claims to show the purpose of this unitary and intelligible natural order, as the creation of a community of love which is also a participation in the Divine love. It is a striking fact that many theories of modern cosmology and the central assertions of Christian revelation cohere and illuminate each other in this way, disclosing an intelligibility and purpose inherent in the structure of the universe which point to its foundation in a deeply interfused spiritual reality.

The laws of the physical universe should not be set in opposition to God, as inviolable general rules which God, as an external power, would have to violate in order to act. The laws give the structure within which the purposes of God are brought to realisation; and at every point there is the possibility of a creatively free initiative or response both from creatures and from God. The existence of a general rational structure in nature in no way inhibits the possibility of discontinuous emergent events which disclose the underlying character of the Divine presence and prefigure the consummation of value which is the goal of creation. It is better to construe miracles as such transformations of the physical to disclose its spiritual foundation and goal than to think of them as violations of inflexible and purposeless laws of nature.[27] In overturning old mechanistic and deterministic models of laws of nature, modern science helps towards a more satisfactory formation of a conception of Divine action as the creative realisation of purposes potential in the physical structure itself, not as interferences from some alien power wholly outside the system. Not all potentials can be realised, so there remains much scope for creative choice. Nor are potentials realised in a wholly predetermined way, so there remains much scope for imaginative elaboration and specification. Yet the model of the universe as directed towards a future which is partly open to creative choice is very different from the mechanistic model of it as predetermined in every detail, and it allows of Divine and human action in much more intelligible and specific ways.

Modern cosmology may lead one to see the physical cosmos as an emergent value-oriented totality which is the optimal solution of a highly ordered and elegant set of boundary conditions. To the extent that it does so it is consistent with and even suggestive of the belief that the physical universe is intentionally brought about by a self-existent being of supreme value. It emphasises that the maximal form of explanation is that postulated by theism; and it helps to show the way in which the universe can be understood as the creative act of God. In these ways theism can be seen as an implication of the scientific attitude itself, and the pursuit of scientific understanding may be seen as converging upon the religious quest for self-transforming knowledge of God rather than as being opposed to it. As modern science sprang from the context of Christian belief, so now it seems to be leading back to its roots, the apprehension of the physical cosmos as the visible expression of the mind of God.

27 Cp. David Hume's vastly popular definition of miracle as 'a violation of a law of nature' in 'Of Miracles,' from *Enquiry Concerning Human Understanding*, Section 10 (first published 1748).

5

Is God a Person?

Vincent Brümmer, in a number of writings, has expounded a form of personalistic theism which is both attractive to the person of faith and masterly in philosophical lucidity and argument. There is no doubt that Christians are encouraged to call God 'Father' and to relate to God as to a person who loves and cares for them. The idea of a personal God is often contrasted with an alleged 'Eastern' idea of ultimate reality as an impersonal reality which is fundamentally monistic in character. Thus one can contrast a Christian idea of God as a moral agent who is properly a person, with an Eastern idea of Brahman as Absolute Reality, with which all finite things are identical and which does not relate as a moral person to human beings. I am not suggesting that Professor Brümmer would be happy with such a contrast; but it is worth exploring whether and to what extent this really is a contrast between 'East' and 'West' or between two distinct and incompatible concepts of the Divine Being. I shall suggest that Professor Brümmer's stress on the personhood of God does not serve to underpin any such contrast, and that an examination of more impersonal-sounding models can be a useful complement to Christian personalism.

One needs to ask, first, what might be meant by calling God 'a person.' The term 'person' is itself very ill defined. We know what persons are in practice. They are human beings. Further than that, however, things quickly become rather unclear. It may be disputed whether all members of the human species are persons; and this brings to the fore the thought that a person is distinguished by having some form of rational or moral consciousness. If a conscious being, even of human form and parentage, is totally non-rational and non-moral (for instance, if it is a very early embryo), some might hesitate to call it a person, though others would be very insistent that it is a person. In such discussions, it usually becomes apparent that there is a grey area about the notion of personhood. But any being which belongs to a class the members of which properly have rational consciousness is apt to be called a person, even if that individual shows no sign of such rationality. This accords with a traditional Christian view, though one deriving from Aristotle, that persons are distinguished from animals by having a rational soul, or the capacity for abstract understanding.

Having broadened the notion of personhood beyond the class of human beings, per se, it is clearly possible to have non-human persons. This again seems to be rather a grey area, for people disagree about whether intelligent machines would be persons. But it is quite widely thought that any being which can consider abstract conceptual questions, which has a sense of moral responsibility, which can feel itself to be under obligation, to be guilty for wrong-doing and capable of doing things on purpose, is properly called a person. If there is a spiritual or non-embodied being with the full set of these properties, it would seem quite reasonable to call it a person, even if it had no genetic structure, no gender and no physical embodiment. If there can be spiritual beings at all, it seems reasonable to think that they can be persons, and that their personhood would consist in their possessing at least a reasonable number of the rational and moral properties that human persons typically possess.

In asking whether God is a person, one is asking whether God possesses the sort of rational and moral properties that human persons possess. At first sight, it may seem obvious that the God referred to in the Bible is a person. God is pleased with the smell of sacrifices; God sometimes repents of what he does; God walks and talks with Abram; and God has thoughts and purposes. There is no doubt that God is spoken of as a person. But there are some Biblical statements which make one pause in this belief. God is also said to be unlike anything that is created; God cannot be seen by human eyes; no image can be made of God. The anthropomorphic descriptions of God, giving him eyes, feet and body, are so heavily qualified that it seems clear they must be taken as metaphorical. That is, they are literally false, though they convey something true about God in a form humans can understand – as long as they do not misunderstand, by taking them literally.

Few Christians would seriously suppose that God the Father has a physical body, or that God is literally father, in the sense of being a male carrier of human genes. Such statements are readily characterised as metaphor. But is it any less metaphorical to speak of God as a non-embodied mind? The Church Fathers very rarely speak of God as a cosmic mind (*nous*); and if the physical properties ascribed to God in the Bible should be taken as metaphorical because of God's transcendence of all human images, why should not the mental properties also be taken as metaphorical, because of God's transcendence of all human concepts?

The obvious reply is that God cannot transcend *all* human concepts, since then nothing at all could be said of God; not even that God exists. Some concepts must apply to God in a literal sense, or we would literally not know what we were talking about. And it does seem that among the things we must say literally of God are such things as that God knows all things, God cares about the good of creatures and God freely gives good things to those who love him. Knowing, caring and freely giving are all things that persons do; so does it not follow immediately that God is a person?

It does not, and the mistake in thinking that it does can very readily be shown. Suppose I suggest that possessing weight, position and velocity are properties that molecules have; that I possess weight, position and velocity; and that therefore I am a molecule. The fallacy is clear. It does not follow that because two objects possess the same kinds of property, they are therefore objects of the same kind. It all depends upon what other properties they possess. Persons are capable of knowing, caring and giving. So is God. But it does not follow that God is a person; for other things than persons may possess such properties. To put it briefly, God may possess person-properties without thereby being a person.

It may be objected that, if I possess weight, I may not be a molecule, but I am at least a physical object, for while not everything that has weight is a molecule, everything that has weight is necessarily a physical object. I have now made that an analytical statement; only physical objects have weight; so anything with that property is, by definition, a physical object. Similarly with God, if it is the case that only persons have knowledge (that is, I call something a person if and only if it has knowledge, or if it is a member of the class of things which have knowledge), and if God has knowledge, then God is a person.

The argument is now valid; but only because I have made it a matter of definition that anything which knows is a person, a member of the class of persons. The question is whether such a definition is plausible. It is almost certainly not, as the following case shows. When I say that anything which has weight is a physical object, I mean that it is a sufficient condition of being a physical object that something has weight. So, if I define it so that anything which has knowledge is a person, I mean that it is a sufficient condition of being a person that something has knowledge. Many animals have knowledge; but we would not ordinarily call them persons, because they lack some other properties (perhaps the capacity for abstract thought or for free moral action) that we consider necessary conditions for being a person.

In general, if one tries to list the sufficient conditions for being a person, one is immediately involved in all those disputes about grey areas which I have briefly mentioned. Suppose one takes it that a sufficient condition is that one is member of the class of things which is a child of human parents, and is capable of abstract thought, emotional response and moral agency. God most certainly would not fall under such a definition.

Suppose one drops the requirement of being a child of human parents. Is God capable of abstract thought? Almost certainly not. God's thoughts are not our thoughts. We form thoughts by abstracting features from sense-perceptions, going through laborious processes of deduction and inference and rehearsing long chains of argument in the words of some natural language. Divine knowledge is complete and intuitive, not abstract and discursive. It does not take place in concepts, let alone some human language (not even Hebrew or Greek). Whatever we mean when we say God thinks, we do not mean that he deploys concepts as we do. We probably mean something like the thought that God has perfect knowledge. But is that something that persons have? Not any persons we know about, if by a person we really do mean a rational (i.e. an inferring, calculating) agent. Strange as it may seem, one good reason for saying God is not a person is that God lacks some of the necessary conditions for calling something a person; and the person-properties God does possess are not sufficient for calling God a person.

This is true also of the properties of emotional response and moral agency, at least for reasonably traditional theists. The impassibility of God is well-entrenched in Christian tradition. And even if one does wish God somehow to share in human feelings, even in the Divine nature, it would be no excellence in God to react as human beings do, in shock, horror, despair, anger and resentment, to what happens in the world. Again, the degree of difference between Divine feelings, if there are any, and human feelings, is so great that there is an oddity about thinking of them as belonging to the same kind of thing.

It is equally odd to think of God as a moral agent, under obligation, trying to do what is right, and to be applauded for effort when he succeeds. Whatever the relation between God and the moral law, it is not such that God can be said to be under obligation to obey the law. For most theists, God is necessarily good, and is unable to do evil. He is not therefore to be praised for being a good moral agent (when he might easily have been an evil one), but for giving the particular good things he has given to the particular people to whom he has given them – things he might not have done. God may be free, but he is not peccable; and in that respect he is quite different from what we ordinarily call a moral agent.

It may be conceded that God fails to meet the sufficient conditions of being a person, in the sense in which humans are persons. But he still meets some of the necessary conditions for being a person – he knows, wills and acts. Would it not therefore be most adequate to say that God is a person, in an extended sense of the word? This amounts to saying that some main properties that apply to persons also apply to God, in an extended sense. Terms expressing these properties may literally apply to God and thus provide the requisite description for identifying what sort of things God is. Precisely at this point, however, a major doubt arises. Even if some key person-properties literally apply to God in an extended sense, do they provide the important core of a description which enables us to say with some adequacy what God is?

Consider the case of a human person. It is undoubtedly the case that some key physical-object properties literally apply to human persons. Such persons possess weight, position and velocity; they are indeed physical objects. But it would be very misleading, if asked what sort of thing a human person was, to say that it is a physical object. Human persons are normally physical objects, though perhaps not essentially so (if they exist after death, they are certainly not essentially so). And to say that they are physical objects is to omit precisely what is of importance about human personhood, their conscious rational agency. It would, then, be very misleading to say that a human person is a physical object. It would be better to say that a human person is a rational agent which normally, or perhaps even essentially for some of the time, but not necessarily for all the time, possesses physical properties.

In a similar way, it may be very misleading to say that God is a person, just because God possesses person-properties. If some person-properties literally apply to him, he will indeed be personal; but to say that is not to say what sort of thing God is. What is important about God is that God is a supremely perfect being, the creator of everything other than itself. God is the sole independent and self-existent reality, of supreme unrestricted consciousness and bliss. Just as things which are more than physical objects can possess physical properties, so God can be more than a person, but possess person-properties. At least some of God's person-properties will only be possessed in relation to the created world – his knowledge of and care for creatures and his response to them. So, if the created world is not essential to God, the possession of those properties is not essential to God either. Some properties are essential to God; but they are basically the properties of self-existence, metaphysical perfection and ultimate causal priority over all things. Persons, as we know them, possess none of these attributes. So our choice is between saying that God is a quite unique sort of person, and that he is not a person at all, though he possesses many person-properties.

There may not seem to be much to choose between these alternative descriptions. But I think there are four main reasons for denying that God is a person which are strongly rooted in the Christian tradition. First there is the belief in Divine ineffability. I have said, this cannot mean that we know nothing at all about God. There must be certain things we can say which are literally true of God, by means of which we can identify what God is. To say that God is ineffable is to say that the essential nature of God, that which is truly definitive of what God is, is beyond the range of any human concepts. To use a distinction formulated by the Cappadocian Fathers, we can identify god in terms of Divine *energeia*, the Divine activities. But the Divine *ousia*, the Divine essence, is not only hard for us to understand, it is totally beyond the range of our mental capacities. It is the same God who is known in his activities and hidden from conceptual knowledge in his being. If one asks how it is known that there is a hidden Divine essence, and that it is that essence which appears to us in the Divine activities, the answer is, from revelation and from experience of contemplative prayer. God's revelation to Moses not only revealed that it was God who spoke, and who appeared truly under certain personal attributes; but also that there was that in God, and the most essential and definitive part, which did not appear; which was forever hidden and could only be grasped by a sort of wordless communion. This is not the place to defend this conception of God. But it is clear enough that it is a central part of the Orthodox and Catholic interpretations of God's self-revelation, and it places God far beyond any limited conceptual categories, including, obviously, that of 'being a person.' From such a viewpoint, a person concept of God is just a subtle form of anthropomorphism; and it derogates from the mystery, the infinity and the ineffability of the Divine nature in an undesirable way.

This has its effects on prayer and spirituality. Those who see God as a person are likely to see prayer as primarily a matter of conversing with, or being in personal relation with, one who is other and greater than themselves. Those who see God as the ineffable origin of all things are more likely to see prayer as primarily a matter of achieving a wordless participation in that uncomprehended infinity. Both words and models of interpersonal relationship are apt to be regarded as very partial, even if correct, forms of conceiving the relation of God and rational creatures, which aims ideally at a union beyond knowledge. Perhaps these are just alternative paths of spirituality. If they are, the contemplative model sponsored by the doctrine of ineffability is just as deeply rooted in Christian tradition as the personal relationship model. Perhaps both are needed for an adequate view. The Father of Our Lord Jesus Christ is also the High and Holy One inhabiting eternity whom no human eye can see and no human mind conceive.

A second reason for denying that God is a person is based on a perception that the relation of persons to one another is a relation of distinct beings of the same sort. However closely persons come together, they remain distinct; each person is alone, and each must respect the 'apartness' of the other. But the relation of God and the soul is not like that. God is closer to the heart of each of us than any other person can ever be. Indeed, God, in the *hypostasis* of the Spirit, is within us, uniting us to himself by giving us a share in his being. The person model is too 'external' to cope with much Christian imagery which uses models of inclusion and union. We are in Christ, and Christ is in us. We are to be one, as Christ is one with the Father. God's presence within us is much closer and more intimate than that of one person relating to another. Here again, much Christian spirituality requires us to go beyond thinking of God as a person in relation to us, and asks us also to think of God as present and at work within us, as the true centre of our own beings. This transcends and complements the person model, without altogether contradicting it.

The third and fourth reasons for regarding a person model as too partial and restrictive are to be found in the specifically Christian doctrines of the Trinity and the incarnation. It is well known that orthodox Christianity holds that God is three persons in one substance. Jesus Christ is a person; but he is only one of three; so any view which sees God simply as a person is too Unitarian for the orthodox tradition. I am not suggesting that *hypostasis* means 'person,' in any sense so far construed in this essay. But it does convey the idea of three subsistent beings, of whom Christ is one, inseparably united in a unitary reality which includes them within itself. It seems fairly clear that if God really is Trinitarian in being, to construe him as 'a person' will be a very partial view of a reality far greater and more mysterious.

Similarly, a person concept of God seems constrained to interpret the incarnation as the enfleshment of the Divine person in a human person. It is then hardly to avoid the idea that either the Divine mind will simply replace the human mind, or that one will have two minds locked in a sort of schizophrenic relationship. These views have always been regarded as unsatisfactory, since it has been held important both to assert the human reality of Jesus' mind and to deny that there are two persons present in the incarnate Lord. However difficult it is to construe this situation, it moves one away from thinking of God as a person of the same sort as a human person, however much greater God is. If one thinks of God as a totally different sort of thing from a human person or mind, it is less difficult to think of that ineffable Divine reality, in one of its *hypostases,* assuming a complete human person to itself. For there is no battle of two persons for supremacy. There is the infinite Divine reality and a finite human person, two quite different sorts of reality, and the assertion of an indissoluble union between them. A fairly traditional view of incarnation therefore inclines one further to deny that God is a person, precisely to support the intelligibility of the contention that God can manifest his being most fully in space and time in the form of a person.

The conclusion of these reflections is that God may be properly manifested in a person; that he may be truly thought of as a person; and that he may be related to as a person in prayer. Yet God is as far beyond being a person as the infinite is beyond the infinite. And, in the Christian tradition, we may better say that God can be worshipped as Father, seen in the life of Jesus, and experienced as the power of the Spirit; so that the Divine being both includes and transcends these different personal forms in a reality which may best be described as supra-personal and utterly unique in kind.

This having been said, one can return to the alleged contrast between East and West with which I began, and ask if the gap is really as wide as it is sometimes made to appear. The standard interpretation of the *Upanishads,* the most important part of basic Hindu scripture, is that there is only one self-existent absolute reality, of supreme consciousness and bliss. It is wholly beyond description, but it appears, for the sake of its devotees, as a personal Lord of glory, possessing all the properties which belong to personal perfection. Moreover, when the believer, through intense meditation, penetrates beyond his or her individual personality and centre of agency and enjoyment, there is to be found in the innermost cave of the heart a Self which is unborn, unchanging and deathless; and that is in fact the supreme Reality itself, which therefore lies at the true heart of every person, waiting to be found.

Is this, I wonder, rightly construed as an impersonal monism which contrasts strongly with the personal theism of the West; or is it very much the same thing in a rather different dress? Is this alleged Western personal theism rather the result of neglecting a great part of the Christian tradition, and adopting a much too anthropomorphic and relational view of the God who is infinite and ineffable in being, and present at the heart of all created things, which he wills to unite to himself in Christ, thus sanctifying the whole of creation? My question is obviously rhetorical and my own preference must be clear. But it is true that the supra-personal view, as I would prefer to call it, can understate the ethical challenge of theism, and that it can miss the vital element of personal devotion which a more personalistic conception stresses. Perhaps what is needed, then, is the constant interplay and dialogue of these conceptions, so that each can complement and criticise the other, in that process of dialectic which always reminds us of the importance of seeking the truth and the danger of ever claiming that our search is at an end.

6

Cosmos and Kenosis

[In the progress of love] each step is a precarious step into the unknown, in which each triumph contains new potential for tragedy, and each tragedy can be redeemed into a wider triumph.

Love's Endeavour, Love's Expense, p. 63

The theology of kenosis is associated primarily with the work of some Lutheran theologians in Germany and with Charles Gore in England. In a way that has not always been noticed, it posed a radical challenge to the traditional concept of God, which had been developed by a long line of Christian theologians, most notably perhaps Augustine, Anselm, and Aquinas.

The traditional concept of God in Christianity is that God is eternal, in the sense of being timeless – that is, without temporal relation to anything in time, and without internal relations of a temporal nature. It follows from this that God is strictly immutable. Whatever happens in the created cosmos makes no difference to God, and does not change God in any way. The cosmos is created by a non-temporal act, and God creates every moment of time, from first to last, in one and the same act of intentional causation.

This in turn entails that the incarnation of the second hypostasis of the Triune being of God is effected by God in the very same non-temporal act by which God also creates and consummates the created order. The incarnation causes no change in God, but lies in a particular relation of the created nature of Jesus to the creator. It is not literally true that 'the Word became flesh' (John 1:14), since the eternal Word cannot become anything. It must always remain timelessly and changelessly what it is. The situation is rather that the human nature of Jesus has a unique relation to the eternal Word, a relation of enosis, unity, by which it expresses in time the nature of the Word and manifests in a uniquely direct way the salvific intentions of the Triune God. The human nature is said to be 'assumed' by the divine person of the Word, but exactly what that assumption consists in remains a mystery of faith. While it can be imagined as a possibility, the human mind cannot gain a clear comprehension of it.

Important points for the traditional account are that the incarnation causes no change in the nature of God, and that it is not a new idea which occurred to God subsequently to his creating the universe. It is part of the one creative divine act, and thus may rightly be said to have been willed from the beginning of creation.

The nineteenth-century Lutheran idea[1] of kenosis radically challenged this traditional account. Basing their theology of incarnation on Philippians 2:7 ('Christ Jesus, though he was in the form of God ...emptied himself, taking the form of a servant'), kenotic theologians held that the incarnation brought about a radical change in the eternal Word. The Word, being in the form of God, is properly omnipotent, omniscient, and perfectly good. When the Word becomes flesh, however, he empties himself of some of these divine attributes. Generally speaking, when the Word takes the form of a man, he gives up omnipotence and omniscience. He actually renounces those divine properties, though he receives them back from the Father after the ascension.

It may seem that Jesus would at least retain the divine property of perfect goodness, and many kenotic theologians held that the Word retains the 'moral attributes' of God. But even that is doubtful. For divine goodness is such that God is incapable of sin, not subject to obligation and not subject to temptation. But even the greatest human goodness is capable of sin, even if it never actually sins. It is subject to obligation and it can be tempted, as Jesus was. In that case, Jesus as the incarnate Word would not even retain the property of divine goodness. He might possess perfect human goodness, but that would be different in kind from the divine goodness, which is not capable of sin or obligation. In the same way, Jesus might possess the greatest possible human power and knowledge, but this would not be divine omnipotence and omniscience, which are outside the reach of human nature.

So it was held that if God is truly to become man, he must set aside or radically curtail his divine properties. Such properties are retained, how-

1 Jurgen Moltmann says something about earlier Lutheran theologians in 'God's kenosis in the creation and consummation' in *The Work of Love: Creation As Kenosis*. J. C. Polkinghorne (ed.) (London: SPCK, 2001).

ever, by the Father and by the Holy Spirit, and can be restored to Christ at the proper time. Such a kenotic view entails that there is change in God, and therefore that there is time, which alone makes change possible, in God. If the Word really became a human being, it also entails that there is suffering in God, so that God is passible, changed by what happens in the created cosmos.

For the traditional view, the divine nature does not suffer, though it can be said that 'God suffers', in the sense that the human nature which is assumed by the Word suffers. For the kenotic view, it is not the case that a human nature is assumed by an eternal Word. The Word really changes and limits himself to become human, and so really suffers and dies as human, before taking up his divine properties again (if, indeed, he can ever really do that so long as he remains in human form).

Why did the Lutheran theologians make this change in the concept of God? Part of the impetus for a kenotic Christology lies in the desire to preserve the sense that God enters fully into the human situation, understands it from the inside, and shares the human condition. Many people have the feeling that if a changeless God simply assumes a human nature to the divine nature, the sense in which God shares in human suffering is purely verbal, and that something of the pathos and depth of the incarnation is lost. Luther's strong sense of the importance of the passion and the cross in Christianity led him to an insistence that the divine nature of the Word must truly share in suffering, and thus enter fully into the human situation.

Another reason for adopting a kenotic Christology is, to put it in the broadest theological terms, the rejection of a Platonic concept of God. In Platonic philosophy the timeless is superior to the temporal, the changeless to the changing, and the intelligible and universal is superior to the material and particular. The classical Christian concept of God was constructed on Platonic lines, so that God was seen as timeless, changeless, intelligible, and universal (a subsistent Form). In modern times Platonism has been generally rejected as a worldview. Since the rise of the sciences, especially, the material and particular have been seen as the truly 'real', while the universal is an abstraction. So time and change, aspects of the material, become important aspects of reality, not simply illusory or merely apparent.

Interestingly, there has been a partial reversal of this change in modern cosmology. Quantum cosmologists are apt to talk of time and space as just four dimensions of a multidimensional reality in which time does not 'flow', and timelessness becomes again the ultimate reality, of which the 'arrow of time' is a phenomenal 'arrow of time' is a phenomenal appearance. This remains a highly controversial topic, but it must be noted that these quasi-Platonic speculations do not usually find much use for the notion of God, positing instead a myth of self-existent mathematical structures (quantum fluctuations) without intrinsic value or purpose. It is Platonism without 'the Good', and therefore of little theological help. In the early modern period, however (in Newtonian physics, for example), the existence of particulars in an objectively existing time was widely accepted as characterizing ultimate reality. Partly in accordance with such views, some Protestant, especially Lutheran, theologians developed a much more personalist view of God, which would be free of Platonic influences.

This is associated also with a greater stress, since the Renaissance, on human freedom, creativity, and individuality. Individuals are seen as having an ultimate moral freedom, a uniqueness that cannot be dissolved into some greater cosmic unity, and a genuine creativity that can change the world, either for better or for worse. In the light of such changes in worldview, God is reconceived as the most creative, free, changing, and individual reality, rather than being seen as a timeless pure Form.

All these changes worked together to produce a kenotic view of God and of the incarnation, particularly in Lutheran theology. In that tradition, the main views developed. The Tubingen school held that the incarnate Word possesses the divine attributes but does not use them. Such possession without manifestation is sometimes called krypsis (hiding). The Giessen theologians held, more radically, that the logos incarnate emptied himself of the divine attributes – that is, kenosis.

Against the kenotic view, traditional theologians feel that for God, even for the second hypostasis of a Triune God, to lose some essential divine properties, even temporarily, is simply for God to cease to be God, and to change into something else, so that proper worship for the divine Word, which is due to him even in his incarnate state, is undermined. The krypsis view is not subject to this criticism, though it is widely rejected on the ground that it involves some form of change in God.

What is at stake in this dispute? I would be hesitant to draw immediate links between such theories and Christian practice. Yet some link might be drawn between an ideal of god as an impassible changeless being and a

Christian practice that seeks the cultivation of an attitude of impassibility and disconnection from temporal things as ideals of human life. And a link might be drawn between the ideal of God as a relational, passionate being and a Christian practice that seeks to be involved creatively in worldly action with others, and that sees change in terms of positive possibility.

In any case I think that kenotic theologians are right in thinking that God truly shares in the human condition, and so feels the suffering of every suffering creature, as well as sharing the joy of every finite happiness. But if that is so, one might well think that the divine sharing in finite experience and action cannot be confined to just one case on the planet earth, the case of Jesus. God must share in all finite experience, wherever in the universe it is. Such sharing does not require incarnation as its necessary condition. What it requires is that God truly feels, by a direct and empathetic apprehension, every experience that creatures have. One may feel such a thing is involved in the possession of true omniscience – not merely a factual registering by God that something is the case, but God's acquaintance with what each experience is like.

For classical notions of divine omniscience, God's knowledge consists of a sort of intellectual knowledge of every true proposition. It is quasi-propositional knowledge, and excludes feeling or passion, which were regarded as defects in a perfect being. Nevertheless, God was said to exist in a state of perfect bliss, and so some analogy to feeling existed in God. It just was not considered to be of cognitive significance, and it was certainly not dependent upon the world in any way.

It may well be thought, however, that no being is truly omniscient if it lacks knowledge of what it feels like to experience suffering or happiness. If I know that the proposition 'You are in pain' is true, but I do not know what it feels for you to be in pain, then there is something I do not know – and that something, you may well think is the most important thing of all. If that is so, then any omniscient being must know what it feels like for creatures to feel as they do. That may be called affective knowledge, a much more involving and intense thing than propositional knowledge.

The classical theist may say that it is just not possible for God to know what pains feel like (at least in the divine nature). God can only have propositional, not affective, knowledge. It is noteworthy that classical theologians do place restrictions on what is possible for God at this point. Omniscience, even for the classical theologian must be interpreted to mean: knowledge of everything that is logically possible for a being with the divine nature to know. There is no such thing as logically unqualified omniscience. We all place restrictions on divine possibilities at some point (that will become important when considering divine omnipotence). But are there really good reasons for denying the possibility of divine affective knowledge? I think the main reason offered is that it would be a defect for a maximally valuable being to feel pain, even by empathetic knowledge. But that is precisely what has been strongly questioned in post-nineteenth-century theology.

The crucial nature of the change is this: in classical theories, God is considered in isolation, as it were, as a being of completely self-contained perfection. Perfection is a state of God, whatever else exists or occurs, and it cannot suffer diminution or change in any way. God is exclusively infinite and perfect. All that is finite or imperfect lies outside of God, and does not affect God in anyway. For post-classical theories (and Hegel is perhaps the major influence here), God is inclusively infinite, and the divine perfection must include relationship to whatever other realities exist. So God relates to finite creatures in ways which make the divine reality different than it would have been had there been no such creatures. For such a more relational or participative view of God, it would be an imperfection not to know affectively what creaturely experiences are like. Any being that co-exists with suffering creatures would be less perfect if it failed to have affective knowledge of what those creatures experience. If one takes that seriously, then one may say that not just the incarnation, but the creation of conscious and rational beings itself is a kenotic act on God's part. For it will involve a giving up of pure divine bliss, and accepting many experiences of pain and suffering. It will involve a giving up of complete control, and accepting the freedom of created beings to make their own decisions, however misdirected. It will involve giving up complete knowledge, and accepting that much about the future must be unknown until it is determined by the actions of creatures. These are real limitations, and this may be thought of as a sort of kenosis, a giving up of some great goods, in order that free creatures may exist in independence, community, and creativity.

This is not, however, kenosis in the sense of giving up divine properties in order just to allow others to possess the values of freedom and community. It is also a way of adding new and distinctive values to the divine being itself. For the creation of finite agents with a real degree of autonomy adds to God himself the possibility of cooperating with them in creative action, of delighting in their existence and in the values they bring into being, and of bringing the cosmic process to a final consummation in which all the values it has brought forth in the long course of its existence will be conserved and apprehended in God forever.

In other words, this sort of kenosis is not just self-giving. It is also, and equally importantly, a self-realisation, a way in which God realises possibilities that are eternally present in the divine being, and comes to experience new forms of value that otherwise would never have been actualised. When God gives up pure bliss, he obtains in return many new sorts of values that could only be actualised in a cosmic process from which finite agents emerge. When God gives up total control, he obtains relationship in community with creatures. When God gives up full knowledge of the future, he obtains the possibility of genuinely new creativity, undetermined even by his own previous nature.

By self-limitation, God obtains many new sorts of values that would not otherwise be obtainable. Of course, these values are mixed with many sorts of disvalues. Along with the values finite agents create are all the forms of suffering they endure. Along with the positive cooperation God can experience with finite agents, are the many forms of obstruction to the divine will that such agents realise. Along with new creativity go possibilities for destruction and conflict within the cosmos. Nevertheless, theists are committed to believing that the good will far outweigh the bad, and that the bad can itself in some way be redeemed, both in the experience of God and, ultimately, for the creatures God can unite to the divine experience.

God, on this view, does not just limit the divine being in order that free finite agents might exist. God realises, makes actual, aspects of the divine being that otherwise would have remained potential. Entering into relationship and communion, and cooperating in realizing new forms of finite value, are realisations of great values in and for the divine nature itself. Perhaps some such realisation is essential to the divine nature, so that God necessarily creates other personal agents. If one thinks that 'God is love' (1 John 4: 16), that love is an essential property of the divine nature, and that love can only be properly exercised in relation to others who are free to reciprocate love or not, then the creation of some universe containing free finite agents seems to be an implication of the divine nature. However, trying to say what is or is not essential to the divine nature is a rather presumptuous exercise, and perhaps the most one can do here is to draw attention to a range of implications that follow from various interpretations of the idea of God.

Some would hold that God could have remained in unchanging bliss, all-determining power, and unrestricted knowledge, but freely chose not to do so in order to create a universe of finite persons. Some would hold that God can realise love adequately in the inner relationships of the persons of the Trinity, but chooses to realise a different form of love in relation to creatures. And some would hold that a truly loving God must create a universe of genuinely other persons in order to realise the essential divine nature. It is hard to know how to decide what is essential to the divine nature. Perhaps we could be content to say that God certainly has the greatest possible power and knowledge that any being could have, and has in fact chosen to realise it in the creation of a universe of free persons which entails certain restrictions on those powers – restrictions that are necessary to enable genuinely free finite persons to exist.

Those restrictions are such that some actual and much possible suffering is necessarily entailed in creation. The type and extent of suffering will depend largely on the choices free creatures make, though some element of suffering seems inevitable in any universe in which there is an evolutionary emergence of potentially self-aware and self-directing agents. Having very little knowledge of the inner structure of the physical cosmos, and even less knowledge of the essential nature of God, we are quite unable to say just what those necessities are that cause conflict and suffering to arise in the world. We view them as necessities because it is unacceptable to say that God would positively intend suffering to exist, and yet all suffering must arise from the divine nature as its only ultimate source. We are thus logically compelled to say that while all suffering arises from God, it must do so, not as intended by God, but as necessarily implied in the sort of universe God has created – a universe in which many great goods exist that otherwise could not have existed, and in which all evil will ultimately be overcome by divine goodness, which is what God positively intends.

This picture involves a double reversal of the classical view that God is wholly immutable. God limits the divine properties in order that a cosmos of free finite agents should exist. But God thereby realises new aspects of the divine nature as God enters into real relationship with creatures. God not only suffers new things. God also enjoys and delights in new things. And in the end all those good things are to be conserved in God, and perhaps shared with creatures, forever. There is an addition to the divine being as well as a limitation of it, and the two are essentially bound together. So if we can speak of a kenosis in God, a renunciation of his absolute and unmixed perfection, we must also speak of a pleroma, or fulfillment, in God, by which new forms of perfection are added by creatures to the divine being.

This is in accordance with the continuation of the passage in Philippians 2:5–11, which says that, because of Christ's self-emptying, 'God has highly exalted him.' The moment of self-emptying is followed by the moment of divine exaltation, in which the whole of creation is ultimately to be included (Eph. 1:10).

This form of kenosis is not a loss of such essential divine properties as omnipotence and omniscience. Indeed, it is the way in which they are exercised. There is nothing wrong with speaking of 'kenosis', as long as it is understood to mean a self-limitation that makes possible new forms of divine glory. It may seem that God could exist in perfect bliss, but in fact God has affective knowledge of a world in which pain and suffering exist. It may seem that God could control all things unilaterally, but in fact God acts in such a way as to make creaturely freedom possible. It may seem that God could know the future completely and in every detail, but in fact God renounces such knowledge in order to let creaturely creativity exist. There are necessities of the divine nature which mean that God cannot exist in a state of unmixed bliss, of all-determining power and unrestricted knowledge, if there is to be a world of free and creative personal agents.

God wills to realise the divine nature in creation, relationship, and cooperation. Without such a willed self-realisation God would not be the God known to be revealed in Jesus. Whether or not there was a real alternative to some such creation, we have no way of telling. Even if there was not, one can reasonably say that God truly wills creation. For 'willing' does not need to imply some alternative that might have been willed instead. Such willing may itself be, as the classical tradition affirmed, an essential part of the divine nature, which is necessarily what it is. Thus God may will kenosis, not as something that might not have been willed, but as something that truly expresses the divine nature as love.

It may be held that such a view of kenosis, not as divine loss but as divinely willed restraint, is a more accurate reflection of the passage in Philippians. For what that passage says is not that Jesus gave up some of his divine or human attributes, but that he did not insist on status and power. Instead, he became a servant, and 'humbled himself.' That is a matter, not primarily of what attributes one has, but of how one exercises them. Jesus could perhaps have claimed instant obedience, and ordered the apostles to serve him. Instead, he washed their feet and gave his life for them. The New Testament scholar James Dunn has proposed an influential interpretation of the Philippians passage which denies that it refers to some decision of a pre-existing Christ, deciding to become incarnate on earth. Rather, he argues, it speaks only of the human Jesus who, like the first Adam, had the form of God by being a perfect image of God. The passage then would be asserting that Jesus did not take advantage of his superiority over virtually all other humans in status and ability. Instead, he showed what the image of God truly is by serving others, by healing, forgiving, and submitting in love to the power of evil.

The lesson of kenosis is a moral one. It does not speak of a renunciation of ontological powers, but of a way of exercising those powers in love rather than in pride. This is how Jesus' human life was lived, and it gives a true picture of the nature of the God who seeks to help humans in love rather than to dominate them. Whether one accepts Dunn's interpretation or the more traditional view that the Philippians passage is about the eternal Word becoming flesh, the important point remains that one is not speaking so much of a literal renunciation of certain divine powers, but of the choice of a way of exercising those powers that empowers creatures to enter into conscious relationship with God. This is a sort of self-limitation, but one that I have suggested might be seen as both divinely willed and as necessarily implicit in the divine nature. If this is a true picture of God, one might say that God does not compel all rational creatures to obey him, but seeks by the persuasion of love to draw them to himself. Kenosis, then, belongs to the creation of rational creatures even before it belongs to incarnation. And because rational creatures are integral parts of the physical universe, that universe must from the first possess an autonomy and openness that will prepare an appropriate environment in which free and rational creatures can emerge. One can thus see a form of kenosis in the creation of the universe, inasmuch as God restrains the divine power to allow an autonomous universe to develop. There is a cosmological self-limitation of infinite divine power, which makes possible the existence of an autonomous cosmos wherein freedom and creativity can in due course emerge and flourish, but in which they can also be impeded by the existence of communities of finite created agents.

The incarnation is not a necessary condition of cosmic kenosis. God can will to cooperate with creatures, share in their experiences, and inspire their new and creative actions, whether, or not there is an incarnation. The Christian belief, however, is that God the Word did become incarnate as man, and that incarnation is an eminently appropriate form of divine self-revelation. The life of Jesus is important because it shows the nature of what God always and everywhere is. It is the revelation of the nature of God in a human person. The life of Jesus is not only the place where God acts in persuasive, self-giving love to draw creatures to the divine. It is the place where God's universal salvific action is disclosed in a paradigmatic way to human beings.

For this to be true, the life of Jesus must be plausibly seen to be completely informed and freely directed by the Spirit of God. There is here a sort of double kenosis – the kenosis of Jesus is that he empties himself of pride and egoism, so that he may be filled with the Spirit of God. The kenosis of God is that the divine being is emptied of perfect bliss and all-determining power, so that the passion of Jesus and the creative action of Jesus can become true expressions of the divine nature in time. Neither form of kenosis is a loss of essential human or divine attributes. In this mutual self-limitation one human life and the divine life are bound together in an ultimate and inexpressible way, so that they may be said to be one: Jesus is the Christ, the eternal Word of God in time.

This is not what has been usually called a kenotic christology, for the Word does not change into a man. In some ways it is more like the traditional christology, for which the Word assumes to itself a human nature. Yet what is different from the traditional view is that the Word is a passionate, related, and therefore temporal hypostasis of the divine being. In the life of Jesus, the Word obtains a clear and full expression within history. The kenosis of Jesus makes possible the manifestation at a particular point of earthly history of that cosmic kenosis of the divine being which makes creation itself possible.

The incarnation is also a specific act of God that accomplishes in a human person the saving destiny God wills for all. In Jesus there may be seen a threefold manifestation of the nature and activity of God in relation to the created universe. The first moment of this divine activity is kenosis, the self-limiting expression of divine power that brings it into relation with a universe containing finite moral agents. In this relation, God does not order all things by divine fiat, but seeks to help and empower moral agents to formulate and attain their own objectives, insofar as they promise to realise good. This means that God will have affective knowledge of forms of suffering and evil, which constitutes a real renunciation of unmixed divine bliss. It means that God will constitute the divine being in relation to others who may to some extent frustrate the divine will. This is a real form of self-limitation, even though it is a true expression and self-manifestation of the divine nature, not a renunciation of that nature.

Jesus' life of healing the sick, forgiving the guilt-ridden, befriending social outcasts, and undermining hypocrisy, is a very good image of the compassionate and persuasive love of God. Because of this disclosure, God can be worshipped not only as the all-powerful source and sustainer of all beings, but as a Father (or indeed a Mother) who cares for finite persons as his children, and wishes them to become fully conscious of his loving presence. In the moment of kenosis, God relates the divine being to creatures who have a proper autonomy and otherness, which it is the divine will not to infringe.

The second moment of the divine relation to the cosmos is that of enosis, a mysterious but intimate uniting of divine personhood and finite personhood, so that finite lives can become true images of the divine nature and mediators of divine power, so that divine and creaturely persons become one. It is through the activity of the Holy Spirit that God acts on this planet within human persons to transform them into transparent images and effective instruments of the divine being. In this relation, creatures do not remain as beings separate and distinct from their heavenly Father, however closely related to him they are in love and respect. Their lives are interpenetrated by the divine Spirit, so that they may, at their best, say with St Paul, 'Not I live, but Christ lives in me' (Gal. 2:20).

The Spirit that found exemplary fulfillment in Jesus Christ can also be in the lives of his disciples, to the extent that a person may find it almost impossible to distinguish what she does and what the Spirit does in her. The inward unity between divine and human was fully realised in the life of Jesus, but it is part of Christian faith to hope that it will be partly realised, at least, in the lives of all believers. God not only limits divine power to relate to finite persons as if he were a person (so Christians believe that God relates to us in and through the person of the risen Christ). God also actively empowers finite persons, so as to give them a share in the divine reconciling and redeeming activity in the creation. In the moment of enosis, exemplified supremely in the person of Jesus, God enters into the being of those who freely consent to such mediating action, and acts in and through them to make them living sacraments of the divine presence.

The third moment of the cosmic divine activity is theosis, that unity with or sharing in the divine life (2 Peter 1:4) which is the final purpose of God for creation. As the Spirit unites with human nature to effect the divine purposes in creation, so human nature is ultimately raised to find its final destiny in sharing in the glory of God. The Christian tradition embodies the view that the whole of creation is in some way to be consummated in a 'new creation'. It is not to be merely relegated to a forgotten and transcended past. It is not to be continued in the same entropic way. It is to be taken into the eternal life of God, and there transfigured into a new life. Paul describes that life as like wheat blossoming in the light of the sun, after its birth in the darkness of earth (1 Cor. 15). On that analogy, this cosmos is the soil in which the seeds of eternal life are sown. Its future will be unlike its present, and yet causally related to it – a consummation and not a cancellation of history.

It is extremely difficult for anyone to envisage such ultimate possibilities. But I can think of nothing more important for Christian faith in our day than to recover the truly cosmic sense of redemption that was characteristic both of the biblical writings and of the Church Fathers. Redemption will not be seen as the saving of a few human beings from the destruction of one small planet. It will be seen as a reconstituting of the whole cosmos in the presence of God, in a more glorious form. When Jesus proclaimed that the kingdom (the rule) of God was at hand, present and active in his own person, one way of understanding this is as an attempt to evoke a vision of each present moment as standing before the possibility of its own eternalization in God. For any theist, it is true that God knows each present moment in the most intimate way. But as each finite moment is taken into the divine experience, it is transformed so that its negative qualities are mitigated and its positive qualities enhanced by the wider context of the divine experience. God's experience is of the world seen in the light of eternity, and so God knows things as no other being is able to know.

Belief in theosis is belief that finite agents will be given a share in God's experience, so far as that is possible for them. They too will see temporal things in the light of eternity, and so see the events of history as having a purpose and pattern that is largely hidden in via. But this may still sound too much like a purely personal experience. It must be remembered that Christian belief is in the 'resurrection of the body'. It is not some form of disembodied experience of God that finite agents have. The forms of time and space themselves will be reiterated, but in a transformed way, free of decay and suffering. When the whole universe is so transformed that it manifests in an unrestricted way the beauty and goodness of God, and when personal beings, including human beings, are able to give conscious expression to this transformation, then the cosmos may indeed be said to share in the life of God.

For a Christian view, history is important. The resurrection world is not one that could just have been created perfect, without all the struggle and suffering that formed part of cosmic history. The resurrection world is precisely a world formed out of struggle and conflict, a world perfected and not simply a world created perfect.

It may not be the case, as some Indian traditions hold, that the cosmos is the body of God. It is perhaps too autonomous and its conscious agencies too self-willed for that. Yet its destiny is to be the body of God. For those who have lived and died with Christ will be raised in Christ (Col. 2:12). All things will be united in Christ (Eph. 1:10). Thus at that stage God will be all in all (1 Cor. 15:28), and there will no longer be a distinction between the church and the world. There will be no church, and no separated world. The cosmos will be fully integrated into the life of God, as the vehicle of divine action and the manifestation of divine glory. In the moment of theosis, the cosmos is transfigured to become the unrestricted manifestation of God's glory, and all rational creatures become the instruments of his praise.

God in Jesus foreshadows in one human person the divine purpose for all creation. But that purpose is to be gradually worked out in the history of this planet, by the inclusion of many persons within that divine-human unity. The Holy Spirit, forming the new community of the church, works in a new way, a way that is explicitly patterned on the life of Jesus, and incorporates people into 'the body of Christ'. Thus the new way of redemption that God begins in the incarnation is continued through the Holy Spirit in the life of the church. Even though the incarnation was not perhaps necessary for the realisation of God's purpose, it is in fact that way, and a richly appropriate way, in which God is carrying out that purpose on this planet. Kenosis is one important aspect of the realisation of that purpose. It gives a special and distinctive vision of the character of the creator, as one who leaves us free, shares in our freedom, and will fulfill that freedom in the conscious loving relationship to the divine. It also gives a powerful moral insight into the way in which creatures should seek to implement the divine purpose in their own lives.

There is a very definite cosmic vision implicit in a Christian view of creation as a kenotic and pleromal process. As the beginning of creation is kenosis, so the end or consummation of creation is theosis. God shares in the pain and permits the wayward freedom of creatures in order that, finally, creatures should share in the bliss and become vehicles of the truly creative freedom of the divine nature. It is that cosmic movement from divine self-emptying to creaturely fulfillment in God which is the sacred history of the cosmos, and, it seems to me, the deepest meaning of the Christian gospel for this planet in the middle of its journey through the mystery of time.

7

Creation and the Trinity

Theologians have tried in various ways to articulate the basic idea of a reality of supreme power and value, thought to reveal its nature in a special way in their own religious traditions. They broadly agree on the supreme perfections that are ascribable to God. Power, wisdom, knowledge, bliss, and compassion are ascribed to God in both Indian and Semitic traditions. There have nevertheless been many different ways of spelling out what such perfections imply, and how they relate to the universe. A common theme has been the desire to exclude from God any hint of imperfection or limitation. This has led to a concept of God which is strongly distinguished from time, finitude, suffering, ignorance, and passibility. God must be absolutely beyond change by any created being, an untouched and immutable reality. Yet in various ways, all religious traditions have had to account for change, suffering, development, and ignorance in the universe.

The Buddhist schools, which have not been treated in this volume,[1] in so far as they accept the existence of a pure reality of wisdom and compassion beyond space and time, make the strongest demarcation by denying any causal relation between such a reality and the realm of *samsara*. This world exists because of desire, and it is by the cessation of desire that the realm of changeless bliss will remain in its purity. Such a view preserves perfection in inviolable purity, though it excludes from the idea of the origin of the universe any action of a personal being. The Vedantic schools involve Brahman in time as the inner Self of all. In some

1 Keith Ward, *Religion and Creation* (Oxford: Clarendon Press, 1996).

manner, Brahman enters into finitude, ignorance, and suffering. Yet in itself it remains unchanged, and the goal of religious life is to realise one's inner unity with that unchanging reality. Aurobindo gives to the temporal process a positive role, as the expression of the relational and emergent being of Brahman.

Thus Brahman has a dual reality, being both infinite and time-transcending and temporally emergent. The relation between them is that the temporal necessarily manifests the timeless. The Vedantic view shares with neo-Platonism and with Hegelian philosophers a vision of the finite universe as eternally emanating from the timeless One. Where Brahman is the sole reality, suffering and ignorance must in a sense be properties of the Supreme itself, though they are somehow sublated in the completed and timeless experience of the One.

Theologians in the Semitic tradition began from a much firmer distinction between God, as Creator, and the created universe. They were thus inclined from the first to attribute suffering and ignorance to the finite created realm alone, and exclude it from the being of God. This tendency was strengthened by the influence of Greek philosophical ideas of divine perfection, which tended to separate the material world from the divine mind, as two distinct forms of reality. Jewish, Christian and Muslim philosophers classically developed a concept of divine perfection which saw it as timeless, immutable, simple, impassible, and untouched by suffering or real relationship to the created order.

I have suggested that belief in creation was always in tension with such a radical distinction between creator and creatures. The tension is seen at its sharpest in Islam, where, as Fazlur Rahman has put it, 'The theory of the eternity of the world is the hallmark of all Muslim philosophers except al-Kindi, while all theologians in Islam are voluntarists and place their entire weight on the side of God's power and will.'[2] An eternal emanation of the universe from God makes it possible to see the world as a sort of 'overflow' from the divine being, which leaves God truly unchanged. A contingently willed creation of space-time, however, introduces an active and contingent element into the divine being which suggests that the existence of the world makes a difference to God. The 'theologians', of

2 Fazlur Rahman, 'Ibn Sina's Theory of the God-World Relationship', in D. B. Burrell and B. McGinn (eds.), *God and Creation* (Notre Dame, Ind.: Notre Dame University Press, 1990), 51B.

course, did not admit such a contingent element in God, as they were, ironically, influenced by the philosophers to the extent that they could not see divine perfection as allowing any change (thus any temporality) at all. If the theologians had emancipated themselves further from the classical Greek philosophers, they might have achieved a different view of divine perfection.

A number of twentieth-century theologians, including those I have considered here – Iqbal, Heschel, and Barth – have sought precisely such a further emancipation. They stress, in different ways, a real relationship of God to creatures, in an empathetic and responsive fellowship with created persons. Such a stress, well rooted in the Semitic scriptures, makes possible a reconception of perfection as essentially involving creativity, affectivity, and relationship. The perfect is not the immutably solitary, excluding all finite limitations, but a supremely creative and affective reality which includes and transcends all finite goods. Its infinity is not a sheer boundlessness whose emptiness of content excludes every particular good, but an endlessly creative and universally inclusive infinity of values. Suffering and ignorance do not have to be ascribed to God since they may be properties of created beings, to which God can relate in appropriate ways without being subject to them, as creatures are. Of course, the theist must give some account of how suffering arises, and of how a supremely perfect being will respond to it.

In the Semitic traditions, suffering is in general attributed to a failure or corruption of created wills, and God, while permitting it for the sake of an end which is good, will eventually eliminate it from creation to enable the purpose of creating finite goods to be fully realised. Judaism, Christianity, and Islam propose diverse views of how God, as perfect being, responds creatively to the corruption of created wills, and of how such corruption can be overcome. Contemporary theologians in each faith, however, are much more open than were classical theologians to seeing God as permitting real creaturely freedom, as responding affectively, in sorrow as well as in delight, to created beings, and as exhibiting a co-operative creativity in working out the divine purposes for good in the world.

The Necessity of Creation

A Christian theologian might find that such a more dynamic and inclusive idea of divine infinity and perfection is particularly well suited to articulate the distinctive Christian idea of God as Trinity. For the Christian gospel is that God enters into time ('becomes incarnate'), shares in human suffering so as to liberate human wills from corruption, and continues to act inwardly and by the persuasion of love in order to make human persons sharers in the divine being, and to make human lives the vehicles and mediators of the divine life. God is manifest in Christ as redemptive love, and that must be the central image which governs Christian reflection about the divine being.

It may be an essential part of the divine nature to be loving. If that is so, it will be essential to God to create beings other than the divine self, with which God can enter into fellowship, as a way of realizing the divine nature in creative and relational action. This is no lack in God, but it is to say that the divine nature is essentially self-expressing – which means that it is essentially other-creating and unitively loving. If it is better for God to be merely capable of loving, it will follow that this is the case.

Paul Helm, in commenting on a previous book of mine, attributes to me the view that God must create a universe if God is to be loving, together with the view that there is no necessity for God to create the universe.[3] He suggests that this is a contradictory position; but it is not, as long as one holds that God is contingently loving. My way of construing this was to hold that God is essentially good, but, since creation is contingent, that divine goodness should relate to others in love is contingent.[4] God would have been good without any universe, but could only be loving with one. It is good that God is actually loving; and, of course, in a sense, God would be eternally loving, namely, in the sense that God would love the divine self wholly and, if God created a universe, would relate to it in love. But God was under no compulsion to realise that disposition, and thus would not be called actually loving with any degree of plausibility, just because God had the capacity to love under unrealised circumstances.

As Helm points out, we do not complain at the thought that God has to be good or wise or happy, that it is part of the divine nature to be so. So should it be a defect to create by necessity of one's nature? 'God eternally chooses this universe as the expression of his nature,' says Helm.[5] I suppose the hesitation is connected with a desire to give God as great a

3 Paul Helm, *Eternal God* (Oxford: Clarendon Press, 1988), 193.
4 Keith Ward, *Rational Theology and the Creativity of God* (Oxford: Basil Blackwell, 1982), 85 ff.
5 Helm, *Eternal God*, 193

sovereign freedom as possible. If God restricts the divine self in creation – by not knowing the future, by suffering? – then God must at least voluntarily do so. Perhaps it is also the thought that God must be self-sufficient without any universe, that God cannot depend upon us in any ultimate sense; so God could remain God without a universe.

I do not now think these arguments very strong. If God is not free to be evil or non-existent, why is it important that God be free not to create? As God is essentially good, so God may be essentially a loving creator; and one might expect that God would be, if God is the greatest conceivable being, and loving creativity is one of the greatest perfections. Nor does God's necessarily creating some universe render God self-existent. It is only that the divine self-existence would naturally, essentially, overflow into other forms of existence, and there is no defect in that, but a plenitude of actuality. Thus I am now inclined to think – though with a hesitation prompted by my reluctance to say that I really understand the divine nature – that some creation, and some disposition to creative activity and loving fellowship, necessarily actualised at some time, is necessary to God being what God is.

It need not be true that God always has to be related in love to creatures, as though there must always be non-divine sentient beings in creation (though angels have sometimes been so interpreted). For God is not necessitated to exercise all divine properties maximally – if this notion of a 'maximum' even makes any sense with regard to God's possible relations with creatures. It is rather that God's disposition to give the divine being in love, if it is a genuine disposition, must be actualised to some degree and in some way. It is the same with the divine creativity, which need not be unceasingly exercised, but must be exercised in some way. As far as this point is concerned, then, this may be the only universe God relates to in self-giving love, or there may be many or even an unlimited number. Naturally, we know of only this one, but perhaps we should not limit the divine being in thought, either by assuming it to be the only one, or by asserting categorically that God has to create, and love, beings just like us.

It may be that the specific kind of relational, suffering, reconciling love manifested in this universe is not an essential property of God, but something like a supererogatory power – one that it is good, but not essential, to manifest. However, if Christ is taken to disclose God as God truly is, as self-diffusive love, it seems reasonable to assert that some universe is a necessary expression of divine love, which will involve real relationship to what is other, sympathetic knowledge of the feelings of others, and creative response to the acts of others. It will therefore involve possibility and temporality as essential features of divine love.

The Idea of a Social Trinity

Classical theology accepts that love is an essential characteristic of God, but has often concluded that the Trinity provides the possibility of loving relationship within God, without having to posit the necessity of creation.[6] Yet it is obvious that, within the Trinitarian being of God, there is no real creation of another, and no unitive reconciliation of that other to God. For all the *hypostases* are one God. There can be no real otherness and no need of reconciliation. The Trinity may indeed reflect or prefigure in the nature of God itself those aspects of perfect being, other-creation and unitive reconciliation which will characterise the divine actions in universe. But there will still be no actual redemptive love of the other unless there is some created universe. A fully Christian view of perfection might show it to be, not a self-contemplating unalloyed and unaffected bliss, but a loving, passionate, and relational creativity.

Much contemporary Trinitarian thought deploys the notion of a 'social Trinity', thinking of God as a society of persons in loving relationship. One of the most persuasive accounts of such a 'plurality model' of the Trinity has been given by David Brown.[7] He proposes that we think of the persons of the Trinity as 'three distinct centres of consciousness, each with its own distinctive mental content'.[8] They act in necessary, indivisible, and full co-operation, and thus cannot conflict with one another. Each is an omnipotent, omniscient individual, though some have forms of action (e.g. the Spirit acts internally in human souls) and forms of experience (e.g. Jesus experiences suffering as human) that the others do not. This model enables one to think of God as a communion of persons, each of which is self-giving and constituted by relation to others. So one can think that 'God is Love', even without any relation to created reality. Relationships of giving, receiving, and sharing love exist within the divine being itself, whether or not there is any creation.

6 See Richard of St Victor, *De Trinitate*, bk. ii, ch. 14, ed. J. Ribaillier (Paris: Librairie Philosophique J. Vrin, 1958), 149.
7 David Brown, *The Divine Trinity* (London: Duckworth, 1985).
8 Ibid. 289.

Richard Swinburne develops a rather similar account, suggesting that there is a compelling reason, in the essential divine property of love, for the existence of a Trinity.[9] A loving being must create another to love, which should be of the same perfection as itself. Since it is the nature of love to share, those two divine individuals must generate a third. 'Love must share and love must co-operate in sharing',[10] so there is a good reason why there should be three and only three divine souls, which in their indivisibility constitute the being of God. For these views, there are three omnipotent, omniscient individuals, and together they enable God to be thought of as truly loving, even without any universe.

Attractive as this model seems, it has grave drawbacks. It seems to conflict with what Jesus selected as the most important commandment: 'The Lord our God, the Lord is one.'[11] As Brown concedes, his view could be put by saying that there are three gods, bound together in indivisible unity of action and purpose. This is very much like a form of polytheism; indeed, a rather cozy and harmonious polytheism. The model it relies upon is a community of rational persons, inextricably bound together in mutual love. For this model to work, each person must be an individual, with a distinct consciousness and will of the same sort, yet each must have distinguishing characteristics which make them different persons. This already distinguishes the model from the traditional view that the 'persons' differ only in their relation to one another, and not in any substantial property.[12] It is very hard to say just what love between two persons consists in; but it must include a concern to help the other, an interest in the acts and distinctive characteristics of the other, a co-operation in using complementary gifts to achieve shared actions and experiences. If one is thinking of two (or three) persons who are omnipotent and omniscient, none of them can need help from the others, nothing can be hidden from the others, and no action or experience can be shared which is not already enacted or known by each person anyway. Brown says, 'Though they have separate powers, to know the mind and will of one is to know that of all three.'[13] The persons have diverse mental contents. The Word has, as

---

9 Richard Swinburne, *The Christian God* (Oxford: Clarendon Press, 1994), ch.8.
10 Ibid. 178.
11 Mark 12: 29.
12 The council of Florence (CE 1439) asserted that *'in Deo omnia sunt unum, ubi non obviat relationis oppositio'* H. Denzinger (ed.), *Enchiridion Symbolorum, 23rd edn. (Frieburg: 1963). No. 1330.*
13 Brown, *The Divine Trinity, 293.*

part of its unique mental content, the experience of human suffering. The Father does not have that experience. But, as omniscient, he may know *that* the Word has the experience. In a similar way, every experience of every divine person is completely known by the others.

The divine persons can also have distinctive forms of activity. The Father is the only one whose creative acts are wholly underived from another. The Son is the only one who suffers and atones. The Spirit is the only one who strives within creatures to conform them to the pattern of the Son. It is unavoidable that the three 'persons' have diverse forms of awareness and action. Each may respond to knowledge of the other persons in their own way, by sympathy and encouragement. One may think of a continual interplay of actions and responses, in which each has its own awareness and activity, and all are fully aware of the consciousnesses of the others.

Yet there is something uncomfortable in the thought that one has here three distinct individuals (what Swinburne calls souls), each with its own independent centre of consciousness. Is it not true that, as Rahner puts it, 'There exists in God only one power, one will, only one self-presence'?[14] Is it not the *same* God who creates, who suffers and dies, who guides and sanctifies? What that seems to require is that there is one ultimate subject which possesses three distinct forms of action and awareness. Bernard Lonergan puts it succinctly: 'The three subjects are aware of each other through one consciousness which is possessed in a different way by the three of them.'[15]

One view posits three divine souls who always act indivisibly and know each other completely, and the other posits one divine subject with three forms of consciousness. A problem with the 'three souls' view is that it seems to require a principle of the necessary unity of the three which is superior to the three themselves. How does it come about that the three are necessarily indivisible, omnipotent,and omniscient? It must be more than a fortunate chance, but wherein can such a necessity lie? The obvious move, which Swinburne makes, is to make the Father the ingenerate cause and the root of unity between the three. Wolfhart Pannenberg, in commenting on a similar sounding Cappadocian proposal,

14 Karl Rahner, *The Trinity*, tr. J. Donceel (London: Burns and Oates, 1979), 75.
15 Bernard Lonergan, *De Deo Trino* (2 vols.; Rome: Gregorian University Press, *1964*), ii, 193).

points out that this seems inevitably to lead to subordinationism.[16] For the Father cannot create another being with exactly the same divine properties as he has.

Suppose the Father tries to create another essentially divine being with the same divine properties, namely, the Son. At least one divine property cannot be thus created, the property of being the unoriginated cause of everything other than itself. The Son will owe being wholly to the Father, and will thus be dependent for existence in a way the Father is not. The Son will have no causal power over the Father that the Father does not give to the Son. The Son's action will necessarily have to be compatible with the Father's existence and actions. As Swinburne admits, this will have to be achieved by the Father initiating a plan to which the Son will, as perfectly good, assent. Thus the Father has a clear causal, volitional, and executive priority. It is implausible to suppose that the Father causally depends upon the Son in the way that the Son depends upon the Father. The upshot is that these two beings do not share the same divine properties. The Son is more like an archangel, after all, than like another god.

Pannenberg's own way to avoid subordinationism is to find the desired principle of divine unity in love which, as 'the power that manifests itself in the mutual relations of the Trinitarian persons, is identical with the divine essence'. The divine essence is 'the power and fire of love glowing through the divine persons, uniting them and radiating from them as the light of the glory of God'.[17] However, this also seems uncomfortably to depersonalise and hypostatise love, as a force superior to the persons in which it is actualised. The divine essence is not an abstract property, even as high-sounding as love, which actualises itself in precisely three individuals. Love is the disposition of a being to create and delight in goodness, to create other subjects who can do so, to co-create and co-experience with them, and to care for their well-being and proper fulfillment. It is a power, but it is essentially the power of a personal subject, and must be embodied in a particular subject. Pannenberg's proposal does not really solve the problem of the divine unity, since one has to ask why the power of love should be embodied in three co-equal subjects, especially when one of them (the Father) is admitted to be the real *arche*, or origin, of the other

16 Wolfhart Pannenberg, *Systematic Theology*, tr. G. W. Bromiley (2 vols. Edinburgh: T. & T. Clark, 1991-), i. 321.
17 Ibid. 427.

two. Either love is the underived property of the Father, given derivatively to Son and the Spirit, which reintroduces the sort of subordination which Pannenberg feels uneasy with, or love must be the property of the Trinitarian God, who must therefore be seen as one subject. Certainly, in the idea of the Trinity one transcends the idea of self-centred or solitary individuality, but not by positing a society of similar divine souls. In the idea of coinhering willing and knowing one has the root of love as delight, giving, receiving, sharing, and co-operating. Yet God is love, not as three loving individuals, but as a unity of three coinherent modes of action of one supreme being. That is to say God does not contain within the divine unity a true otherness, a plurality of similar and relatively autonomous subjects. As Rahner puts it, 'Within the Trinity there is no reciprocal "Thou".'[18] Again, 'There is properly no mutual love between Father and Son.'[19]

I do not think that it is possible to construct such a view of God simply from reflection on what love as such is. One may however find in many theistic traditions, as I have tried to show a sense that a simple understanding of God as a loving person misses some of the complexity of an adequate account of the Divine as Creator. The Christian claim is that by reflection on the person and role of Jesus, a profound understanding of divine and therefore of true human love can be formed. As Sarah Coakley has suggested, Christian experience of prayer suggests a basis for Trinitarian thought for which the Trinity 'is the graced ways of God with the creation, alluring and conforming that creation into the life of the "Son".'[20] But such prayer itself depends for its precise form on acceptance of the role of the Spirit as the one who 'intercedes for us with sighs too deep for words',[21] and who is sent as 'Comforter' by the Son.

The problem of incipient tritheism arises from thinking of the persons of the Trinity as separate minds, which have intra-divine relations, apart from any relationship to created reality. Jurgen Moltmann, who also develops a social view of the Trinity, evinces some reservations about this model. He does insist that 'Father Son and Spirit are in fact subjects with a will and understanding.'[22] They are not, he insists, 'modes of being' of a

18 Rahner, *The Trinity*, 176 n.

19 Ibid. 106.

20 Sarah Coakley, 'Why Three?', in S. Coakley and D. Pailin (eds), *The Making and Remaking of Christian Doctrine* (Oxford: Clarendon Press, 1993), 37.

21 Rom. 8: 26.

22 Jurgen Moltmann, *History and the Triune God*, tr. J. Bourden (London: SCM, 1991), 84.

single divine subject. The main reason he gives is that, if one begins from a biblical perspective, the Father, Son, and Spirit seem to be treated as different subjects, the Son praying to the Father, the Father grieving over the suffering of the Son, and the Spirit glorifying both. So Moltmann asserts that 'the Trinity supersedes theism.'[23] At the same time, he qualifies this social model by suggesting that the three hypostases of the Trinity are not of the same kind at all.[24] 'No subsuming generic terms may be used in the doctrine of the Trinity', he writes, which must mean that the 'persons' cannot properly be conceived as three mental beings after all.

Moltmann seems to me entirely right to insist that all talk of the Trinity must be rooted in the biblical history of salvation. But when he says that Father, Son, and Spirit do not belong to some common genus, he provides the best reason for denying that they are all independent subjects of the same kind, with will and understanding (the genus of 'person'). New Testament exegesis very rarely, if ever, comes up with an analysis of the texts which suggests that there are three divine individuals in continuing conversation throughout the Gospels. It is usually agreed that the idea of the Trinity only exists embryonically in the Gospels, and that what needs to be worked out is the exact relation between Jesus as Lord, God as Creator, and the Spirit as life-renewing and inspiring power in the early Church. Such working out is a complicated and delicate task, but I judge that Moltmann is mistaken to say that 'Those who begin from this salvation history begin with the recognition of these three indivisible and different subjects and their one, unique collaboration in their history.'[25] They begin, as the Apostles began, from belief in the one God of monotheism, who is somehow mediated to them through Jesus and intimately present in the power of the Spirit. The idea of the Trinity does not supersede monotheism; it interprets it, in the light of a specific set of revelatory events and experiences.

A plurality model of the Trinity has not been accepted by the main traditions in the West. The main alternative model, largely adopted, with some amendments, by Anselm and Aquinas, is that of Augustine's *De Trinitate*. As is often pointed out, the psychological analogies appealed to

23 Ibid. 24.
24 Ibid. 88.
25 Ibid. 83.

by this model again seem to commit one to thinking of God as a cosmic mind, though this time not three minds but one mind, operating in three different ways. If one thinks of the Trinity as something like the *memoria, intelligentia,* and *voluntas* of a human mind,[26] and one thinks of the many ways in which mental activity can be analysed, this might, as David Brown says, 'make one doubt what it could mean to say that a mind might have internal divisions that are non-arbitrary'.[27] Augustine interpreted intra-divine love as a delight in one's own perfection; but that cancels out the social aspect completely, and makes divine love a matter of self-contemplation. While it has some appeal to think of Father and Son as lover and beloved, it is quite unsatisfactory to think of the Spirit as the love which binds them together, since that depersonalises the Spirit, perhaps helping to give rise to the rather mechanical theories of the operations of grace which permeate late medieval theology. What makes both plurality and unity accounts seem unsatisfactory is their determination to think of God as a sort of disembodied mind or triumvirate of minds, coupled with their separation of the timeless intra-divine life of God from the economy of salvation in which Trinitarian talk was originally rooted.

Catherine Lacugna has argued that 'the divine processions, "being begotten" and "being breathed", are inconceivable apart from the divine missions: the life and ministry of Jesus and the sending of the Spirit to his followers.'[28] The basic Christian perception about God is that God never existed as a solitary figure. 'God is ecstatic, fecund, self-emptying out of love for another, a personal God who comes to self through another.'[29] The 'social Trinitarians' are quite right to try to explore this insight. But this cannot be done by making the communion of divine persons somehow intra-divine, which retains a slightly extended self-absorption in the divine being, after all. Any model of love within the Trinity must be, in the end, simply the love of God for the divine self, and not the love of another who may pose a real otherness and distance, and in some sense an opposition, to the lover, and who may then stand in need of reconciliation. 'The communion of divine life is God's communion with us in Christ and as

26 Augustine *De Trinitate* bk. ix, ch. I, tr. E. Hill (New York: New City Press) 271.
27 Brown, *The Divine Trinity, 275.*
28 Catherine Mowry Lacugna, *God For Us* (San Francisco: Harper, 1991), 6.
29 Ibid. 15.

Spirit.'[30] Thus 'an ontological distinction between God *in se* and God *pro nobis* is, finally, inconsistent with biblical revelation.'[31]

To take such a view is not to reduce the Trinity to a merely economic role, as though it was a matter of different ways in which God acts towards creation, while the *theologia,* the inner being of God, remains non-Trinitarian. One can insist – indeed one can insist with increased emphasis – that the economic Trinity, God as known to us historically through Christ and in the power of the Spirit, gives an insight into what God truly is. It is our only access to what has been called the immanent Trinity, the inner Trinitarian being of God, and such access is authentic and reliable. What one cannot do is to take the hypostases of Father, Son, and Spirit out of all historical relations and present them as internal goings-on within a wholly self-contained and self-sufficient Godhead. That would ironically, betray precisely the fundamental insight into God's ecstatic, overflowing goodness into a realm of genuine otherness, responsiveness, and dynamic creativity. The Divine threefoldness is a real quality of God *in se.* But that *'in se'* is not existent out of relation to creation. It is manifested in its true and essential character in creation and in the return of creation to God, a *Patre ad Patrem,* which is always through Christ and in the power of the Spirit.

This should not be interpreted to mean that there is no immanent Trinity, that God is only Trinitarian in relation to creation. It means that the intra-Trinitarian being is given to us only in revelation. Our speaking of it is a conceptual abstraction and inference from the revelation in Christ, not an independent metaphysical hypothesis. In this restricted sense, 'Rahner's Rule', that the economic Trinity is the immanent Trinity,[32] can be endorsed. It is not that there is no more to God than what is revealed to us, nor that we know exactly what God's inner being is like when we speak of the Trinity. It is rather that God essentially is such as to be authentically revealed as a Trinitarian God. Nonetheless, the Christian theologian must beware of reducing the infinite divine being to the compass of any human mind, however inspired, and also of constructing a speculative theory of the divine being in itself which makes human history and divine relation to it virtually irrelevant. God is what God is in relation to creation, a God of

30 Ibid. 15
31 Ibid. 6.
32 Rahner, *The Trinity;* 27.

self-giving, suffering, redemptive and reconciling love. God remains for us, of course, a mystery hidden in uncreated light, but is, Christians claim, revealed for human understanding in a threefold – ecstatic, incarnate, and unitive – form. The doctrine of the Trinity is not founded on pure speculation, but on the belief that God has truly revealed the divine self in the life and teaching of Jesus and the advent of the Spirit at Pentecost.

The Basis of Trinitarian Doctrine

The doctrine of the Trinity is firmly rooted in the apostolic experience of Jesus as the one who makes God present and who inaugurates the rule of God in the world. The Gospels suggest that some at least partly misunderstood Jesus' message and role during his lifetime, expecting him to rule over a liberated Israel in a new historical era.[33] But Jesus inaugurated a spiritual, not a political, kingdom.[34] He did proclaim the inauguration of the Kingdom of God, and he claimed by his deeds that he was the King who was to rule in a new Israel and a new era.[35] That rule is foreshadowed by the outpouring of the Spirit upon the young Church community. It is too crude, however, to see the expectation of the Kingdom as belief in an end of history in the near future. It is truer to the subtlety of apocalyptic and eschatological imagery to see the Kingdom as something which remains always future to every historical time; though it is always imminent at every historical time, as each temporal moment is integrated into the eternal life of God. The 'end of history' is imminent at every time, as its inner purpose and intended consummation, yet it does not put a stop to history, wherein the Spirit continually makes present its foreshadowed realisation, by making the Christ who was present in Jesus present again in the community of the Church.

Jesus comes to be seen as himself the end or goal of history, and his death and ascension to God unveils the inner meaning of the whole historical process, the drama of conflict with evil, victory by self-giving, and union with God in which the whole human race participates. Though he is the exemplar of perfected humanity, he is not only a paradigm of human life. He is also the temporal image of the eternal love of God, embodied in a human life, as the word of grace which invites all earthly

33 Luke 24: 21.
34 John 18: 36.
35 e.g. Mark 11: 1–10.

beings into communion with God. In the early Church community, God comes to be seen primarily as the Father of Jesus Christ, the one who sends the Spirit to empower Jesus' life with grace, who remains the object of Jesus' prayers and obedience, and who is the final goal, to union with which Jesus leads all earthly beings. Jesus is the obedient Son, who, in perfectly obeying the Father's will to make him the King of the redeemed earth, becomes the visible image of the invisible God. Together with the Father, Jesus sends the Spirit upon those who follow him, to make them holy and incorporate them into a life of indivisible community with one another and with God.

In the first four centuries of the Church's existence, these new strands of religious thought were gradually woven into an elaborate doctrine of God as Trinity. But the simple historical source of this doctrine is the apostolic experience of God as loving Father, Jesus as the obedient Son, the Father's image on earth, and the Spirit as the one who makes Jesus present to every time and place, and unites all in him. The experience of new life, the foreshadowing of salvation, came to the Christians from the Father, through the Son, and in the Holy Spirit. That experience began with the acceptance of Jesus as Lord, of his testimony that God was his Father, and of the Spirit as the inner power which he sent in a sort of spiritual baptism upon their community.

There is here a sort of simple primitive Trinity, preceding the formulae of later Church councils. The father is God the transcendent Creator of all, who loves creation so much that God calls Jesus to be the express image of Divinity and to manifest redemptive love on earth. Jesus is God in Wisdom, embodied in a human life, revealing the mystery of redemption, which is the uniting of all things in the Spirit. The Spirit is God working within the heart, realizing a redemptive purpose and bringing humans to wholeness of being. Father, Son, and Spirit picture God the transcendent Creator, beyond all history; God the redeeming Saviour, manifesting the divine being decisively at one historical time to inaugurate the rule of the Spirit; and God the empowering Spirit within, present at every earthly time to prepare and complete the process of redemption.

The Development of Trinitarian Doctrine

In one way, Christian belief in the Trinity need never move beyond this fairly simple picture. It captures what is essential in the distinctively

Christian view of God. Yet it soon became clear that Christian thought could not remain content with a purely historical, and therefore relatively local, account of the God who had become known in a new way in and through Jesus. From the earliest times, Jesus was naturally interpreted in the context of the ideas of God which can be found in the Hebrew Bible. God the Father was not only the Father of Jesus. God was the Father of Israel, creator of heaven and earth, making a covenant with humanity to bring it into a relationship of love. The Spirit is not only the new power known in the apostolic community. Spirit is the power of creativity, courage, and vision who had rested upon the prophets of Israel and who moved over the waters at creation. Jesus himself cannot be seen just as a man who is empowered by God. He manifests the Torah, the Wisdom of God, which had existed before all time, and who as such expresses the pattern for all creation and the final goal towards which all things move. In the rabbinic tradition, the attributes of God were often hypostasised to become virtually distinct spiritual beings. One key text is found in Proverbs 8:22 ff., which makes Wisdom into a personal being, the 'child of God': 'The Lord created me at the beginning of his work, the first of his acts and old.'[36] This Wisdom was identified with Torah by some rabbis, and with the *cosmos noetos* by Philo. It is that through which the universe was created, which delights in creation, and which is itself the first word of God. It can easily be identified with that primal creative word of God by which all things came into being, when 'God said', and things came to be.[37]

For Christians, the idea that this primal Word or Wisdom was created, and was thus different in being from God, was ruled out after the defeat of Arianism. There is good conceptual reason for ruling it out, since it is odd to speak of the Wisdom of God as something created by God, as though God had no wisdom before God created it, and so must have created it unwisely. On the other hand, it also seems odd at first to speak of Wisdom as a personal reality, instead of simply as a property of the divine being. One can think of wisdom, in one way, as the content of the divine thought. Wisdom, as in part the plan of this universe or the archetypal model of true humanity (the eternal Torah), might be created, in the sense of being conceived in the mind of God by a creative act of thought. A

36 Prov. 8:30
37 Gen. 1:3.

standard account of the 'days of creation' in Jewish thought was that they did not provide a temporal ordering, but a logical ordering.[38] Thus to say that Wisdom was the 'first' divine act does not have to imply that it came at the first moment of time, but only that it is logically the primary turning of God towards a created order, or towards the conception of such an order. In that way, Wisdom can be an eternal thought of God, engendered by something analogous to a creative act of intellection, though not coming into being when once it was not. In so far as Wisdom is in the mind of God, it is not different in being from God. In fact, it can intelligibly be said to form an essential part of what God is, so that without it, God would not be God, an intellective agent. The divine thought could be called 'consubstantial with' God, since it is part of the one divine substance, without which that substance would lack something essential to its existence.

Yet neither as a disposition of God nor as the eternal content of divine thinking is Wisdom a person, which can 'delight in' creation or be with God like a little child. It is significant, nonetheless, that rabbinic thought did hypostatise Wisdom,[39] and that the sense in which Wisdom is created by God is very different from the sense in which the universe is created, since the former, but not the latter, may well be said to be necessary to the divine being and to be part of the divine mind rather than a separate or distinct consciousness. The Christian view of Wisdom obviously requires that it not be considered as simply a passive content of the divine thinking, but asa reality which has some form of conscious relationship to its *arche*, or creative source in the divine nature. At this point the neo-Platonic tradition of emanations within the divine nature inevitably comes to mind. In Plotinus' influential version, the ultimate source, the One, generates from itself the intellective world, *Nous,* which in turn generates the World-Soul. From this triple being the universe emanates, as a sort of overflowing of being, down to the last dim echo of positive reality, infected with unreality, fading into nothingness.[40]

Such an emanationist view qualifies any straightforward account of God as a divine person, containing thoughts (Wisdom) and bringing things

38 See Ch. 12.

39 See Solomon Schechter, *Aspects of Rabbinic Theology* (New York: Schocken Books, 1961), ch. 9.

40 Plotinus, *The Enneads,* v. i. 3–12, trans. S. MacKenna (Harmondsworth: Penguin, 1991), 350–60.

into being by creative fiat (so that 'the Spirit', too, is just a term for the creative activity of one divine person). The concept of a divine person is, in the end, too restrictive for the infinity of the divine reality – an infinity and mystery which, as has been noted, Jewish thought is very keen to stress. One might then think of the Wisdom of God as possessing its own proper form of intellective activity, with its own mode of acting and its own generative nature. Wisdom was hypostatised by the rabbis partly because it was not seen as a purely passive content of thought in the mind of a divine subject. It was seen as an active and substantial intelligible principle, though one which received its form of being from a reality beyond itself.

What seems to be essential to such a development of thought about God is that the Creator and Wisdom are not to be conceived as two things of the same sort (e.g. as two 'persons' in anything like the modern sense). Nor are they to be conceived as a person and one of its activities. They must be conceived as two distinct forms of existence within the divine reality. There is the primal source of all being, the 'depth of being', which is almost wholly beyond our conceptual grasp. And there is the relatively concrete, 'formed', active intellectual being which, as intelligible, generates the structures of this universe on the pattern of its own reality. Wisdom is hypostatised because it is dimly grasped that the intelligible Lord and pattern of this universe is itself grounded in an infinite reality which is beyond human comprehension. In neo-Platonic thought and in the Hebrew wisdom tradition, belief in the infinity of the divine being led to various hypostatizations or emanations from the ultimate divine source, which could connect it to this universe by a sort of chain of intermediaries. The hymn to Wisdom in Proverbs 8 leaves the status of Wisdom indeterminate, a creature and yet a child of God. In Plotinus, the hypostases of the Divine emanate from greater to lesser. Plotinus holds that 'the offspring is always minor'[41] but the Council of Constantinople (CE 381) condemned the view that Son and Spirit are subordinate to the Father. It is analytically true that, if the Father generates Son and Spirit, and if effects are always subordinate to their causes, then in one way Son and Spirit are subordinate to the Father. What the Council condemned was the view that the Father freely creates Son and Spirit as different beings. The most plausible view of the Christian tradition on this issue is that Son and Spirit are generated necessarily, as ways in which the one

41 Plotinus, *The Enneads*, v. i. 6: 354.

God exists. Divine omnipotence is necessarily and only exercised by Father, Son, and Spirit together. The Father can be called omnipotent, but only with the proviso that his power is exercised through the Son and in the Spirit, as essential aspects of the one divine being.

Thus in Christian theology, Wisdom became fully consubstantial with God, not created but procreated or 'begotten', a distinct active and substantial source (an hypostasis), receiving its reality from the image-less origin of all. The letter to the Colossians contains what is thought to be an early hymn, saying of Christ, 'He is the ... first born of all creation; for in him all things were created ... through him and for him.'[42]

Christians added a third form of being to the divine nature, again prompted primarily by reflection on the impact of Jesus on the apostolic community and modelled on concepts suggested in the Hebrew Bible. In Genesis, the Spirit of God moved over the face of the waters,[43] and throughout the Hebrew Bible the Spirit inspires and gives life, as a dynamic power. If one may think of the Divine Wisdom as an 'active intellect' within the divine nature, one may perhaps think of the Spirit as the creative energy of God. This energy, as a creative Power or hypostasis, has its source in the 'unoriginate One' and finds the forms which direct and pattern its activity in the Divine Wisdom. The Spirit is not simply an inchoate energy. It works according to a particular form and pattern, and it works to generate new particular forms, realizing the divine archetypes in new particular ways. Spirit requires Word to give it form, and Word requires Spirit to give it life. They are bound together, as an infinite generation of living forms, originating from one source generating self-expressive order and creative bliss in their dynamic harmony. Such a notion lies beyond the reach of human thought. It is simply an extrapolation from the triadic model of God which is rooted in the human experience of Jesus, through the Spirit. It stumblingly affirms that in the God beyond thought and time there is that which is the true and authentic ground of the God who endlessly relates in love to creatures. God is not adequately thought of as a solitary cosmic mind. Neither should God be conceived as a society of similar beings, inextricably bound together. The nearest human imagination, prompted by revelation, can get is to say that God is the infinite and boundless ocean of being, within whom there is

42 Col. 1:16
43 Gen. 1:2.

both intelligible contemplation and creative life. Far beyond both individual mind and any society of finite beings, the divine nature may be conceived as the archetypal perfection of both individual and communal personal being. In a triadic unity of being, creativity, and intelligible form, that changeless and perfectly actualised reality exists which is the sole foundation of every created universe. Thus Cyril of Alexandria could say that '*Everything* is from the Father, through the Son, in the Holy Spirit.'[44]

At the end of this process of reflection on the mystery of God revealed in Jesus, one may speak, in the most fundamental and yet in the most abstract way, of a Triad of the depth of being, the power of being, and the manifestation of being. The depth of being is that beyond all words, the ground of all beings, the infinite potency of all things which is also a wholly and unimaginably unrestricted actuality, beyond conceptual grasp. The power of being is the creative activity which expresses the divine being, actualizing from the abyss of potency endless particular forms, without end in its creative energy. The manifestation of being is the archetypal pattern and the completed image, the matrix and completion of creative activity, fully apprehended and appreciated within the divine life. These are not three distinct subjects of awareness, but three forms of the being of God, in each of which its whole being is expressed in a different manner. 'The one God subsists in three distinct manners of subsisting.'[45]

As triadic being, God can be said to exist from the divine being alone, Without dependence on any other thing. God is the supreme self-power, seeing the divine self as truth in the divine image.[46] God is supremely creative, a principle of energy and life, not of static aloofness, yet without having any lack or discontent which needs to be remedied by action, moving in *ek-stasis* out from itself to express itself in creativity.

In the terminology developed in the fourth century, the Trinity is three hypostases in one *ousia*. On the account just given, the best way of interpreting this rather vague description is to say, using the term suggested by Barth, that there are three modes of being of the one omnipotent and omniscient will and awareness who is God. The primal being, the manifested being, and the creative being are all ways in which the one God experiences and acts. All of these coinhere, forming one Subject in three

44 Cyril, *Contra Julianum*, 3, in *Patrologia Cursus Completus*, ed. J.P. Migne, Series Graeca (Paris, 1957–66), lxxvi. 649.
45 Rahner, *The Trinity*, 109.
46 Athanasius, *Contra Arianos*, i. 20–1, ed. W. Bright (Oxford: Oxford University Press, 1873).

centres of awareness and will, indivisibly co-acting and experiencing, each in its own way, and with its own form of awareness of other centres. Each hypostasis of the same consciousness and will interpenetrates the others, being aware of them in its own appropriate mode and willing with them in its own distinctive modality.

The Threefold God

It can now be seen how this developed doctrine of God as Trinity has strong and sometimes unexpected points of resemblance with views of God in other religious traditions, while it remains quite distinctive. Heschel, Iqbal, and Aurobindo all speak of God as an ineffable and infinite source of all being. They all hold that, though in one sense that source is self-existent and in need of nothing, yet it does not remain alone and self-sufficient. It makes itself known in particular forms of relation to created reality, and thus constitutes itself in some way as a personal reality, though that personal relationship does not change or detract from the infinite nature itself in any way. So, for Christian Trinitarian thought, the Father is the incomprehensible abyss of being, which is also ecstatic being, going out through the internal generosity of love to the creation of other forms of goodness. God manifests the primal divine reality as the Lord and Bridegroom of Israel and as the Father of Jesus Christ, entering into responsive and personal relationship with creatures. God also receives all things into the divine self, as God delights in the completed experience of redeemed creation.

Iqbal speaks of God as the Cosmic Ego, realizing its character in the progressive unfolding of history, and Aurobindo speaks of God as the Supermind, which expresses itself in the temporal evolution of the universe. The Christian idea of the Son or eternal Wisdom of God, as an intelligible agent who conceives the particular forms of created being in archetypal form, the *Nous Haplos,* expresses part of that notion. Christians do not quite see the whole process of history as realizing the archetypal pattern present in the Divine Wisdom, since individuals frustrate and deflect the primal divine plan to some degree. Nevertheless, that Wisdom is manifested in one perfect exemplar, Jesus of Nazareth, who incarnates the pattern of human loving responsiveness in time. Thereafter the destiny of creation is to be united in Christ,[47] so that Christ might in that sense be seen as the Cosmic Mind or Self in which the universe is completed and reconciled. All finite realities are to be included in the Christ, and it is in that all-including life that they are offered to the Father, the ultimate source of all and goal to which all things must return.

Iqbal speaks of God as co-operating with creatures in bringing new forms of reality into being. Aurobindo speaks of *Shakti* as the primal energy of emergent creation, and of *Sachchidananda* as emerging through time to realise its inner potentiality. One can find here echoes of the Christian idea of the Spirit of God as the immanent creativity of God, projected as the creative energy which forms this space-time universe, as the co-operative and inner power who forms Christ in the lives of believers, and as the one who actively unites all things in Christ, making them whole and bringing them to the fullness of the stature of mature humanity.

The Christian idea of the Trinity is thus not wholly at odds with the sorts of reflection that take place in other religious traditions. But it does articulate the concept of God in a way which is most unlikely to have taken the exact form it has without a dependence upon what is taken to be a decisive divine self-disclosure in the person of Jesus. Once posited, this concept may be thought to have a coherence that provides a rationale for Christian devotion and suggests a fruitful basis for understanding the structure of created being and history. It can be seen as developing logically in a fourfold form, which expresses the eternal-primordial, originative-expressive, historical-responsive, and eschatological-unitive character of the divine being as it is revealed in Jesus Christ.

The timeless and primordial pure actuality of being, creativity, and form, which is the immanent Trinity, remains unchanging and unchanged in an active and self-sufficient perfection. It is the primordial aspect of the divine, the source of all beings, the absolutely unoriginated, possessing indivisible unity and self-existence, It is not, as in Whitehead, an unconsciously envisaged conceptual realm of abstract objects,[48] but an objectless intelligence (having its own activity as object), an unchanging activity and a completeness of being that must remain hidden from human comprehension in inaccessible light. Nor is it, as in Neo-Platonic thought, an

47 Eph. 1: 10.
48 A. N. Whitehead, *Process and Reality* (New York: The Free Press, 1978) 521.

undifferentiated One,[49] since even in its primordial character it retains an internal richness and complexity which Christian reflection expresses in triadic form. The infinite and primal death of being, through the timeless exercise of the power of being, will actualise a supremely valuable set of states which manifest supreme beauty. It will do so by the actualization of value from the intelligible pattern of being which is, logically, its first self-expression.

Thus one may think of the depth of being (the Father) generating an intelligible self-expression and pattern of being (the Son), with its own form of consciousness of all possibilities. Together, they generate, through the power of being (the Spirit), with its own actualizing and evaluating consciousness, a set of supreme values, which forms the changelessly completed awareness of the Father.

So there is, in the Trinity, a giving of primal being, expressing itself in an objectified form of consciousness, and taking that back into primal being as realised experience, by the power of an evaluating, actualizing, and unitive form of consciousness. This is not a temporal process, but an always completed and immutable relational unity in which infinite depth, intelligible expression, and unitive creativity are bound together in blissful communion of being.

This account has unmistakable echoes of the Hegelian explication of Absolute Spirit as being in-itself, for-itself, and consciously in-and-for-itself.[50] Hegel has, in my view, illuminated the way in which one may give temporality a real function in the self-expression of God, while retaining a notion of the ultimate transtemporal reality of God. It should be borne in mind, however, that accepting the usefulness of this terminology does not commit one to the philosophy of Absolute Idealism. In particular, a Christian may wish to stress the otherness of God and the autonomy of creatures more than Hegel did, and to insist that to talk of an immanent, timeless Trinity is not to disclose the philosophical truth of which religious doctrines give only a pictorial representation.[51] It is rather to accept the religious insight that the divine being has a timeless, fully actual, and perfect aspect as well as a temporally expressive aspect. Further, the doctrine of the economic Trinity, while it is the starting point and sub-

49 Plotinus, *Enneads,* v.i. 7:355 f.
50 Hegel, *Phenomenology of Spirit,* trans. A. V. Miller (Oxford: Oxford University Press, 1977; 1st pub. 1807), 465.
51 Ibid. 463.

stance of Christian prayer and practice, will be reflected in the immanent being of God, though in a form which all human concepts must fall far short of representing adequately. The doctrine of the immanent Trinity is not a speculative philosophical basis for Christian belief. It is a stumbling attempt to say what the primordial aspect of God may be, if the economic revelation of God as Trinity is an authentic self-disclosure of the Divine.

The primordial being of God gives rise to the origin of worlds in a distinctively threefold pattern. The ecstatic abyss of potentiality engenders the archetypal intellect which forms the pattern for a particular universe, and the power of creativity which embodies that form materially. The world is created through the Divine Wisdom, the Christ, in the power of the Spirit. 'In him were all things created ... through him and for him.'[52] In a movement beyond the divine being itself, through the power of the Spirit which moves over the waters of chaos, and through the intelligible forms of beauty which are inherent in the image of the Son, the universe is brought into being by the will of the Father. The Spirit proceeds from the Father in creative energy, and proceeds from the Father and the Son together as the Spirit shapes particular created things into the image of the archetypal Son. This is the creative aspect of the Divine, the dynamic infinity of the self-existent, as it manifests the divine being by an overflowing of its goodness. This creativity leaves the primordial nature unchanged, yet classical Thomist accounts of the Divine fail fully to acknowledge the reality of this changing and creative aspect of God, a reality which does not impair the divine perfection, but extends its scope.

Throughout the process which is the history of the universe, the primal source constitutes itself in relation to the world as Father, as transcendent Judge and Deliverer. This Father calls a particular people into fellowship. God becomes known as a transcendent but loving presence, who calls a particular people into covenant relationship. God sends the Spirit to inspire the prophets and make known the divine will. The divine being is embodied, first in Torah and then in the person of Jesus, as the incarnation of the cosmic image upon which all things are patterned. The Christ is incarnated on earth as the particular historical image of divine love, responsive to created human beings, whom he guides and teaches. The Spirit, in relation to the historical process, becomes the one who makes the love of Christ present within creatures. 'God has sent the Spirit of his Son

52 Col. 1:15

into our hearts.'[53] This is the responsive aspect of the Divine, which interacts with created beings to check tendencies to disintegration and guide them actively towards perfection. This is the aspect which Whitehead most markedly fails to deal with, reducing the guiding function of God to that of a 'lure', which is only ambiguously responsive at best.[54]

Finally, as creation returns to its source, the Spirit sanctifies,reconciles, and unites all things within the perfected and actualised form which is the cosmic Christ. In the Spirit and through Christ, allthings return to the Father, and all the values of temporal existence are conserved in a completed experience, in which all sentient creatures can share in an appropriate way. 'His purpose is to unite all things in him, things in heaven and things on earth.'[55] At the end of this historical time, all created life which is responsive to God's call is taken into fellowship with the life of God, who will be all in all. The goal of all things is the *apokatastasis,* the return of all created things in the Spirit, through Christ as the body of the completed cosmos, to the Father. This is the consequential aspect of the Divine, incorporating into its being all the completed realizations of value which comprise the history of the universe, purged of evil and corruption. Process theology has great difficulty in thinking of a final elimination of evil from the unending process of reality, in which finite 'actual occasions' may always conflict. Where creativity is placed more firmly in the omnipotent being of God, and the laws of this space-time are given a finite duration, it becomes possible to think of a final triumph of the divine will, in a new heaven and earth', which is the transfiguration of present physical reality by its completed union with the Divine. 'Then comes the end, when he delivers the Kingdom to God the Father ... that God may be everything to everyone.'[56]

Concluding Remarks

This volume began by outlining four twentieth century doctrines of God as the creator of the universe, each claiming to be an authentic yet original exposition of the scriptures of Judaism, Christianity, Islam, and Hinduism,

53 Gal. 4:6.
54 This problem in Whitehead is pointed out and discussed in J. Cobb and D. Griffin, *Process Theology* (Philadelphia: Westminster Press, 1976), ch. 4, and a more positive responsive role is given to God.
55 Eph. I: 10.
56 I Cor. 15:24.

respectively. Abraham Heschel expounded the Jewish, 'prophetic', concept of God as that of a passionate, morally demanding, responsive, and liberating power which underlies the processes of history. Karl Barth drew from the New Testament an idea of God as essentially self-giving love, creating others, entering into their alienated condition, and uniting them in the divine life. Mohammed Iqbal elaborated a Muslim idea of God as dynamically creative, and of the universe as the self-unfolding of a Cosmic Self, guiding a community of finite selves into final union with Itself. Aurobindo Ghose developed the Upanishadic doctrine of Brahman to show the universe as the evolving, dynamic expression of Brahman, and its goal as the full manifestation in time of the divine life. Heschel, Barth, Iqbal, and Aurobindo all modify their classical traditions by stressing the affectivity, creativity, relationality, and temporality of the Divine. For all the differences of their scriptural sources, they agree in seeing the Supreme Being as creatively powerful, wise, expressing goodness in relational love, affectively knowing, and blissful. Those five essential characteristics modify, but do not replace, the traditional theologians' idea of God as a timeless and self-sufficient reality. They do, however, clearly make creation central to the being of God, and claim, not only that the character of God makes a difference to the sort of universe this is, but also that creation makes a difference to the sort of reality God is.

In Part 2, the coherence and plausibility of speaking about God as Creator was defended. It was argued that non-realist theologians are right in seeing theism as primarily a way of expressing and evoking attitudes such as those of awe, gratitude, and hope, grounded in a basic search for self-transformation in the realisation of value. But they are wrong in thinking that such a form of life can be appropriate without a metaphysical commitment to beliefs about what the universe is like in its general nature. It was also argued that there must be some literal, if analogical, statements about God, and that theistic speech cannot coherently be regarded as wholly symbolic or metaphorical.

In Part 3, an exposition of the five essential characteristics of God, brought to light in Part I, was offered. Though written from a Christian viewpoint, the exposition tried to take the range of views considered in the first part into account. It aimed to produce a doctrine of God as Creator which would be broadly acceptable to all four traditions (and to others, not mentioned here), and which has learned from each of them. It is, however, not uncontroversial, and will be contested by defenders of more classical interpretations of their traditions. Nevertheless, it is defensible on scriptural grounds in each tradition, and provides a coherent and theologically fruitful account from a theistic perspective of the nature and purpose of creation.

Anselm's definition of God as 'that than which no greater can be conceived' was accepted as suggesting a helpful way of setting out the notion of a being of supreme power and value, which is at least implicit in all four scriptures. A supremely powerful being, it was suggested, would be the one and only creator of everything other than itself, though it could limit the exercise of its power so that other beings could exercise a limited autonomy. The most valuable aspect of power is creativity, which is itself a great value. Divine perfection is not the complete coexistence of all values in one being – a dubiously coherent idea – but the endless creative realisation of many sorts of goodness, which is the supreme exercise of power. Power is a necessarily possessed dispositional state which issues in infinite contingent realisations of creatively envisaged possibility. Divine power is thus better conceived as divine creativity, and this in turn is an expression of divine love.

The wisdom of God is shown in the intelligibility of the universe. God is an absolute explanation of the universe, as the depth of being, the ontological foundation of all possibility; the power of being, not deriving its existence from another; and the manifestation of being, actualizing a set of possible states for the sake of their goodness. God is not just a sufficient cause of the universe, as though it flowed from a changeless, purely actual being by pure necessity. God freely and intentionally creates the universe out of infinite potentiality. The universe is intelligible, both in the elegance and economy of its basic laws and as an expression of free creativity for the sake of goodness.

The goodness of God follows necessarily from the fact that a powerful all-knowing being will choose maximally desirable states for itself, and will create what is desirable to others and to itself. God's goodness is inherently self-diffusive, sharing action and experience with others. In that sense, the creation of some universe may be necessary to God, as an expression of the divine nature as love. The creation of a community of rational agents who can share in creating and appreciating goodness increases the quantity and variety of the forms of existent goodness, and so flows from the divine nature as a free expression of self-diffusive love. Expressive creativity and relationship are both great values, which can be possessed by the divine being as possessed by the divine being as it brings created persons into existence and relates to them in an ever-growing community of being.

The affectivity of God consists in that experiential knowledge by which God finds delight in goodness and beauty. But in a world of free agents, God will also feel compassion for suffering and revulsion from evil. Thus God's knowledge will be fully responsive and affective. It will express a real relationship to creatures, and will partly depend on the free actions of creatures. It follows that God will not have a complete knowledge of a future which is truly open, but God will still be omniscient, as knowing everything it is logically possible for any being to know at any time. However, the future is not wholly unknown to God, since God orders all things to good, wills that all creatures should find a proper fulfillment, and determines that evil will finally be eliminated and goodness fully realised. This is what is meant by speaking of God's predestinating knowledge and efficacious grace.

God is supremely blissful, since the being of God itself contains infinite actualised perfections, and since all created evil will be turned to good or eliminated. Sorrow will exist in God, but it is redeemed by its integration into a wider experience of goodness and beauty. There is an immutable and transtemporal divine perfection and bliss. But that primordial aspect of the divine being is expressed in the temporal process of value-creation which is the history of the created universe. By the *kenosis* and *koinonia* of love, by divine self-giving and sharing in fellowship with creatures, God is supremely affected by creation. But God ensures that creation will find fulfillment in supreme beatitude, and the creative, affective, relational, and unitive acts of God impart a character to the joy of the divine being which only the creation of communities of free co-agents and experients could realise.

Part 4 sought to locate this general concept of God in relation to the picture of the physical universe which modern cosmology provides. It also sought to show how the Christian doctrine of God as Trinity has many complex overlaps with elements of non-Christian traditions, while taking a distinctive form as it is shaped around the mystery of God revealed in Jesus Christ.

The universe disclosed by modern cosmology is a non-mechanistic, highly interconnected, emergent whole whose boundary conditions are highly ordered and finely tuned for the genesis of sentient life. The universe seems to be a contingent but efficient and mathematically elegant process issuing in states of intrinsic and distinctive value. The theistic claim that the purpose of this universe is the creation of a community of love takes on plausibility as one sees the whole process as one of creative emergence, in which the material order becomes gradually self-aware and self-directing. God sets the basic parameters of the universe and continuously influences it towards the goal of communal sentient life, ensuring that finally a transformed material order will become a luminous sacrament of spiritual being.

In the final chapter, a number of strands of thought which had emerged throughout the volume were gathered up to provide a Christian doctrine of God as a Trinitarian being, the depth and pattern and power of love. The primordial depth of being (the Father) moves outwards in love to generate creatures and to respond to them in loving-kindness and judgment, through the archetypal pattern of Divine Wisdom (the Son), which takes particular form in human history, and in the power of the creative Spirit, which makes that form present throughout history. Then the Spirit gathers up and unites all creation in the completed form of the cosmic Christ and returns it to the Father as the transfigured fulfillment and goal of the original creative purpose.

This concept of the Trinitarian God is a Christian description of the idea of a creator of the universe, and it is given its distinctive form by reflection on the life and person of Jesus as an authentic revelation of God. It is one of many traditions which interpret the suprasensory reality with which the religious life is concerned in terms of a being supreme in power and value, the creator of everything other than itself. I have examined the idea of creation in four such traditions, and the way in which those traditions have been reinterpreted in the light of developments in scientific and historical knowledge. Such reinterpretations involve a stress on the creative, relational, and unitive involvement of God in the temporal structure of the created universe, and on the importance of that temporal structure to the self-expression of the divine being. These reinterpretations show how each tradition may hope to preserve the main elements of its own distinctive witness, while engaging in positive interaction both with other traditions and with developments in scientific views of the universe. This volume is written from within the Christian tradition, illuminated and deepened by the teachings of a number of revelatory traditions, and by recent advances in the physical sciences. As such, it has aimed to present an intelligible and defensible doctrine of creation, which can enable one to see the physical universe as the expression of the mind and heart of God. With such an understanding, religious faith, in its theistic form, may be understood, not as an irrational leap into the unknown, or as a satisfaction of some purely emotional needs, but as a reasoned commitment to seek personal union with a reality of supreme value and power, which gives to the universe and to sentient lives within it objective purpose and significance.

III

Science and Religion

8

Believing in Miracles

Pope Benedict XIV (1738) defined a miracle as an event whose occurrence exceeds the power of visible and corporeal nature. It follows that if miracles occur they must be brought about by spiritual and incorporeal beings. Human persons might perform miracles, however, if they were given powers beyond their nature by a superior spirit, whether angel or God. This definition is slightly more relaxed than that of Thomas Aquinas, who argued that God alone can work miracles, inasmuch is a miracle must occur 'outside the natural run of things' and be beyond any natural power – even that of an angel – to bring about (Aquinas 1276, Ia, 110,4). There are two main elements in these definitions. A miracle must be an extraordinary event, one that is not part of the normal or regular operation of things, and must be beyond the power of either a corporeal or a natural, created being to bring about. If one allows the operation of the general causal principle that no event occurs without any cause, then the occurrence of a miracle requires an incorporeal or supernatural cause, perhaps the action of the Creator of the natural order.

If there is a God, a Creator of the universe, it is plainly possible that God might perform miracles, might bring about events that no created cause has the power of itself to bring about. Any argument that miracles are impossible simply begs the question by assuming that there is no God. Thus, David Hume, who at one point unguardedly speaks of 'the absolute impossibility' of miraculous events (Hume [1748] 1902, 125), makes an assumption of atheism to which he is not entitled, by his own professed agnostic principles. An agnostic does not know whether or not there is a God and is bound to admit that miracles are possible. Therefore, miracles could be reliably reported and justifiably believed. And if they were, they would constitute evidence that there is indeed a God.

Hume famously denies that miracles could ever constitute such evidence, but his arguments are exceptionally poor and are found acceptable only by those who are (rightly) impressed by his general philosophical acuteness – an acuteness that does not carry over into his remarks on miracles.

Everything begins to go wrong for Hume when he revises the classical Christian definitions of miracle. Hume's definition of a miracle as a 'violation of a law of nature' differs from the definitions of Benedict and Aquinas, and of Augustine, too, in that he introduces the idea of 'a law of nature' and sees miracles as violations of the rule of law in the universe. Of course Aquinas was aware that the natural world behaves in an orderly way most of the time. He speaks of the natural, normal, or regular operation of things and is quite clear that a condition of the rational intelligibility of nature is that there are such regular operations. He speaks of the 'natural powers' of objects, their tendency or disposition, in appropriate circumstances and in relation to other objects, to behave in regular and largely predictable ways. There is no reason that such regular tendencies to act should not be formulated and conceived of as 'laws of nature,' general principles of the exercise of the natural powers of objects as they have been created by God.

Hume, however, is introducing a hyperinflated sense of a 'law' of nature, which views such laws as unbreakable and as absolute principles that govern the occurrence of each and every possible event in the history of the universe. Where such laws are still connected to theism, it can come to seem that it would be an imperfection in God's work for God to interfere in the presumably perfect order of laws that God has ordained. Among Christian theologians, Friedrich Schleiermacher, D. F. Strauss, and Rudolf Bultmann propound this argument (see Swinburne 1989 and Houston 1994 for good discussions of this issue). It is, I think, an extremely odd argument for those who believe in a personal God to put forth.

It is possible that a personal God might create a universe in which events always and only occur in accordance with a set of absolute and universal laws, laid down unalterably from the beginning. Yet it would be very odd for a person to say, 'I intend to act only in accordance with universal laws, not altering them for any reason.' Among philosophers, Immanuel Kant perhaps came nearest to such a view, in thinking that all actions should be capable of being generalised as laws for all rational agents. But even he did not think that every human action had to conform to laws that were already laid down in the structure of things, so that no new relationships or creative decisions could be ever be made. And Kant's account of human action is notably lacking in those features of feeling, interpersonal relationship, and uniquely individual initiative and response that make human acts fully personal.

Why should a personal God confine divine action to a set of absolute laws? If appeal is made to the desirability of having an intelligible and predictable structure to the universe, such a structure is in no way undermined by the occurrence of some events that, for good reason, transcend that general structure. Rare exceptions do not undermine useful general principles. Even if we accept Hume's tendentious talk of 'violating' laws of nature, occasional violations do not destroy the advantage of having general principles, especially when such violations can for all practical purposes be ignored.

The Humean tendency is to think that any variation from a law of nature is improper, untidy, or arbitrary. That is the connotation of the word *violation*. But if we think of laws as having been created by God, the laws themselves must exist for some reason – and if God is a personal agent, that reason could well justify some occurrences that transcend general law-like principles. Suppose God's purpose is, as the New Testament suggests, that there should come into being finite persons who come to know and love God and enjoy the divine presence forever. In that case an integral part of the structure of created being will be that finite persons should come to be aware of and have some personal relationship with a reality beyond all created being, with God. If that relationship is to involve some sort of personal relation on God's part – for instance, God's making the divine presence known to a finite person or comforting or strengthening that person – there will be some causal power exercised by God that affects the way things happen in the universe, if only in the minds of finite persons. A full causal account of what happens will require reference to the presence and causal action of God, a supernatural and spiritual being.

It seems that any self-revealing act of God in human experience will be, according to Benedict's definition, a miracle. It will be, or will entail, an occurrence in some human chain of events that can be brought about only by God and so are quite beyond the powers of any natural object. We would not call such an event a miracle, however, because it might be considered to be part of the normal or regular exercise of human powers.

Nevertheless, the occurrence of such an event entails that a closed and complete account of events in terms of laws of nature is insufficient if there is a personal God. By a 'closed and complete account' I mean one that wholly explains the occurrence of all aspects of physical events without reference to anything outside a set of (in principle) specifiable general laws of nature.

This line of reasoning does not show that miracles are likely to occur if there is a God, but it gets the camel's nose inside the tent. That is, it shows that any causal account of the natural world must include reference to divine actions as part of complete explanation of why things happen as they do. The reason this goes to affect the physical sciences is that such sciences simply do not mention or concern themselves with these divine actions (of revealing, forgiving, comforting, and strengthening). They do not even have to concern themselves with, the question of whether such divine actions leave all of the laws of physical nature intact or whether they modify them in some way that can for all practical purposes be discounted.

A theist will see God as continuously acting in the physical cosmos in order to realise the divine purpose of enabling persons to know and love God. The cosmos will not be a closed causal system that requires no reference to God as a causal agent at any point. Divine acts will not generally 'violate' the law of nature. Nor will they 'interfere' with an otherwise complete set of laws. Rather, such fairly frequent divine actions will be seen as integral and 'natural' parts of the regular operations of nature, at least in such complex integrated structures as the human brain.

In this context the question of miracles is the question of whether a God who is constantly causally active in the cosmos sometimes acts in ways that wholly transcend the regular operations of nature for a sufficiently good reason – for instance, to forward in a conspicuous way the purpose of bringing persons to know and love God. At the very least, such extraordinary acts would not be improper or arbitrary. The occurrence of a miracle would be largely a matter of degree, of the extent to which a divine action transcends the normal powers of natural objects and functions as a disclosure and realisation of a divine purpose.

Suppose God wills that persons should be transformed into a form of existence beyond this space-time, that they should know this to be possible, and that they should know that Jesus was not a failed prophet and understand that the way to their own transformation is through the Spirit who filled the life of Jesus. In that case, the resurrection of Jesus, though it transcends all known regularities leading to the natural decomposition of bodies, would be deeply intelligible, a divine act conspicuously manifesting and foreshadowing the destiny of the physical cosmos itself. It would be no violation of nature but rather a disclosure of the final goal of the whole natural creation, when all nature's laws will be transcended by a more intimate and conscious relation to their divine source.

Hume's Argument Against Believing in Miracles

Hume has two rather weak arguments against believing in miracles, and they can be quickly disposed of. First, he maintains that the evidence for the existence of laws of nature will always outweigh any claim that a miracle (something that breaks such a law) has occurred (Hume [1748] 1902,114). This is plainly not so. In both cases, observation is the ultimate court of appeal. Even an enormous amount of testimony that events have always obeyed regular laws of succession in the past cannot count at all against a well-grounded claim that there has been an exception to such regularity. How can we be sure that the future will be like the past? Hume himself admits that it is basically a matter of custom or habit: we just expect it to be so. Observation, however, can confound our greatest expectations. If we ask for evidence for the claim that laws of nature allow of no possible exceptions, it is hard to see that we can get any at all. One good case of reliable observation provides the only required counter example. Therefore, reliable testimony to observed miracles should rationally outweigh claims that laws of nature allow of no exceptions.

Hume's second argument is that there can be no reliable testimony to miracles. For us to accept such testimony, he says, the probability that the testimony is false must be less than the probability that the miracle occurred. But for Hume the probability that miracles occur is zero, whereas there is always some probability that testimony is false – that misobservation, deceit, delusion, or hallucination have occurred. In reply to Hume, it may be said that there is always some probability that miracles occur, if one cannot definitively rule out the existence of God, and the probability that one is deluded or deceived in observation is sometimes extremely low – in good conditions and with a number of unbiased observers and careful and cautious reporters.

Hume argues that the more unusual an occurrence is, the less we can trust reports that it happened. But that is false. There is no correlation between the unusualness of an occurrence and the unreliability of a report. 'No one has ever before experienced events like *X*' is not a strong argument against a claim that 'I have just seen an event of type *X*.' A more reasonable statement would be that, in the case of reports of events of a certain sort that are very commonly found to be delusory or deceitful – as in reports of UFO sightings – one should scrutinise them very carefully. It is not the unusualness of the reported events that makes us think them unreliable but the usualness of delusion in such cases.

We should scrutinise reports of miracles carefully, because people are known to exaggerate, be deluded, or be victims of deceit where miraculous events are concerned. We should not, however, discount seemingly strong testimony just because, much less to the extent that, the events reported are very unusual. A report of a maximally unusual event can be rationally accepted if the report meets the tests of delusion and deceit that we usually apply. And miracles, for a theist, are not even maximally unusual; they are irregular, rare, and exceptional. But good reasons might be found for their occurrence, insofar as they fit into a general web of beliefs that leads one to expect physical-law-transcending actions, unusual or not, from a Creator whose purpose is to lead people beyond the physical cosmos into conscious relationship with a higher spiritual reality. And if events that look like miracles are reported by reliable observers, that might in itself raise the probability that there is a God. If I am wondering whether God exists, reliable and life-transforming reports of the resurrection of one claimed to be the Son of God might reasonably lead me to believe that there is a God who can raise from the dead.

Miracles and Laws of Nature

What goes awry with a Humean account of miracles is that the laws of nature are taken to be absolutely changeless and universally operative. Acts of God, then, are taken to be interferences with or violations of the system. The antidote to this view is to see that if there is a personal Creator of all things, the physical cosmos will be partly instrumental in the realisation of a purpose that begins with but transcends it – eternal life. Laws of nature are the general principle of intelligible regularity that govern the physical cosmos, but there is every reason for a theist to think that there are higher principles than laws of nature – principles that draw finite persons into conscious relationship with the Creator. Miracles, events that transcend the regularities of nature, result from the application of such intelligible principles. In extraordinary circumstances, and for reasons connected with the realisation of the Creator's ultimate purpose, miracles are partial completions of the intelligible purpose that underlies the very existence of a physical universe. Insofar as they disclose personal purpose and its foreshadowing in the history of this cosmos, miracles vindicate, not violate, the rational unity of the cosmos.

There are good reasons why miracles should not be considered part of a scientific account of the universe or fall under formulable scientific laws. Carl Hempel's account of laws of nature as either deductive-nomological or inductive-statistical (1962) still often finds favour with philosophers of science. Deductive laws set up axioms from which laws can be deductively derived, and they state that whenever event of type *X* occurs, other things being equal, there is a general law that an event of type *Y* will follow. The effect follows deductively from the cause, given that the covering law applies. Since miracles are events caused directly by God, they do not follow from any prior physical state in accordance with a general law. We cannot give any physical account of why God acts as God does, because God is not a physical being. So we cannot in principle formulate any deductive covering laws for the activity of God.

Inductive Hempelian laws assign probabilities to events, such that, if an event of type *X* occurs, there is an exactly specifiable probability that an event of type *Y* will follow. The effect follows from the cause with a specific probability, but some other effect, whose probability is also specifiable, may follow instead. Some interpretations of quantum mechanics maintain that there is an objective probabilistic indeterminacy in nature that makes exact prediction of specific states impossible, though general, quite deterministic equations can be formulated.

There is perhaps some leeway for God to act here, determining the indeterminate. But God would still be confined by the limits of probability, and of course any divine action of this sort would not be miraculous, inasmuch as it would concur with the natural powers of objects. A miracle would not be physically probable – that is, it would not be predictable as a probable outcome of a prior physical state alone. Because a miracle is unpredictable (I assume that prophecies are not predictions but promises to act), Hempel would hold that to say God performs miracles is not an explanation.

At that point, however, many philosophers of science are prepared to reject Hempel's principle of structural identity, which maintains that all explanations must be predictive or must have predictive power (for one alternative account, see Cartwright 1983). It seems sensible to abandon it, since it does not work for Darwinian evolution explanations anyway. And it would certainly explain the resurrection to say that there was a personal agent with the power and a reason to raise Jesus from the dead, even though no one could predict the resurrection from the previous history of the universe. One could see why it happened, what its meaning was, and how it forms part of a wider web of beliefs about the nature of the universe. Such an explanation, however, is not part of any natural science.It can be provided only if one believes that there is, or could be, a God with a purpose to raise the dead and to raise this particular person in a unique way. There is no way that sense observation and experiment can detect such particular intentions of a spiritual being. Therefore, miracles can occur, and can properly explain the divine purpose, without forming part of any scientific, physical, partly predictive account of the universe.

The only sort of explanation that can be given of miracles is personal or value explanation – explaining an event as existing in order to help one realise a personal purpose or intention, to realise a goal that is of value in itself. We normally assume that value explanations are complementary to, or can run concurrently with, covering-law explanations, which derive events from prior conditions together with general laws of regular succession. I can say both that my arm went up because of the movements of electrons in my brain and nervous system, and that I raised my arm – it went up because I intended it to do so for some reason. It is plain that these explanations are separable in principle. My arm may go up involuntarily or I may intend to raise my arm and nothing happens. It is logically possible that my intending to do something may bring it about, even though no covering-law explanation of the event be found. That is how things used to be before the rise of modern science, though we now often assume that covering-law explanations always can be found. It may be, however,that covering-law explanations never completely explain human actions,that there is always some sort of 'gap' in the purely physical account that needs to be filled by intention. The assumption of full complementarity may turn out not to apply in some cases. Whether or not it applies will depend on empirical investigation.

The case is similar with miracles. It is logically possible that God could bring an event about by direct intention, then no covering-law explanations of the event can be given. That would be a miracle. God is a wholly spiritual being, unlike humans, who are embodied physical beings. God is also the ordainer of the natural order, able to direct it to God's purposes, whereas humans are parts of the natural order and cannot order it as they desire. For these reasons, intentional acts not falling under covering laws are much more likely to be modes of divine action than of human action.

In the question of whether miracles occur, then, the prestige and success of the natural sciences is of no avail. The sciences cannot, of themselves, make the possibility that miracles occur more or less likely. In assessing whether a miracle has occurred, we have to pay close attention, first of all, to the reliability and wisdom and knowledge of those who report its occurrence. Then we have to assess the sort of value explanation that can be given of its occurrence. Does it, for instance, contribute to the realisation of a good and intelligible purpose that points to a transcending of physical conditions as their fulfilling destiny? Or is it just an odd event that seems to have no particular spiritual point? If the testimony is reliable, and the event transcends the normal powers of objects, which is disclosive of divine power and helps to realise a divine purpose in a conspicuous way, it is wholly reasonable to accept that a miracle has occurred. The occurrence of miracles, then, will be a proper part of a many-stranded argument for the existence of a personal ground of being, a Creator of the universe.

I may have given the impression that science has nothing at all to say about miracles. That is not quite right. An event cannot properly be called a miracle unless it does transcend the ordinary powers of natural objects. It is for competent scientists in the appropriate field to say whether a given event transcends the normal operation of the laws of nature. If it does not, however statistically improbable the event may be, it is not a miracle. Where miracles can be subjected to scientific examination – as in the most often claimed cases, cases of healing – they should be, and competent scientific authorities should declare whether an event is a candidate for a miracle or not.

Science is important not only as a set of laws, methods, and assured experimental results but also as suggesting a rational and reflective approach to the world in which we live, a general view of the universe and the place of humans within it. If proper scientific method requires an exceptionless rule of general laws and an absence of any events that are not completely explicable in physical terms, then scientific method, if not scientific fact, will be at odds with a religious view. At that level a Humean view of science will find miracles absolutely impossible; they simply do not lie within the realm of physically possible events this view legislates.

The sort of scientific worldview into which miracles comfortably fit is one in which personal explanation plays an important and inexponible part, in which the powers and capacities of objects are variously realised in contexts of varying complexity and degrees and types of consciousness and in which the whole cosmos can be seen as expressing the purposes of a personal ground of being, purposes whose ultimate realisation may well-transcend the physical existence of the cosmos itself.

The investigations of scientists into the physical structure of the cosmos are highly relevant to the formation of such different worldviews. They are relevant in many informal and cumulative ways, in strengthening or weakening webs of belief about the most general nature of the cosmos. I have not argued that miracles occur, I have argued that they could occur, be reliably reported, and be justifiably believed. I have suggested that decisions about their occurrence will depend on a serious assessment of evidence and testimony and, wherever possible, on a scientific assessment of the availability of a natural explanation of the events. Decisions will also depend on the judicious formation of worldviews that scientific investigations support but that need also to take into account the status of personal or value explanations and of the data of conscious experience to which such explanations primarily apply. One is certainly justified in basing a view about miracles on one's own reflections on such matters. Until such investigations have been much more seriously undertaken, however, one might be wise not to be too dogmatic about what they will reveal to an (imaginary) unbiased observer.

References

Aquinas, Thomas. 1276. *Summa Theologiae.*

Benedict XIV. 1738. *De Servorum Dei: Beatificatione et Bertorum Canonizations iv. De Miraculis* I

Cartwright, Nancy. 1983. *How the Laws of Physics Lie.* Oxford: Clarendon Press.

Hempel, Carl, 1962. 'Deductive-Nomological versus Statistical Explanation.' In *Scientific Explanation, Space and Time,* vol. 2; *Minnesota Studies in Philosophy of Science,* H. Feigl and G. Maxwell (eds). Minneapolis: University of Minnesota Press.

Houston, Joseph. 1994. *Reported Miracles.* Cambridge: Cambridge University Press.

Hume, David. [1748] 1902. *An Enquiry Concerning Human Understanding.* A. Selby-Bigge (ed.). Oxford: Oxford University Press.

Swinburne, Richard. 1989. *Miracles.* London: Macmillan.

9

Christianity and Evolution: A Case Study

Introduction

Since the sixteenth century there has been an explosive expansion of human knowledge of the universe. It has been caused largely by commitment to an ideal of scientific knowledge, which was made possible by a combination of the invention of new means of controlled observation and the development of sophisticated mathematical techniques. The results have been spectacular and totally unforeseen, and have revolutionised human thought about the universe.

It may be said that Christian belief is not primarily about the nature of the physical universe. But the Bible does contain remarks about the creation of the universe, about the first human beings, about the origin of death, about the role of angels and demons in human life, about the probable course of human history, and about the end of the universe. Christianity makes the life of Jesus of central importance to its account of the whole of the created order. Its iconography gives human beings, especially in the persons of Jesus, Mary and the saints, a privileged place in heaven. Its creed apparently places a young human being, Jesus, as co-equal with the creator of heaven and earth. In other words, the Christian story seems to make humans central to the existence of the universe, and the life of Jesus is seen as a culminating event very near the end of that story.

It is this placing of the one human life at the culminating point of cosmic history which the modern scientific view of the universe has put in question. There was always a 'scandal of particularity' in Christianity. Why should God act in just this one human person, when there are so many other human cultures and histories? But that scandal fades to insignificance in the light of the vast universe which science has discovered.

The universe is fifteen thousand million years old. The earth is one tiny planet on the edge of one galaxy out of millions. This planet will probably continue to exist for five thousand million years, before the dying and expanding sun in its death throes renders it uninhabitable. Humans are the results of millions of years of the gradual evolution of life-forms, and humans will eventually evolve into something else, or die out without causing more than a ripple in the universe as a whole.

The stage on which the Christian story was first thought to be played out has expanded so amazingly that it has, for many, become imaginatively impossible to see this planet, let alone one human life, as of any particular importance in cosmic history. In the face of such a revolution in perception, the question of how far Christianity can adapt, while retaining its identity, is a real and pressing one.

The challenge of the cosmic perspective of science faces virtually all religions, most of which originated in pre-scientific times. I shall, however, confine my attention here to Christianity. I shall also select for consideration just one rather crucial aspect of the scientific theory of cosmic evolution, the Darwinian theory of the evolution of life-forms by natural selection. That is because the Darwinian theory generates in a particularly sharp form the opposition that can arise between religious and scientific views. It thus focuses particularly acutely the issue of how far religious beliefs can change in the light of new knowledge.

I shall take it for granted that new scientific knowledge renders some traditional Christian beliefs false – a literal interpretation of the story of Adam and Eve, for example. The interesting question is whether the new perspective can add depth to some fairly central beliefs, so that new interpretations may plausibly be seen as part of a coherent re-organisation of the whole belief-system, rather than as merely *ad hoc*, slightly desperate adjustments. I shall defend the view that the scientific vision of cosmic evolution forces a coherent and interconnected set of changes on traditional Christian beliefs. In the course of doing that, I hope to clarify one sense in which a set of religious beliefs may be revised and develop, while continuing to constitute one religious tradition.

The Theory Of Evolution and the Existence Of God

It is a fairly safe assumption that the writers of the New Testament documents had not come across the theory of evolution. That theory was not invented by Charles Darwin, but his book, *The Origin Of Species,*[1] published in 1859, presented it in what may be called its classical form. Darwin did not have access to modern knowledge of genetics, but with its aid we can state his basic theory in four simple propositions. Organisms reproduce. In the course of such reproduction, various mutations occur, now often called 'mistakes' in the copying process whereby DNA replicates itself. Organisms compete for scarce resources, and many of them are eliminated by the environment or by their competitors. Some mutations are naturally selected by this process, simply because they survive and reproduce more effectively than others. Given these four propositions, one is able to see the whole history of organic life on earth as a process of random mutation, in which natural forces continually act to select some mutations in preference to others and so different species evolve over thousands of years. Homo Sapiens is a species which has evolved by millions of tiny mutations over millions of generations as our non-human ancestors proved able to survive the hazards of their environments and continued to produce mutated forms which were favoured by natural selection.

The four basic propositions of the theory have been experimentally well established. There can be no doubt that DNA replicates and produces continual mutations and the process of natural selection has been repeatedly observed in relatively isolated animal populations. A simple example is that fluffy mice are selected in cold winters in preference to short-haired mice, so that the weather in this case naturally selects fluffy mice, which originally mutated from short-haired mice. The theory of evolution is a generalisation from these truths, which claims that they provide the basis for a general understanding of why organic life on earth today takes the very varied forms it does.

There is much room for dispute about the adequacy and implications of such a generalisation. Stephen Jay Gould takes it to imply that the history of life on earth is a matter of pure chance, an immensely improbable series of accidents which could very easily have taken a very different course. For him, there is no reason why conscious beings should have evolved at

1 Charles Darwin, *The Origin of Species by Means of Natural Selection* (rpt. Harmondsworth 1985).

all, and humans are an accidental growth at which we should be extremely surprised, but which is in no sense a result of some plan or purpose.[2]

For Richard Dawkins, however, mutations will almost inevitably give rise to conscious organisms at some stage, and once they exist they will quickly eliminate possible competitors. There is an inbuilt tendency to complexity and consciousness. 'But there is still no purpose or need for a designer, since the process accounts for itself quite adequately, and the introduction of a designer would only complicate matters unduly.'[3]

It is difficult to adjudicate between these differing interpretations. To know whether the process of evolution is inevitable or not one would have to know what mutations were liable to occur, and what selective pressures might exist which could be guaranteed to keep the process going in the direction of complexity. It is hard to see how one could know such things. But there is one way in which one could guarantee an evolutionary movement towards complexity and consciousness. That is if the system was planned so that mutations of the right kind would occur, and so that selective pressures would favour complex life-forms. Such a plan would require vast intelligence and power over the laws of nature. But it is clearly possible that an evolutionary process could be set up by such an intelligence which would inevitably result, after millions of generations, in human beings, or at least in conscious, rational moral agents very like human beings.

Since this is so, any claim that the theory of evolution does away with the necessity for God, or that it shows that humans evolved by pure chance, is quite unjustified. Gould's interpretation claims that human life could evolve by chance, but that it is extremely improbable that it ever would. Dawkins' interpretation claims that, given the system, something like human life is bound to evolve, but the system itself, with its complex and highly integrated process of relations between mutations and selective natural conditions, just exists by chance. It is obvious, however, that such a system could also be intelligently designed. And the hypothesis of intelligent design makes the existence of the process much more probable than the hypothesis of pure chance. Dawkins may say that the theory does not need God, but it remains true that God is a much better explanation of

---

2 Stephen Jay Gould, *Wonderful Life: The Burgess Shale and the Nature of History* (London: Vintage, 1989).

3 Richard Dawkins, *The Blind Watchmaker* (1986; rpt. Harmondsworth: Penguin, 1991).

the process than is chance (which is in fact no explanation at all). In this sense, God may not be necessary to the theory of evolution. But the theory of evolution is much more plausible if there is a God – and that is what Charles Darwin himself thought.

This conclusion may come as a surprise to those who have been accustomed to regard the theory of evolution with suspicion, as somehow in conflict with biblical truth. But that is partly because the theory has sometimes been presented as though it requires the 'pure chance' interpretation, or as though it subordinates the providential acts of God to some sort of impersonal or random process. I have tried to suggest that is just not true.

God and the Cosmic Process

In some popular presentations, science and religion are portrayed as enemies which can never be reconciled, but such a view would be wildly inaccurate from a historical point of view. Just to take the most obvious example, Isaac Newton was a pious Christian (though it is true he did not accept what he took to be the orthodox doctrine of the Trinity), and he records that he was able to formulate the basic laws of mechanics by postulating that the universe was created by a wise and powerful God. He asked himself the question what general laws such a God would create, and decided that they would be the simplest, most elegant laws, capable of giving rise to complex sets of effects. He turned out to be right, as everyone knows, and so not only did he discover the basic laws of nature, he also vindicated his postulate of a wise creator God.

Perhaps one could pursue Newton's question a little further, in a different form, and ask why a wise creator God might set up a process of evolution by natural selection. Putting it in an even wider context, why would God create a universe which evolves, as a whole, from the primordial Big Bang, an ultimate simplicity of infinite density, without complexity or consciousness, through the emergence of elementary particles, the formation of galaxies and planetary systems, to the evolution of those very complex forms of organic life with central nervous systems and brains that generate awareness and autonomous action?

I suggest that, from a Christian viewpoint, the first clue to answering this question is to see the distinctive value of a process of creative and co-operative realisation and comprehension of new forms of truth, beauty and loving relationships, within a community of sentient moral agents. For Christians, the goal of human existence is the realisation of the 'kingdom of God,' a community in which goodness can be actualised in a society of truth, fidelity, justice and peace. That community is a finite image of the Creator, who is the final truth, the utterly faithful and just, the supremely beautiful and the loving source of all things.

This is a goal which is depicted in Christian revelation, but which is worthwhile in itself, and which could be chosen by an intelligent creator. It would involve the creation of moral agents who could interact with one another in seeking to realise many forms of goodness, to understand their world and shape it in accordance with their imaginative ideals. In other words, a worthwhile goal of creation would be the existence of a community of moral agents, united in the pursuit of goodness.

It may be thought that fifteen thousand million years of cosmic evolution is a very roundabout way to achieve such a goal, when God could presumably create it directly, as many Christians used to think God did. But perhaps the goal is not just the culmination of the process, but the whole process itself, which is one of generating from within a material cosmos the ability of that cosmos to understand and take control of its own being. Human beings are parts of the cosmic process at which one can see this understanding and control begin to exist.

They are not mature conscious agents without a history, who just begin to exist, with the whole material cosmos as an unnecessary backdrop to their activity. They are highly complex material structures, carrying within themselves the history of their development, integral parts of a wider material order. It is that order which they can understand and help to control and human life should be seen as just one part of a wider process of creative development.

The process is one of creative emergence, as new forms of intelligibility and beauty successively come into existence out of earlier and simpler structures. From the explosive destruction of primordial undifferentiated energy emerge the elements of hydrogen and helium. From the interaction of those elements emerge the stars and galaxies, and the more complex formation of carbon atoms. From the complex organisation of carbon atoms emerge RNA and DNA, the primal structures making self-replication possible. From the recombinations of nucleotides emerge self-sustaining organic structures which produce central nervous systems and primitive brains. And from the elementary forms of perception and semi-automatic response to stimuli emerge the capacities for abstract understanding and free action which characterise human beings.

One can see this whole process as if it were a work of creative imagination, continually building complex structures out of simpler elements, and always moving towards the capacity of the process to know and shape itself. If it is such a work, the whole process will have a beauty, intelligibility and imaginative flair that will be of great value to the creative intelligence which creates it and continues to move it towards that final goal, which has been implicit in it from the first. Humans are not, in other words, spiritual substances dropped into the material world as alien intruders. They are parts of a continuum of growing complexity in the material order, realising possibilities implicit in that order from the beginning.

God values the whole cosmic process for its imaginative beauty, its continual realisation of new actualities out of the indefinite array of possibilities which are implicit in its origin. The whole process is of value to God. It is in itself an expression of the imaginative and creative activity of God. But the process of creative emergence is one which generates from itself communities of beings who can know and shape its future. Such beings come to share in the delight and imaginative creativity of God. They can become fellow-workers with God, co-operating with the divine creative Spirit in the task of making the material world a sacrament of the divine Spirit, a world in which wisdom, creativity, and friendship can be celebrated and enjoyed.

One might envisage three stages of such a created cosmic process. First is the stage of imaginative creativity, in which the creator shapes ever more complex emergent forms out of the primordial energy, the 'great deep' of potentiality. The Genesis picture of the creative Spirit moving over the waters of the great deep, the sea of primal chaos, expresses this stage well. Next is the stage at which consciousness emerges as a property of the cosmos, and begins to co-operate with God in shaping the cosmos to a form in which it can express the divine Spirit itself. Again the Genesis picture of humans being given dominion over the earth, with the responsibility of making it fruitful is a very apt one. Third is the consummation of the cosmos, in which it becomes a sacrament of perfect beauty, without conflict or defect, fully expressive of the divine nature as love, shaped by communities of love which share in the expression of the divine love. The New Testament picture of a people united in Christ depicts such a fulfilled universe.

In this way one can think and see why a creator God might originate an emergent, evolutionary cosmic process. It would be a process culminating in the goal of a sacramental community of love, but the process leading to that goal would be an important factor in the value of the goal itself. In that final consummation, the whole process could be summed up and seen as having from the first been directed towards a partly self-shaped conscious union with the creator.

The Theistic Hypothesis and the Consummation of the Cosmos

I have suggested that the hypothesis of God makes the emergence of moral life in the cosmos by the general mechanism of Darwinian evolution much more probable than the hypothesis that it occurs by pure chance. But for the God hypothesis to be fully satisfactory, it has to be true that the third stage, the emergence of a community which fully expresses the divine life, will be realised. From a scientific point of view, we do not know whether or not it will be. Scientific optimists do look for a continued increase in knowledge and sensitivity, which will result in a just and peaceful society, free of disease and even of death. Scientific pessimists point out that humans are liable to exterminate themselves at any moment, and that the universe will run down anyway in the end, eliminating any possibility of a final goal of evolution.

Scientific optimists hold that we will be able to control our genetic constitution, thus eliminating the elements of randomness in evolution, with its consequences of disease and death. We will, they say, be able to replace the struggle for survival by co-operation, when we have the technology to ensure abundance of goods for all. Scientific pessimists, however, point out that the people trying to exercise genetic control will themselves be in the grip of the passions of greed and hatred, and are likely to create genetic monstrosities which will probably get wholly out of control. And technology does not make for abundance. On the contrary, it uses up energy resources at an alarming rate, so human conflict over scarce resources is liable to become universally destructive.

Atheists do not have much reason for optimism. It is highly unlikely that blind processes of ruthless competition will issue in the existence of a stable moral community of justice and peace. On the theistic hypothesis, however, the mutational process is not blind or wholly indiscriminate. It involves elements of randomness, but is set up to move inevitably to greater complexity and integrated order. One theistic explanation for the existence of such randomness is that it provides a necessary physical basis for the later development of responsible freedom, which in time is necessary for the existence of fully personal relationships of love.[4] This requires that the universe is not completely determined, and so, at pre-rational stages, must be partly random.

Nor, for a theist, is the evolutionary process one of less competition. On the contrary, it essentially involves intricate co-operation to produce and maintain living organisms. If evolution is to take place, there must be a replacement of lower by higher forms, but once the stage of rational reflection has been reached, co-operation can increasingly take over from competition, as a driving force for further development.

It looks as though theists will be optimists, expecting evolution to produce responsibly free and co-operative agents, who can subordinate their non-rational and competitive dispositions to more reflective and altruistic intentions. But the story is slightly more complicated. Evolution has produced such agents, but the price of producing them and leaving them free is that they can fail to rise to reflective altruism, and may choose rather to oppress and destroy others than to encourage and sustain them. Theists have to take freely chosen selfishness into account, and that qualifies any over-easy optimism about the future.

In fact, since the earth will be swallowed up by the sun in about one billion years, and the whole universe will eventually run down, it is fairly clear that any ultimate goal for the cosmos must lie beyond this physical space-time. This leads to the conclusion that the final stage will probably be beyond the confines of this cosmos, though it must also be the consummation and recapitulation of this cosmic process. Thus theists are committed to being trans-cosmic optimists. They are committed to believing that there will exist a community of wisdom, joy and love, from which all evil and egoism is excluded. From that viewpoint, the history of this cosmos can be seen as the preparation of sentient beings for existence in the perfected community, though that history has its own distinctive value as the arena of the creative activity of God and the place where

4 Cf. Vincent Brümmer, *Speaking of a Personal God* (Cambridge 1992), 139–45.

created souls can either prepare themselves to share in the love of God or fall into the destructive patterns of egoistic existence.

Evolution and the Moral Order

It follows that the theistic hypothesis is the best explanation of the evolutionary process as we see it (making the evolution of sentient beings from initial unconscious states more likely than any other hypothesis). But it does require that one sees the process as not wholly morally indiscriminate (not morally random) and as not one solely of ruthless competition.

I think that one's evaluation of these matters will depend largely on personal judgments about the moral value of human life. I would say that the evolutionary process does not look blind to moral values – it does issue in the existence of moral agents, who can shape the world to good or evil by their own choices. But it necessitates much conflict and suffering, and thus seems, considered on its own, to suggest a God who wills to create goodness through suffering, and is thus far from being a wholly kind and gentle God. We might recall, however, that the biblical God is one who inspires terror, who destroys as well as heals, and whose goodness is more awe-inspiring than tender-hearted. It may be that some modern Christian ideas of God fail to preserve the sense of terror and awe of which the Bible is well aware, and which depict the creator as one who wounds and heals, kills and makes alive, but who in the end offers an overwhelming good to those who persevere.

I also think that Darwin's gloomy view of nature as a continual struggle for survival is unduly one-sided. There is a struggle for survival, but most of that struggle does not involve the suffering that characterises organisms with highly developed nervous systems. And the evolutionary process also requires co-operation and self-sacrifice, a creative striving after fuller life and experience, not just a desperate attempt to stay alive at any cost. It is more a 'striving for fuller life' than a ruthless 'struggle for survival': The process is well-fitted to implant dispositions both to selfish and to altruistic behaviour in the higher conscious animals. Seeing how evolution implants both survival and sacrificial dispositions in complex organisms gives a helpful explanation of why humans should be tempted to evil, and yet obligated to goodness. As the early theologian Irenaeus said, primitive humans were placed between good and evil, so that they might grow to maturity, whether for good or ill, through the responsible choices they made.[5] In the course of evolution, there must have been a first moment of conscious moral choice. That is the point at which the 'Fall of humanity' began, and humans were estranged from that natural fellowship with God which should have been theirs.

It seems to me, then, that the theory of evolution does not require that the process is blindly random, morally indiscriminate, and one of a ruthless war of all against all. These are evaluations, not parts of the scientific theory. The process can be plausibly seen as probabilistic, yet ordered to the realisation of good, and as promoting co-operation and altruism as well as a selfish will to survive. As such, it is best explained by a God with the power to establish such a probabilistic order, and with the will to create morally autonomous conscious agents. Yet the theistic hypothesis will only be fully confirmed if there comes to exist a community of souls born in this cosmos but finding their final goal in a trans-cosmic state of unity with God.

That is only to say what most Christians have always said, that the purpose of God will only be fully realised beyond this world. The gospel on which Christianity is founded is that there is such a realisation, and that it has received its confirmation in the resurrection of Jesus. Such confirmation is beyond the investigative techniques of science. It is a matter of faith, but not some sort of irrational leap in the dark. It is a faith based on present experience of a God who promises good, and on the apostolic testimony to Jesus' resurrection as the foreshadowing of the creation of a new heaven and earth!

No scientific theory claims any knowledge of the existence of God and of life after death. Christian revelation is a primary source in history for such claims. It is Jesus who teaches, and shows by his life, that God is a personal God of love, who offers that love endlessly to those who respond to it. One would not expect a scientific description of the physical universe to discover such things. Nevertheless, the scientific description must be consistent with these truths, and one might expect that it may, at least in an indirect way, point towards them.

Some proponents of the theory of evolution may speak of mutation as random, yet it is undeniable that the process has led to the existence of conscious, intentional, morally reflective agents. They may speak of a battle for the survival of the fittest, but it is only by co-operation and

5 See John Hick, *Evil and the God of Love* (1966; reissue London 1985).

inter-dependence that anything survives at all, and the end-state of the process so far is one where consciousness of truth, beauty and friendship have become conscious goals of at least a great many living beings.

Such facts are consistent with the Christian belief that humans are free agents who have trapped themselves in self-will, but are still capable of turning to goodness when it appears to them. The facts of evolution plausibly suggest a universe which is ordered by a wise creator towards the realisation of freely chosen goodness, which has been deflected from that aim by its own misused freedom, and which may yet be open to a restoration of its primal aim by the reconciling action of the creator. If the postulate of a creator is the best explanation of the facts of evolution (making its actual history much more probable than chance), and if the myopic choice of self is the best explanation of much of the suffering on this planet, then one might reasonably hope for some effective action by the creator to make the original goal possible. It is in that way that the scientific description of the universe may actually point towards the possibility of a historical disclosure of the creator, which would reveal the way to the realisation of the creator's goal in an estranged world.

Christian Faith and Cosmic Evolution

At this point the surprising consonance of Christian revelation with the theory of evolution is apparent. Biblical revelation leads us to see God as the creator of all things. It leads us to see the cosmos as created through Wisdom, which delights in the creative process (Proverbs 8). It sees the cosmos as developing from primal chaos to ordered creation (Genesis 1:2) through the creative activity of the Spirit, patterned on the archetypal Word of God. Human beings are not seen as disembodied souls inserted into alien matter, but as formed of matter (dust), which is shaped to become a finite image of God, to be self-aware and self-directing.

Moreover, the whole created cosmos moves towards a goal, not yet realised but foreshadowed in Christ – 'He has made known to us the mystery of his will … to unite all things in him [Christ], things in heaven and things on earth' (Ephesians 1:9–10). The Christ in which the whole cosmos is to be united is the eternal Word of God, 'the image of the invisible God, the first-born of all creation,' and 'in him all things were created' (Colossians 1:15–16). That eternal Word assumed human nature and was manifest on earth as Jesus, but in itself the Word is infinitely greater than any human life. He is the pattern of all creation, and according to Paul he is the completion of creation, within whose reality all things will be united.

At that time, 'the creation itself will be set free from its bondage to decay and obtain the glorious liberty of the children of God' (Romans 8:21). The Christian hope is not for personal immortality. It is for the transformation of the whole creation into a perfect sacrament of God. The New Testament even holds that this will be an inclusion of creation 'in Christ,' an assumption of the creation into the life of God, a state that some early theologians called 'theosis,' a sharing, by grace, in God.

The biblical picture of the cosmos is thus from the first an evolutionary one, according to which primal matter, the chaos of the 'great deep' is shaped by the Spirit on the pattern of the eternal wisdom or Word of God, until it becomes finally united in the being of the one who is the perfect image of God, until it becomes the body of Christ, and we are compelled to say, the body of God. The history of the cosmos is the history of a development from the inert chaos of primal matter to the fulfillment of its proper function as an embodiment and personal manifestation of the life of God.

The New Testament writers see this development as having been corrupted by the doomed attempt of sentient creatures to turn away from obedience to God. The created cosmos falls away from its intended goal, and becomes subject to futility and spiritual death. The wages of sin is death, existence in estrangement from God, the only source of life. Within this estranged world, the divine Word takes human nature in order to heal the sickness of self, manifest the divine love, and lead humanity back to its proper destiny. When the first Christians looked for the *parousia* of Christ, the manifest presence of the eternal Word, they were looking for a future in which all creation will be renewed in the divine Word, restored to its predestined goal.

They may never have heard of the theory of evolution. But that theory fills out the Christian revelation in an enriching and illuminating way. Some early Christians thought the end of the world would come in their own lifetime. They were unaware of the millions of years that had preceded them, and of the millions of galaxies that surrounded them. They did not realise that the end of life on earth would leave the vast spaces of the cosmos virtually untouched. They suffered from a cosmic myopia for which they could hardly be blamed, given the knowledge available to them.

At the same time, they already possessed the cure for their myopia, though they may not have fully recognised it. The good news of liberation from the bondage of self, and the gift of life-giving union with God, was meant for all humanity, not only for a few contemporary Jews. Prompted by Peter's visions and Paul's enthusiasm, a mission to all nations was initiated which implied that the end of all things was not yet. Since the sixteenth century, the remnants of such Christian myopia should have been thoroughly corrected as the full extent of the vision of cosmic redemption which is so central to Paul's recorded teaching has become clear. Humans may or may not have a central role in the redemption of the whole cosmos, but at least it is obvious that the death of this planet will not be the end of creation by any means. Creation will have an end, but it will not coincide with the destruction of the earth, as the New Testament writers almost certainly thought it would. Such knowledge of the vastness of the cosmos does not undermine Christian hope, or the decisiveness of the life of Jesus for the history of planet earth. Its central teaching remains that the ending of the history of the cosmos will be, not a whimpering descent into everlasting darkness, but a recreation of all things in the glorious presence of the divine Word.

This hope does not license a lazy optimism or a relaxation of striving for the good. Our own lives, or life of the whole planet, may indeed end at any time in disaster. For that reason we must indeed stay alert, for we do not know when the end of human life on earth might come. Nevertheless, the vision of contemporary Christianity is a cosmic vision of the reconciliation and uniting of the whole cosmos into a unity in Christ. It is impossible to say how and when God will accomplish that goal, but it is clear that if the divine purpose is not brought to a premature conclusion by human evil, we are as yet a very long way from its realisation.

There can be no doubt that belief in cosmic evolution forces changes on Christian belief. These changes, however, are not as radical as they may seem at first. If it were established that evolution is really random and non-purposive, that would undermine any form of Christian belief which makes objective claims about the nature of the universe. It would force either a radical form of non-realism, or, more plausibly in my view, an abandonment of Christian belief. Despite the efforts of anti-religious neo-Darwinists, I do not think the non-purposive interpretation has been established, and I am prepared to risk the bet that it will not be.

In that case, one plausible interpretation of a Pauline-Johannine Christology transposes quite easily into an evolutionary context. Such an interpretation was, indeed, very like a set of options current in early forms of Christian thought, even though such options have sometimes been officially denied (as recently as the Roman Catholic Encyclical *Rerum Novarum*, which apparently made belief in Adam and Eve binding).

The New Testament shows that there existed an early belief that Jesus would return very soon in glory to save a selected group of humans from imminent Judgment, and found the kingdom of God. Apparently a surprising number of American Christians (a remarkable 48%) still believe this, despite the fact that they have to reinterpret the 'very soon' quite radically.

This belief, however, already received re-interpretation within the New Testament itself, and it was bound to do so as soon as there was time for reflection on the implications of the nature of the Messianic claim made for Jesus. For it was soon seen that Jesus was the universal Saviour, the incarnation of the eternal Word, and that God had a goal for creation and a global mission for the Church. These beliefs are all incompatible with a literal coming in glory to 'save' just a few Jewish disciples and put an end to history within just a few years.

Reflection on the theory of cosmic evolution does little more than continue this process of re-interpretation. It does so in five main ways. First, it leads one to stress that, while Jesus is the incarnation of the Word on this planet, there may be innumerable worlds and forms of non-human incarnation. So it leads to a less anthropocentric view of redemption and of the possible inhabitants of heaven.

Second, it leads one to emphasise that Jesus shows the universal love of God for every sentient being, and so to adopt a less exclusive attitude to non-Christians and a broader view of the universal mission of the Church.

Third, it leads one to reflect on the immensity of the divine goal for creation, and so to adopt a positively world-transforming attitude to the Christian life, rather than quietly wait for the world to end (an attitude which Paul anyway condemned).

Fourth, it leads one to adopt a non-literal reading of much of Scripture, especially the narratives of creation and Final Judgment, and so encourages one to explore metaphor and symbol in a way which would have been familiar to Jewish commentators.

Fifth, and perhaps more controversially, it leads one to accept a great degree of chance in nature, and a great degree of relatively autonomous freedom in created beings. Thus it stands in some degree of opposition to accounts of a total divine determination of all things. That reverses the tradition of Augustinian interpretation which was broadly accepted in many Christian churches, but it has strong support in many biblical texts.

Strange and unexpected as it may at first seem, Darwin's discovery may be seen as a valuable extension of our knowledge of the nature of God's creation, putting Christian faith in a wider context in space and time. It can give a greater appreciation of the wisdom of God which is shown in the complexity and beauty of the evolutionary plan, in the disclosure of the true goal of the cosmic process, and in the hope for the whole universe that is foreshadowed in Jesus Christ.

None of this could have been envisaged in this form by the first generations of Christians. It moves Jesus from being the last major event in history to being a proleptic disclosure on earth of a million-year process towards a cosmic goal. This revision can be seen as a development because its core beliefs of a revelation in Jesus of God as love, of the human goal as sharing in that love, and of the means to the goal as participating in the life of the Spirit are preserved. The Christian religion remains the same, because it continues to trace its originative and canonical disclosure of the divine to the person of Jesus. It must continually change, because growing knowledge of the context of that disclosure must change its meaning and significance. The impact of evolutionary theory on Christian beliefs is one case which shows how large-scale interpretative changes can plausibly be seen as developments, not repudiations, of a set of canonical and authoritative beliefs.

10

The Soul and the Brain

One of the most persuasive attacks on the idea of the soul comes from those who would claim that the soul depends wholly for its existence on the brain, which can be understood in straightforward physical terms. The brain, it might be said, is just like a rather complex computer, and it can be predicted, modified or controlled in the same sort of way. We do not talk about computers having souls; so we need not talk about human beings having souls, either. Souls are superfluous; we should just see the brain as a complicated electrochemical computer, and treat it accordingly. There is no 'ghost in the machine', it might be said; no need to talk about hidden or secret spiritual entities. There is just the machine, and we will soon be able to understand and control that with the aid of science.

Neurophysiology, the analysis of the physical structure of the brain, is still an infant science. But it has already reached a stage at which certain sorts of experiences can be chemically induced, or certain personality traits surgically altered. The rather drastic operation of prefrontal leucotomy, for example, which separates the frontal lobes from the rest of the brain, has consequences that include major personality changes. It seems that we can change character by tampering with the brain. Monkeys have been sexually stimulated by passing electric currents to exposed parts of the cortex. By the same methods, bulls can be halted in the middle of an aggressive charge, hens can be made to fly in panic or display sexually. Further, human subjects with electrodes implanted in their brains can be caused to see such things as red patches when they are electrically stimulated, and by stimulating different parts of the cortex, different sorts of sensations can be caused.

From such facts as these, it may seem that conscious experiences are all caused by electrical stimulation of parts of the brain, and that they could in principle be artificially produced by such stimulation. As well as electrical stimulation, many chemicals are regularly used by psychiatrists in the course of their daily work, in order to relieve depressive illnesses or acute anxiety states. The use of stimulants and depressants is almost normal in our society. And it is probable that more extensive control of moods, of bad temper and aggression, of happiness or misery, could be induced by more efficient methods of drug control. We may have here a much more effective method of controlling human behaviour than our present course of moral persuasion and exhortation. Where, in the past, people may have looked for some spiritual answer to depression, they may find more certain and rapid relief by a simple injection or course of tablets.

The fact that drugs, surgery and electrical stimulation can alter your experiences and character, and that the physical structure of the brain will perhaps be completely understood some day, has great implications for our view of human life. Just as we can now transplant hearts, kidneys or other physical organs, we may learn to transplant brains, and thus transfer a person from one body to another. Not only that, but we might learn to duplicate, artificially, the structure of a person's brain – perhaps making an exact replica of it in metal or silicone – and so give that 'person' immortality. And if we could do that, we could manufacture any number of duplicates of the same person. Then we might be able to control their behaviour from some central computer, so that they would do whatever we want without complaint – since we would control all their thoughts and desires by controlling their brain impulses.

All this is in the realm of science fiction, of course. But some scientists think it is possible. And if it is possible, it seems to show that all our experience is totally dependent on physical states of our brains. That humane thinker Julian Huxley writes, 'I confidently look forward to a time when eugenic improvement will become one of the major aims of mankind'.[1] He is thinking of developing control of the genetic basis of human life, by manipulating the DNA that forms the basis of character, so that we might be able to eliminate aggression, increase intelligence and altruism and so on. But it is clear that such control will be even more effective if we can learn to control the brain directly, and thus cause people to be

1 Julian Huxley, *Man and his Future*, ed. G. Wolstenholme (Churchill Press, 1963), p. 17.

altruistic, aggressive, happy or depressed as we choose, by pressing an array of buttons. In the end, we could insert experiences, emotions and even seeming memories into their minds. The degree of control that will be possible seems frightening. It looks as if the species *homo sapiens* will be able to design and manufacture its own descendants to a planned recipe. Complete conscious control over character and experience may at last become a fact.

What happens, in view of these quite astonishing possibilities, to the idea of the human soul? When we see the possibility of controlling human nature by physical means; of duplicating persons or mixing their memories up, even transferring memories from one person to another; of changing characters, desires and hopes at will – what then happens to the idea of a spiritual, indivisible soul? The more we realise the extent of the dependence of personal consciousness upon physical brain-states, the less plausible seems the idea that we each have one unique and continuing subject of moral will and awareness, which is our soul. So we need to look rather carefully at these claims and possibilities.

In the first place, it is not really surprising that if we interfere with the brain by cutting pieces out of it, putting electric shocks through it or injecting strange chemical substances into it, our personality and experience will be affected. Nobody would be surprised if we reminded them that, if we chopped their heads off, their conscious experience would be badly affected. Similarly, if I lock someone in a dark room for three years, I would expect his character to change for the worse. Do drastic things to people, and they will be affected quite badly. So it is not odd to be told that our experiences and characters depend greatly on our environment, on the states of our bodies and brains. If our bodies lack one chemical, we get diabetes and feel tired and lethargic. If they lack another, we may feel very depressed, and both states can be relieved by taking the necessary chemical artificially.

This is not worrying; it is obvious, when you think about it. The worry only comes in when the claim is made that *all* a person's experiences are determined *solely* by physical states of the brain, and that these states follow inevitable, predictable laws of physics and chemistry alone. B. A. Farrell, who was a psychologist at Oxford University, once said, 'A human being is a modulator of pulse frequencies, and nothing more'.[2] We

2 B. A. Farrell, 'On the Design of a Conscious Device', in *Mind*, July 1970.

have met that 'nothing more' before. This time, man is being seen as a very complex feedback, storage and reaction machine, and nothing more, a computer of a relatively advanced sort; with an organic main-frame.

If this were true, it would, I think, be worrying. If I am able to predict with certainty, by using known physical laws, all subsequent movement of a person's brain, then I would know exactly what he was going to do, and I would know that he could not do otherwise. People may think they are acting 'freely', that they have choices. But in fact all their thoughts and acts would follow inevitably from physical laws alone. Once we know that, we should really give up all notions of responsibility and guilt, of punishment and desert, and simply set out to control deviant behaviour in the most effective way. Law courts would be replaced by panels of psychiatrists and brain surgeons, and the only question to ask would be how to modify the person's behaviour so that he did more acceptable things in future. I think I would find this more worrying than being brought before a jury; the possibilities for social manipulation are enormous.

But the basic question is, are all my experiences caused by brain-states that are wholly predictable according to laws of physics? If we believe that persons are free to direct their own lives, at least to some extent, we will normally think that their actions are not wholly predictable or explicable in physical terms. The quite widely held view that freedom and complete physical predictability are wholly compatible seems to me another version of the double-think view that we can go on assuming that people often could have done otherwise (as we do in English law, for example) even when we know that they could not have done so in fact.

If I am right, there seems to be a test for whether people are free. For if we did manage to predict all a person's acts in physical terms alone, we would have shown that real moral freedom – the physically indeterminate choice of action – did not exist, at least in that case. But in fact we can say with certainty that such a test could never be carried out. The amount of information we would need, to be able to predict all a person's subsequent behaviour, is infinite. It cannot even be quantified exactly enough to form the basis of accurate prediction. We cannot keep people in closely controlled laboratory conditions for long. And we can never be sure we have exhaustively specified all possible causal influences on their behaviour. In view of these severe limitations on our ability to gather adequate data, we will have to retreat to rather vague generalizations about probabilities. We may be able to predict roughly how large masses of people will react to various stimuli (though economists and politicians do not seem to be very good at it). But we will never be able to predict exactly how individuals will behave. We can say what our friends are *likely* to do, but we can never be absolutely sure. So, though at first sight there seems to be a scientific test for whether freedom exists, it turns out that no such test could ever be successfully devised or carried out.

So I could never *prove* that all my brain-states are predictable solely by appeal to the laws of physics. But may they nevertheless *be* so? Perhaps we can begin to consider this by looking at the well-known analogy of a computer. Computers do, of course, obey the laws of physics. If they did not, we could never be sure that they would work. Once the program is loaded, we can predict what the computer will do. But we will nevertheless not understand what it is really doing, if we only know the laws of physics and nothing more. All we will have is a series of physical states, following general sequences. What we can never know, from the laws of physics alone, is what the whole series is *for*; what it *means*; or *why* it was set up in the first place.

Moreover, the initial state of the series of physical events has been determined by a designed program, which is not part of the system, and which, again, can only be understood in terms of human purposes and desires. And, of course, most programs require continuous humanly regulated input, which can then be processed by the hard-wired systems in the computer. So it is not true that all events in the computer can be predicted according to laws of physics alone. The initial design of the system; the more-or-less continuous interface with human input; and the interpretation of the data produced by the system are all non-derivable from a study of the closed physical structure of the computer itself.

The model of complete physical predictability is, it must be stressed, an ideal, hypothetical abstraction from a complex, dynamic, emergent reality. We should not think of mental activity as an 'interference' in a closed mechanistic causal web. It is the idea of such a web that is a pure imaginative construction of the mind. What is being said is this: imagine that the world consists only of so many physical particles, with clearly definable properties, relating to each other according to a few general laws. Nothing else ever interferes with this system – it is closed, in that sense. Since we can know all the laws and properties exhaustively, and there can never be any new ones or any new, unique, truly creative events, everything in that system is perfectly predictable.

In laboratories or very simple environments, like the near vacuum of space, we can come close to having such a closed system. In such places, our ideal model is close to reality. But in environments where things get much more complicated – like the surface of the earth – the model begins to break down. We have to ask: do we really know all the properties of physical particles, exhaustively? We might think of a physical property as a tendency or capacity to react to other forces in specific ways. Thus what we call 'mass' is the capacity to interact with other objects by repelling or attracting them in special ways. Particles may have many properties – sub-atomic physicists seem to discover more patterns of interaction every day. We may think of them as forces locked up in the structure of the particle, ready to be realised if an appropriate interaction occurs. So the properties we perceive a particle to have depend on the sorts of interactions it has with other particles. How can we ever be sure we have catalogued these exhaustively? Quite simply, we cannot. So the first point to make is that we can never know if we have found all the properties even of quite simple physical objects.

But then it gets worse, for physical objects become very complex. They form complex structures, hierarchies of organisation and pattern. May such complexity not call into play new properties, new forms of interaction, which had not previously existed? This possibility certainly cannot be excluded in principle. It is just a dogma that the laws of physics are set immutably the same for ever. I do not mind accepting the dogma that the basic laws of physics will not change drastically. But I do not see why we should believe that there cannot also be other, more complex laws of relationship at higher levels of physical complexity – especially since that is what things actually look like. There is an alternative model for the physical world: that is the model of organic development. On the basis of rather simple and general laws, more complex structures come into existence, with correspondingly more complex patterns of interaction between them. These structures not only exhibit law-like behaviour (which implies regularity and repetitiveness), they also exhibit something analogous to creative response to stimuli (which allows for uniqueness and originality).

For this model, the human brain would be a particularly complex structure, with a dominant organizing position in the body, whose interactions generate new, emergent properties (of consciousness) and correspondingly new and unpredictable forms of response (in terms of desire and purpose). The important point is that conscious states are not just thrown up as a sort of irrelevant by-product of brain-activity, which itself carries on in the same old mechanistic, predictable way. Rather, conscious states will be emergent properties of the physical system, and as such, they will modify radically the nature of the system. They will enter into the pattern of interactions that make up physical reality. Its laws will still, if you like, be physical, but they will not be derivable from the simple general principles of inorganic physics. To understand them, the concepts of intention, interpretation and rational deliberation have to be introduced; otherwise, you simply cannot see what is truly going on.

Consider a person going through a simple deductive argument, like a piece of arithmetic. Obviously, this causes his brain to operate. It seems equally obvious that the brain processes will be guided by states and patterns of interaction that physics does not deal with – states of understanding the concepts of number, patterns of change directed by principles of logical connection, rather than simple causal regularity. Is it not simpler to say that these states and patterns of change are states of the *same* reality that also has physically locatable cells and forces like electromagnetic charge and mass? The fact is simply that when those forces assume the complex form of organisation of the human brain, new emergent states and principles are generated, and these continually modify the total state of the brain, making its states unpredictable from laws of physics alone.

Some people might call this a form of materialism, because we are saying that consciousness and brain are different ways of looking at the same total reality. But, of course, if we are really saying that consciousness and the brain are the same, then we could put this by saying that the brain is the outward expression of consciousness. That is, mind and brain are not two quite different, disconnected realities. They form parts of one integrated whole, in which the brain is the way the soul appears to others. As far as we can see the situation the soul is generated by a particular physical system. At a specific point in time, a subject of rational consciousness comes into being. All conscious states belong to a subject, which is able to understand, deliberate, formulate goals and initiate actions. Its perceptions are perceptions of the physical world; its intentions are enacted within it. As Aquinas said, 'The soul in a certain fashion demands the body in order to act'[3] and in order to get information. Should we say, then, that the soul is the brain? That would probably be too crude a view, for it might mislead us into thinking that all conscious states were determined by predictable laws of physics alone, or by brain-states as thus predictable. All our evidence shows that this is not the case; for our conscious processes often seem to be causally primary. Moreover, the subject of consciousness is capable in principle of substantial existence; and therefore of continued existence in some other form of body.

The most important characteristic of the soul is its capacity for transcendence. It has the capacity to 'exist', to stand outside the physical processes that generate it, and of which it is part. We might see the soul, the subject of awareness, deliberation and intention, as one part of a vast web of interacting processes, at various degrees of complexity, coming to conscious perception of the actions of other forces upon it; and realizing its own capacities in accordance with more or less clearly formulated principles. It is distinguished, not by being quite different in kind from its material environment, but by reflecting and acting in that environment in a more conscious, goal-oriented way. In other words, the soul is not an alien intrusion into a mechanistic world. It is the culmination and realisation of the principles that dimly inform what we call 'matter' at every stage of its existence. Yet, in that culmination, it is able also to transcend the material. The material is limited to a particular location in space and time. It is contained by that location. But the soul by nature 'transcends'; it is orientated away from itself, to what is beyond itself.

When we apprehend a truth we do not simply register sensations, passively. We rather seek by intelligent enquiry to understand something of the nature of things, of how things really are in their characters and relationships. To grasp a truth is to grasp something that transcends particularity and self-concern. It is to grasp what is impartial, objective, universal. Of course truths are uttered in particular languages, from limited viewpoints, but they aim at the universal and comprehensive. Truth always lies beyond us, in its fullness. Yet we discern something of it, as soon as we move beyond the passive and particular, towards an active grasp of properties and relations. In understanding '$E = mc^2$', we move in a realm with its own norms and constraints, transcending what appears, to grasp or move towards what may be and the inner form and structure of what is.

3 Aquinas, *Summa Theologiae*, Ia (Blackfriars ed. 1964) 75, 6.

This apprehension of truth, which is most characteristic of the soul, is far from being aesthetically or morally neutral. In physics, we seek the elegant, the beautiful, the simple and the fruitful theory. The intellectual structures we seek are structures of beauty. And they impose their moral constraints – of impartiality, comprehensiveness, honesty and trust in one another. Without these values, science as a progressive body of knowledge could not exist. They are internal to the activity of truth-seeking, and that activity is a search for a beauty of order, form and structure which we seek to discover, apprehend and contemplate.

The world of 'bare sense-experience', so beloved of the older sort of empiricists, is a world without beauty or value or truth – all these things became conventions or emotional projections. But we may discern a realm in which truth has attracting beauty and compelling value, both repressing self-interest and calling forth a flowering of understanding, an ecstasis of the soul, finding its true fulfillment in the discernment of value.

All this may seem rather intellectualist. But the doctrine of the soul reminds us that it is not only in the supreme creativity of Einstein or Beethoven that we touch the realm of spirit through the veils of sense. They are supreme adventurers of the spirit, but each of us can distinguish, in our own way, between truth and falsehood; beauty and squalor; the worthwhile and the trivial; love and selfishness. We may not be able to do differential calculus, but we can distort the truth by resentment or prejudice, or we can try to be fair and honest. We can litter the country or cherish it. We can get permanently drunk or take a pride in painting the house. We can go all out to make money or look after the old lady next door. It is in such simple ways that we shape our souls, and it is in these ways that our intelligence is exercised morally, that we can all assert our transcendence over impulse and natural inclination. The transcendence of the soul is its self-determination towards the true, the beautiful and the good. Ultimately, it is its determination towards that which is most fully perfect and actual, the supremely real and good.

For all this to be true, it is not necessary that there should be a strange ghost hidden in the machine of the body. The fact is that the brain is not a machine, as most contemporary computers undoubtedly are. However sophisticated our 'expert systems' are, in computer science, these are still basically machines that operate mechanically in accordance with complex purposes, rational programs and final interpretations of results, all of which are external to the computer mechanism, in human operators. In the brain, however, the purpose, deliberation and interpretation are internal to the system; and that means that this 'physical system' includes states and operates in accordance with principles not covered by laws of physics alone. Indeed, in its subjectivity and transcendence, each soul is beyond the reach of any general inductive laws – for each one contains new and unique properties whose effects on surrounding phenomena cannot be exactly predicted from past experience.

What we have to grasp is the vast complexity of reality – the way it surpasses any set of precise laws or descriptions we apply to it; the organic interrelatedness of events – so that every event is affected by and in turn affects every other event in some, maybe infinitesimal, degree; and the creatively emergent character of physical processes – the way their interactions create new, emergent properties, which modify the process of change in future. This general view of nature, which seems to be fully corroborated by such developments in physics as quantum theory and relativity theory, helps us to see mental states and operations as emerging from the physical structure of the brain, and modifying it in new ways. The soul is the subject of these states and operations; and, like a butterfly emerging from a chrysalis, it may be able to disentangle itself from the public spatial properties of the brain and exist either alone or in a different form of materialization.

Immortality is, on this view, a real possibility. It follows from what I have been saying that we could, in theory, make artificial intelligence machines, super-computers, which really would have souls. That is, they would have states of conscious understanding, freedom and moral responsibility, and relationship to God (as I have put it, 'determination towards supreme value'). In fact, I do not see why we should deny that possibility. We bring souls into existence whenever we have children. We can now fertilise embryos in laboratories, so that our control over procreation is increasing. It is possible, in theory, to construct a genetic sequence, which will begin embryonic development and so create a human life artificially. It is not out of the question that we could also construct a replica of such sequences in other forms, and so create quite new sorts of souls.

Of course, if we did so, we would have just the same sorts of responsibility to those souls as we now have to human beings. We would have to respect and care for them, treat them as responsible and ascribe personal rights to them. It would be grossly immoral to treat them simply as machines, even if they looked like machines. They would indeed be persons. So there is nothing much to worry about in the rather science-fiction idea of creating metal computer-persons. If such things were wholly controllable and predictable, because of some program we had put into them, then we know they are not persons at all, however cunningly they may be made to deceive. But if they really are free, rational and responsible, then we cannot wholly control them without infringing their truly personal rights and destroying that freedom.

Of course, there are very good reasons why such beings may never be produced. The sorts of experimentation that would be necessary to make them would be morally abhorrent. And the sort of dictatorship that would be needed to exercise such total control over personal beings is itself so undesirable that it should always be resisted. So we are not likely to get computer-persons in the foreseeable future. But there seems nothing absurd in the idea that souls, persons, could be brought into being by the construction and development of suitable material states. After all, that is just what happens in the growth of every human embryo. Subjects of rational consciousness are generated by material systems, by natural processes of emergent causation; and there is no need for believers to deny it.

What is wrong with materialism is that it takes much too low a view of matter. It sees it just in terms of its simplest, most abstract and repetitive, measurable and publicly observable properties. This analytical approach has, it is true, been of immense value in producing an exact quantitative set of models for explaining and predicting natural processes. But it is very strange that the limits of the approach, which are quite obvious to anyone who tries to apply quantitative predictive models to human affairs (to any economist, for example), have sometimes been ignored. For the truth is that 'matter' has much greater potential, complexity, opacity to quantitative measurement, uniqueness and novelty than can be expressed in any set of scientific models, whether considered singly or together. Indeed, we might say that 'matter' will only be fully understood when it is seen in its innermost tendency towards consciousness and realisation of value. It will only be understood truly in terms of its end or goal; its fullest realisation, and not its simplest initial states.

In this process, human beings stand at the transition-point at which matter turns outwards from itself towards a transcendent source of truth, beauty and goodness. The Bible puts it supremely well when it says, 'The

Lord God took some soil from the ground and formed a man out of it; he breathed life-giving breath into his nostrils and the man began to live'.[4] Man is made of dust; but he is filled with the spirit of God. He emerges from the simplest material forms, but finds his true kinship in the goal and fulfillment of his existence, the supreme Goodness.

The trouble many people have about the soul lies in a particular picture they have of it. They think of God making a complete spiritual thing, with its own personality, and then having to attach it to some physical body. The soul has a purely external relation to the body. Whereas the biblical account is that man is a truly physical entity, touched with God's spirit. It is *this holistic entity* that knows and thinks and decides; yet this entity is more than electrons or chemicals or genes or psychological states or social roles. All those elements enter into what it is, but none of them, singly or together, exhaust what it is. That is why it is, after all, misleading to say that it is this *body* that thinks – because when we think of a body we think of a corpse, not a living thinking thing. So when we speak of the soul, we speak of this physical entity in its capacity for responsible relation to God, or to those values of truth and beauty through which God is present, often unrecognised.

But if this is true, how can the soul exist without a body? The material universe has produced out of itself states of consciousness and processes of reasoning and intentional action. Now many physical properties that are parts of a more complex whole can exist separately, or in another whole that is significantly different. There is no trouble about that – the molecules making up my foot could exist in a chair or tree. So why could conscious states not exist apart from the brain? The difficulty lies in the fact that conscious states are not just strung together, like beads on a thread, each one separate and externally connected to the others. Each experience needs to be placed in the context of many others, recognised and interpreted. It is the experience of some subject, which relates all the various experiences it has, and organises them within a set of projects and aims. Experiences form a unity, in being the experiences of one common subject. They cannot simply be taken out of that unity, and inserted somewhere else, for then their character would be different. It is, therefore, not the conscious states that can exist separately, but the subject that knows and remembers these states and has certain dispositions and

4 Genesis 2:7

goals. This subject is acquainted with physical realities, and its goals are formed by and rooted in physical realities. It has its place in the physical world; it has a locatable viewpoint and field of action, in space. Yet it is itself beyond every spatial and publicly observable description; it is the subject that is never an object, even to itself; the agent that is never itself an event in the world.

It is essential to see that the soul is both a spiritual and an embodied reality. It is not a ghost behind the scenes, and it is not just the physical brain, in its publicly describable properties. It is not an object or event or set of events in the world. It is a point of subjectivity and transcendence, of rational understanding and responsible action, which comes to be at a particular stage of the emergent interactions of spatial, material substances. Once it is generated, it continues to have a place in those physical interactions, to respond to them and realise itself in them, as their 'actuating principle', as Aquinas put it. It would seem that, though it has a real and distinctive form of existence, it must have something to actuate; the 'form' must be the form of something other than itself.

Nevertheless, in its understanding the soul relates itself also to that realm of truth and value that transcends the physical; in its interior life of feeling, and perhaps of prayer and contemplation, it expresses a capacity and natural tendency to relate to a purely spiritual realm. Each subject is one, throughout its known and remembered states, in the continuous development of its projects and its acceptance of responsibility for past acts. The 'bare subject' is an abstraction, which never exists alone. But it is an essential element of the whole, binding together the organic unity within a whole of developing apprehensions and responses. And this subject is not confined by its physical boundaries. In understanding and imagination, it ranges beyond the temporal and actual, considering possibilities and values, capable of discerning the eternal and infinite hidden in the forms of time and place.

Thus, though it is truly material, there is a very real sense in which the soul looks beyond the material world for its proper fulfillment. It looks to a presence and perfection and purpose beyond all material form – to the reality of God, its true source and goal. This is where the real break with old-fashioned materialism comes. For the old-fashioned materialist, the final reality is 'matter' – that is, a collection of particles, possessing the properties of position, velocity, mass, gravitational, electromagnetic and nuclear force, but having no purpose, value, awareness or responsibility.

In such a world, the soul, as a continuous subject of uniquely apprehended experiences and responsible, creative freedom, is an anomaly or illusion. The self or subjectively conceived 'I' is constructed, perhaps, at the behest of society; it is a set of psychic by-products of physical processes in the brain. But there is no place in the materialist world-view for a free, moral, spiritual subject, whose proper destiny is to pursue moral excellence and realise unity with God. We must instead see the brain as a cybernetic system that can be programmed or electronically controlled, or even replaced by more efficient, inorganic thinking machines. All sense of the reality and importance of subjectivity disappears. Moreover, human behaviour will be modified most effectively by neurological engineering. This can replace the less effective idea of 'responsibility', which was a very inefficient conditioning mechanism to make people behave in socially desirable ways.

From a religious point of view, it can be pointed out that it is a denial of the obvious facts of subjectivity and freedom in the name of a very abstract theory for which there is no positive evidence and which there is great difficulty in even formulating coherently. That is not to say it is false; just to point out that it is far from being an obvious truth as it is sometimes taken to be. It is a highly disputable, poorly evidenced and very vaguely stated metaphysical theory.

For theistic believers the most basic reality is spiritual – the only self-sustaining being is God, who is personal, purposive, supremely worthwhile and aware. Believers do not at all deny the reality of the material world, but they would stress its total dependence upon God for its existence; and would not see why the material world, which God has brought into being from nothing, should not develop non-mechanistic, purposive, holistic, emergent and non-law-like characteristics, if God so desires it. In fact, it looks as if those are just the characteristics matter has developed, in the existence of the higher animals, and especially in mankind. Thus the physical structure of the central nervous system and the brain causes the genesis of one continuous subject of experiences, which then interacts in responsible and purposive ways with its material environment, through its own material properties.

The proposal that the brain should be treated just like a computer, modified and tampered with according to someone else's desires, is not a conclusion from any truly scientific theory. It is a proposal to treat persons as objects, to be disposed of and manipulated at will. In other words, it is not a scientific theory, but a basic moral perversion. The interesting thing is that this perversion has to be dressed up as a scientific theory – as what Jacques Monod calls 'the principle of obiectivity'.[5] Of course, Monod does not *wish* to create a morally perverse view, but such is the implication of what he says. How we treat people does depend on how we see them; our actions will be shaped by our vision of how things are. So if we see human beings as collections of purposeless physical particles, we will begin treating them as if they were just more complicated rocks, without inherent dignity or value. Whereas if we see them as transcendent subjects with a unique experience and a responsible freedom, we will have to cherish that uniqueness and respect that freedom in our own actions.

Believers should not wish to deny that the soul is the embodied person we think and see and know in the world. But, in speaking of the soul, they wish to stress that the most important characteristic of the material world is its inherent tendency to realise purposes and values and achieve consciousness of them; it has been purposively created by God to do just that. And the soul, even in its true and full embodiment, finds its deepest fulfillment in seeking a growing union with the spiritual reality of God. God is the true end of the soul, and in this sense, its goal, its proper purpose and true nature, lies beyond the physical universe. That is a strong reason for thinking that the subject embodied in this world may properly find other forms of experience and action, in contexts lying beyond this universe, wherein its God-given goal may be realised, its experiences woven into a meaningful pattern and its responses brought to an appropriate consummation. The semitic faiths speak of the 'resurrection of the body'. By this they mean that the human person will have a fuller life beyond death in community with others and in fulfillment of its own true nature. The Indian faiths speak of 'rebirth'. By this they mean that each person will live after death, perhaps in this world or perhaps in other forms of embodiment, until it works out its destiny – its *karma* – and attains a supreme spiritual goal of knowledge, freedom and bliss. These views are not so different as is sometimes thought, for they both speak of a continued yet new embodiment of the present person, and of an ultimate destiny of freedom from sorrow, ignorance and selfishness. We need have no inkling of what this ultimate state may be. We need only see that this subject-soul finds its true purpose in union with a reality transcending the physical; so

5 Jacques Monod, *Chance and Necessity* (Collins, 1972), 30.

we have no reason to limit it to the present form of its embodiment, and some reason to hope that it may find an appropriate form of fulfillment when this physical body becomes a corpse.

Properly understood, then, the sciences of cybernetics and neurophysiology do not threaten the spirituality of the soul at all. On the contrary, it is only a clear grasp of that spirituality that can prevent such sciences being misused by morally perverse tyrannies. Of course the soul depends on the brain, but the brain is not a machine. And the soul need not always depend on the brain, any more than a man need always depend on the womb that supported his life before birth. The most basic dependence of the soul is upon God, and it is in becoming conscious of the reality of God and learning to love and obey God that the soul discovers what its true nature is. Belief in the dignity of the soul and in a supreme spiritual reality, which theists know as God, go together. And that is why belief in God or in the reality of a supreme spiritual goal is the essential basis of a genuine and rational respect for the dignity and sacredness of the rational soul and of human life.

11

The Open Future

The dominant interpretations of quantum theory are probabilistic – they affirm that the same cause can have different effects. If this is also true at macrocosmic levels, it allows for radical freedom. Physical determinism is not an axiom of science, and quantum theory shows that it cannot be scientifically established. A picture of the cosmos as creatively moving towards an open future yet fundamentally expressing a hidden but intelligible reality is one that is consonant both with quantum physics and with a basic religious vision of reality.

AIM: To show that creative human freedom and responsibility are consistent with a scientific worldview and with the existence of laws of nature.

SUGGESTIONS FROM QUANTUM THEORY: INDETERMINACY

A Probabilistic Universe

Not only is the real world, the unobserved world of wave functions that seems to be revealed by quantum physics, not made up of discrete and atomistic (separable) parts; it appears to show forms of causality that are non-deterministic. The most widely accepted interpretation of quantum mechanics – the Copenhagen interpretation, named after Niels Bohr of Copenhagen – is that there are genuine indeterminacies in nature. It is not just that we cannot predict the future. Some events happen, at the sub-atomic level, which are not completely determined by any previous physical state or by any physical law.

Abner Shimony, former Professor of Physics and Philosophy at Boston University, writes, 'If the quantum state of a system is a complete description of the system, then a quantity that has an indefinite value in that quantum state is objectively indefinite, its value is not merely unknown by the scientist who seeks to describe the system. Furthermore, since the outcome of a measurement of an objectively indeterminate state is the complete bearer of information about the system, the outcome is strictly a matter of objective chance – not just a matter of chance in the sense of unpredictability to the scientist' ('The Reality of the Quantum World', *in Quantum Mechanics*, 1988, p. 5).

Objective chance, on this interpretation, is not just a limitation on human knowledge. It is a feature of the objective world. So a wave function, which gives a complete description of a quantum system, cannot predict the position of an electron exactly, but only with a mathematically assignable probability. An electron will probably be observed at a specific location, but there is a finite probability that it will not. The reason we cannot predict exactly where it will be is that there is nothing to determine precisely where it will be. The future is open – though within very precisely definable limits – and the electron may take one of several possible paths at random (or in quantum formalism it may take all of them).

The Schrodinger equations, which predict the probable outcomes of particle experiments, are deterministic in mathematical form, but they assign only probabilities to the location of observable particles. William Stoeger says, 'In the projection of this quantum world into the macroscopic world of our experience, determinism fails' ('Epistemological and Ontological Issues Arising from Quantum Theory', in *Quantum Mechanics*, p. 89). That is to say, when one of the many possible futures described by the wave function is 'chosen' by making a measurement, it is objectively uncertain which future will be so chosen. For quantum mechanics, the same cause can give rise to different effects. This was a great shock for those who thought that science must assume as a basic axiom that the same cause always produces the same effect. It is, however, welcome to believers in radical freedom, whose view of freedom is that the same initial situation can open up a number of different tracks into the future.

For believers in radical freedom, a paradigm of a morally free decision is when one possible action realises an objectively good state, and another realises the egoistic satisfaction of the agent. Believers in radical freedom, among whom I count myself, think that the ascription of praise and blame to humans depends upon agents being undetermined by anything other than themselves, their knowledge of possibilities open to them, their awareness of right and wrong, and their capacity to choose without compulsion in crucial moments of moral choice.

Determinism is the view that every physical state is the only possible effect of preceding physical states plus the laws of nature. It depends on the axiom that the same cause always produces the same effect. If this axiom is undermined by quantum physics, the postulate of radical freedom becomes much more plausible.

The Principle of Indeterminacy

Some theorists maintain that radical freedom can operate in the indeterministic gap opened up by the collapse of the wave function (William Pollard, *Chance and Providence*, London, Faber, 1958). The mind can choose which possibility to actualise, and that is its area of freedom. But I agree with John Polkinghorne that this seems an unduly 'hole-and-corner way of influencing quantum events' (John Polkinghorne, *Science and Providence*, SPCK, London, 1989, p. 28). Quantum indeterminacies even out over large numbers, so that by the time we get to the level of ordinary experience the processes of nature are governed by quasideterministic Newtonian laws (as has been seen, they are not truly deterministic). We might be unwise to confine human freedom to the realm of quantum indeterminacy.

The importance of quantum theory is not that it proves that radical freedom really exists. It might seem much too restrictive to make morally responsible free acts depend on tiny random events in the sub-atomic realm, which mostly cancel each other out. The principle of indeterminacy does not even strictly prove the world is not deterministic. It certainly sets limits to our ability to predict the future. But the world might be determined, even though we are unable to predict it. There are quantum theorists, from Einstein to David Bohm, who advocate a deterministic substratum for quantum events. Bohm has proposed a deterministic account that envisages a completely different approach to quantum theory, re-establishing particles as a central feature of the unobserved world, but seeing particles in a completely non-Newtonian way, such that their properties cannot be specified independently of a holistic context (that is, a context in which the nature of the parts is partly determined by the structure of the whole). This is determinism of a distinctly non-atomistic and non-mechanistic kind. Whether it is truly deterministic at all is open to question.

It cannot be said that quantum theory has wholly established objective indeterminism, even though most standard interpretations of the theory (especially those deriving from the Copenhagen interpretation) are indeterministic. James Cushing, Professor of Physics and Philosophy at Notre Dame University, remarks that 'considerations of empirical adequacy and logical consistency alone do not force one to accept an indeterministic view of fundamental physical phenomena' ('Determinism and Indeterminism in Quantum Mechanics', in *Quantum Mechanics*, p. 99). The issue, Cushing holds, is probably not empirically decidable.

However, given the success and wide acceptance of a Copenhagen-type interpretation, what quantum theory does show is that full physical determinism is not necessary to good scientific procedure and explanation. Indeterminism within specifiable limits of probability does not undermine scientific explanations. Since the majority interpretation of quantum physics is actually indeterministic, the fact is that much available scientific evidence counts against determinism.

For those who are inclined anyway to believe in radical freedom, such freedom entails a lack of complete physical determinism in the universe. What quantum theory shows, minimally, is that good and fruitful science does not entail such complete determinism. More positively, in what is still its standard, though disputed, interpretation, quantum theory suggests that indeterminism is a basic feature of the physical universe.

This in turn suggests, though it does not entail, that 'even at those macroscopic levels where classical physics gives an adequate account, there is an openness to the future which relaxes the unrelenting grip of mechanical determinism' (Polkinghorne, *Science and Providence*, p. 30). The point is that, once the stern grip of determinism has been loosened at the quantum level, we might be more open to the possibility of a macroscopic universe that is not bound by determinism. Copenhagen-type interpretations of quantum theory do not prove that the macrocosmic universe is not physically determined. But they open up the possibility that it might not be so determined, and that macrocosmic indeterminism, the necessary condition of radical freedom, is wholly compatible with modern science.

Indeterminism and Freedom

There is thus no scientific barrier to indeterminism at the everyday level. No scientific laws will be broken if humans can on some occasions determine by an act of will, not itself scientifically observable, that one future rather than another should become actual. Physical determinism is a dogma of philosophy, not an axiom of science.

This thought is reinforced by the fact that there is no hope of proving that, *on every occasion*, one and only one future outcome of a state of affairs is possible. It is, after all, an extremely ambitious statement to say that there is only one possible future at every stage of the existence of the universe. How could we possibly establish that no other track into the future was even possible? As the philosopher David Hume put it, what strange sort of necessity would it be that ensured that every causal situation could have one and only one outcome?

It does not look as if we could ever establish such a thing scientifically. For a start, we know that we cannot exhaustively specify every causal feature in any real life situation. We do not have the resources to measure all real life situations in a rigorous experimental way. As I shall show in the next section, quantum theory shows that events in the universe are entangled, so that events light years away, and unknown to us, can produce changes of state in phenomena that we are observing. That entails that we cannot have exhaustive knowledge of any local physical state without having exhaustive knowledge of the whole universe, which is impossible (see John Polkinghorne, *The Quantum World*, Longman, London, 1984, chapter 7).

Quantum physics provides another reason why it is impossible to gather exhaustively all possible information about any given state. Heisenberg's uncertainty principle prevents us being able to measure precisely both the position and momentum of a fundamental particle, and so it prohibits complete knowledge of any observed physical state. Thus we cannot know the precise causal conditions of an observed state of affairs at any stage of the universe's existence. That means that we can never be in a position to say precisely what effect is bound to follow from such causal conditions.

The consequence is that we can never conclusively test whether physical determinism is true – whether one and only one precise effect is bound to occur, given any causal state and the laws of physics. That is because we can never establish exactly and exhaustively what any specific causal state is and therefore we can never predict exactly what effect is bound to follow. That does not mean physical determinism is false. But it does mean that its truth cannot be scientifically established.

Physical indeterminism – the view that on at least some occasions, however rare, more than one possible future can follow from a given physical state of affairs, and no physical factor determines the actual future in advance – is thus fully consistent with present science, it is accepted by most quantum physicists and it cannot be scientifically disproved. That is a fairly strong position for a theory that common sense and morality presuppose when they assume that at least some physical organisms – namely, human persons – are sometimes free to choose which track into the future they will take.

Whatever the truth or otherwise of determinism, it is certain that many causal outcomes can only be predicted in a probabilistic or statistical way. This is true, not only at the tiny quantum level, but also at the level of ordinary life. The development of chaos theory shows that dynamic systems far from equilibrium have the property that minute fluctuations can, in the right circumstances, have large-scale effects. We have all heard the story of how the flap of a butterfly's wing can cause a hurricane on the other side of the world. The point is that we cannot predict many ordinary states (like the weather) if they depend on fluctuations in minute sub-atomic conditions. At this point chaos theory connects with quantum theory, because quantum theory shows that there are such tiny fluctuations, which are unpredictable in detail (that is true, whether you believe in 'ontological indeterminacy' or not). If such unpredictable fluctuations give rise to macrocosmic changes, it follows that such changes will be unpredictable too. Therefore deterministic prediction, of the sort Laplace hoped for, is in principle impossible: 'Chaos brings a new challenge to the reductionist view that a system can be understood by breaking it down and studying each piece' (J.P. Crutchfield *et al.*, 'Chaos', *Scientific American*, 225(6), 1986, p. 56). There are significant patterns in the way the world is, but they permit an openness of texture and an access to novelty that 'provides a mechanism that allows for free will within a world governed by deterministic laws' (ibid.).

All this does not prove that freedom and creative spontaneity are objective features of the universe. What it shows is that determinism cannot be proved, that it is not needed for good science and that many scientists these days do not accept it. The standard interpretations of quantum theory posit that the cosmos changes in accordance with causal principles that are stochastic or probabilistic. To many modern scientists, it looks as if the universe at the quantum level continually moves into an open future by probabilistic processes. It is a plausible generalisation from this that similar processes may occur at the atomic and molecular levels. Suitably complex organisms may give rise to acts of creative spontaneity and responsible freedom in a world that lays down a number of alternative tracks into an open and undetermined future. That is a very different picture from that of the heirs of Newton and classical, largely deterministic, physics.

The Quantum World

It must be stressed that this whole area of physics is still a realm of deep disputes. Einstein never accepted that a statistical theory could be complete, and so maintained to the last that 'hidden variables' could one day be found that would eliminate probability. The physical world, he believed, did consist of objective events that could in principle be modelled by a complete physical theory that would be deterministic and would not speak of such strange objective realities as probability waves, superimposed realities, collapses of wave functions and non-physical interactions between fundamental particles.

This does not entail the sort of 'universal physical determinism' that was inspired, however oddly, by Newtonian mechanics. It affirms that there are real physical particles and real nonprobabilistic causal laws, and so restores a generally Newtonian view of the physical world. But it need not deny, any more than Newton did, that there are also non-physical causal factors in reality with which the physical sciences do not deal.

In any case such a theory is not within sight and even the most ardent Einsteinian would have to agree that the hope to find a 'realist' view of fundamental particles that are more or less ordinary physical entities is a matter of faith. God may not play dice with the universe, but it *looks* as if God does!

David Bohm's attempt to develop a theory that would restore determinism to fundamental particles is at the cost of postulating a mysterious 'pilot wave', without energy, probably unobservable, conveying information faster than light. His precise theory has not convinced many physicists, but it shows that quantum physics does not necessarily rule determinism out. It also shows that physicists are nowhere near having a complete knowledge of the bases of matter. Physicists are as yet unable even to reconcile relativity and quantum theory in one coherent explanatory theory. Perhaps determinism is not, after all, dead. But it is absolutely not established by the sciences and remains little more than a philosophical dogma.

Furthermore it looks as though any adequate account of both determinism and matter will be very different from any simple picturing theory of intuitively clear realities. The quantum world is one of virtual particles continually fluctuating in and out of existence, even in a vacuum; of superstrings vibrating and twisting in ten or eleven dimensions, most of which are 'rolled up' and invisible; of a reality in which gravitation, space-time and matter are or were merged in one 'instanton' (a postulate of Hawking and Turok). This is not anything like the classical materialist world of small massy particles bumping into each other for ever.

Determinist or indeterminist, the reality with which modern physics deals is one in which solid things seem to disappear into probability waves, in which space-time can be finite, unbounded and expanding without expanding in anything, and in which new space-times can possibly be generated inside black holes. This is a world far beyond common sense and anything we can picture to ourselves in a simple way. So modern physics shows the world to be a reality that is very different from anything the senses perceive and to be one that is deeply intelligible and mathematically beautiful.

In a sense modern science has, in a strange and unexpected way, returned to a form of Platonism. An important part of Platonism says the senses provide only appearances, whereas reality is purely intelligible and knowable, if at all, only by mind. Platonism, it seems, has returned in triumph, now guided and tested by observation and measurement, but erected on a foundation of intellectual beauty, perceptible only by mind, a world of concepts and numbers appearing to us as a world of material objects constructed by our senses.

This may not be a religious view, but it carries unmistakeable resonances of the basic religious insight that the whole sensory world is an appearance of a deeper spiritual reality. That reality is one of supreme beauty and wisdom and is knowable only by a disciplining of the mind and will. In this world of appearance, human freedom has chosen tracks into the future that have realised suffering and frustration as well as moments of creative insight and altruism. The religious path is one of seeking to re-orient a freedom that has preferred sensory desire back towards the primal beauty from which it has fallen.

Naturally, quantum physics is not concerned with such issues. But, for those who are, the picture suggested by at least some quantum physicists of a probabilistic cosmos, founded on a hidden reality of beauty and wisdom and yet making possible moral freedom and creativity, is one that is deeply consonant with a religious view.

IV

The Bible and Its Interpretation

12
The Nature of Biblical Inspiration

What is the Bible? It is still the world's best-selling book. Some people think it is written more or less literally by God, containing sets of moral instructions and wholly accurate accounts of human history, dictated direct from the creator in person. At the other extreme, some people think it is a set of nationalistic legends and ancient irrational taboos, which ought now to be regarded as obsolete.

It contains some wonderful passages of compassion and hope. Most of the Psalms, Isaiah chapters 40–55 (which scholars tend to call 'second Isaiah'), selected parts of the prophets, parts of the New Testament letters like 1 Corinthians 13 (the hymn to love), and the sermon on the mount (Matt. 5–7), are high points of literary and spiritual writing. But it also contains long lists of seemingly irrelevant laws (almost all the book of Leviticus – though that book does contain the sentence, 'Love your neighbour as yourself' (Lev. 19.18), which is arguably worth pages of boring instructions on bodily discharges and varieties of skin diseases). There are also some pretty gruesome passages on exterminating the Amalekites, calling on God to pour down fire and brimstone on one's enemies, and generally promising a coming day of wrath and terror for almost everybody (everybody else, that is).

So the Bible is a puzzling document, taken as the final guide to life by millions, yet denigrated by and offensive to many others. Perhaps the explanation of this fact is that the Bible is neither a book dictated by God nor just a set of outdated taboos and politically slanted histories. It is a very mixed set of documents by many different writers from many different times, which records the struggle of many people in one particular religious tradition to respond to their discernments of a transcendent spiritual power.

That power is spiritual, meaning that it is not material, not physical. It is more of the nature of mind and consciousness. But it is also transcendent, in that it is much greater than any finite mind. It is beyond the whole of space and time, though it is discerned through the events of space and time. And it is greater in value, in goodness and beauty, than anything in space and time. Many people feel an awareness of such a transcendent spiritual power. It can be a sense of presence, known through the beauty of a desert or of high mountains. It can be a sense of moral demand and obligation which encounters us with compelling force. It can be mediated through the impact of great art or music, through an inner sense of union with a higher self, or through our awareness of the awesome complexity of the physical world. Sometimes, but not always, people call this 'a sense of God', of a mind that has knowledge of the world and a purpose for it, and that has a causal influence in bringing about that purpose.

The patriarchs and prophets of the ancient Hebrew tradition interpreted their sense of transcendence in terms of the power of an active God. They saw that power in different ways – sometimes as a terrifying destructive force: 'Look, the storm of the LORD! Wrath has gone forth, a whirling tempest' (Jer. 23.19) – and sometimes as a compassionate saving and healing power: 'When the poor and needy seek water, and there is none, and their tongue is parched with thirst, I the LORD will … open rivers on the bare heights and fountains in the midst of the valleys' (Isa. 41.17–18) – and sometimes as a bit of both: 'He is like a refiner's fire and like fullers' soap; he will sit as a refiner and purifier of silver, and he will purify the descendants of Levi and refine them like gold and silver' (Mal. 3.2–3). What is quite distinctive about the Bible among the religious books of the world is that the dominant image of transcendence, of spirituality, that slowly develops in its pages is the image of a power that urges and helps humans to seek a moral goal in history even when such a thing seems humanly impossible to achieve: 'Let justice roll down like waters, and righteousness like an ever-flowing stream' (Amos 5.24).

The Bible is a story of repeated moral failure and desperate and sometimes misguided moral striving. The moral goal itself is sometimes seen in a very limited and exclusive way, as something that very few (the 'remnant') will ever attain. But at other times there is a hope that it can eventually be attained by all, despite human greed, pride and folly, with the help of some ultimately overwhelming divine power, the power of grace. It is a record of dreams and failures, ideals and nightmares, heroism and deceit. It is a human document, but it is a document of human interactions with what is believed to be a supreme spiritual power, placing before humans a supreme moral goal. And it is a document which expresses the very varied responses of humans to disclosures of that power, disclosures that have always been mediated through the events and experiences of individual human lives. The Bible is, in short, a spiritual text.

The Bible is, of course, mostly a Jewish book. The Hebrew Bible, the Old Testament, is a record composed by the prophets, historians, poets and lawyers of Israel. Today, interpreted with the aid of the Talmud and of the traditions of the Rabbis of Judaism, religious Jews still find in it an inspiration to seek justice and peace and the rule of goodness in a very unjust and violent world. I think everyone will admit that the search has always been morally ambiguous, mixed with nationalistic and vindictive motives, and it has never been wholly successful – Jerusalem today is hardly the 'city of peace' it was meant to be. Yet underlying it is a vision of transcendence as an ultimate spiritual reality that is itself supremely just and merciful, that calls the children of the covenant to embody such justice in history, and that promises that their moral struggles will not be in vain.

If you add the New Testament to this you get the Christian Bible. While owing almost everything to its Jewish roots, Christian faith puts the whole Bible in a different light by claiming that Jesus of Nazareth both negates and fulfills the Hebrew Bible prophecies and expectations. He negates them by becoming the origin of a new religious set of institutions, the Christian Church, no longer bound by Jewish law, centered on him as the decisive revelation of God. He fulfills them by taking the main strands of Jewish prophecy, law and wisdom, and bringing them to one focal point in his own person.

Christianity inherits all the ambiguities of Judaism. It can be interpreted in a restrictive, judgmental and negative way. Most of the world's population are doomed to hell. Only a few, those who consciously believe in Jesus, are the remnant who will receive eternal life. Urgent missionary efforts are needed to save a few believers from the terrible judgment that is coming upon the world.

But it can also be interpreted in a more universal, compassionate and positive way. There is judgment on human evil and corruption, but everyone without exception is offered a real possibility of forgiveness and eternal life. God wishes everyone to be 'saved' from evil and freed for a life of goodness and love. Missionary efforts exist to spread this 'good news' that all are offered eternal life with God, however miserable or imperfect their lives are. Divine forgiveness is freely offered to all who repent and turn to God. This is a positive gospel of new life, freedom and joy, and of hope for all, including those who may feel their lives are without point or purpose, and who are estranged from any sense of God.

I belong, and have always as a Christian belonged, to this second group. It includes Catholics, Protestants, Orthodox and Anglicans. The positive gospel is that, although humans live in a world dominated by hatred, greed and selfish pride, God has entered this world in Christ in order to forgive sin, free us from the power of self, and unite us to the divine life for ever. None who turn to him will be rejected. Even those who reject him God will not neglect, but will go to the furthest lengths to bring them into companionship with the divine life. That is the message of the cross – God goes to the uttermost lengths to draw us to God. And it is the message of the resurrection – God's love will not be defeated either by evil or by death.

This gospel is not founded on a book, not even on the Bible. It is founded on the liberating power of God, channelled through the presence of Christ in the Church. Yet for us to know what this power is, and what Christ is, we need the Bible.

The New Testament in its letters records the thoughts and experiences of some of the first disciples who responded to this good news of new life and joy in God. In the Gospels it presents memories of the life of Jesus, as that life has been reflected upon in the early Church, and as it has disclosed new facets of God's love to them. These documents, like the whole Bible, contain many different viewpoints, some of them rather petty or prejudiced on occasion, but all of them touched in some way by the grace of Christ. We need to read them with discrimination, with an awareness of human partiality as well as of divine guidance ('inspiration'). We need to be helped to understand them with the aid of the best available biblical scholarship, and of the teachings of wise and saintly readers down the ages. If we do that, the Bible can become what it was meant to be, a record of human discernments of transcendence that has the purpose of evoking in us our own unique discernment of God. Since this discernment will be a response to the self-disclosure of God to us, we may rightly say that the Bible is 'the word of the Lord'. It is a term which has the power of conveying the presence and power of God to us. But we need to remember that, like all 'words' or texts, it carries many layers of meaning, negative as well as positive, and our understanding of it will largely depend upon our personal experience of the Christ to whom it must, for Christians, always point.

We should not expect, then, that the Bible is an inerrant text which provides totally correct information about God from start to finish. I see no reason to think that there are any such texts anywhere in the world. All human knowledge is infected with error and limitations of understanding, and in my opinion religions are not exempt from this universal feature of human knowledge.

Even if some people think there is such an inerrant text, it is only their opinion that it is inerrant, and since they are human, their opinion is not inerrant. They may very well be wrong. So there is no escape from the fallibility of all human knowledge. If someone claims that the Bible is inerrant, we need to ask them, 'How do you know you are right? Might you not be mistaken about that? Do you really need to claim that a text contains no mistakes at all, before you can trust it and take it as a guide to your life?'

There is, after all, another interpretation. We can say that the Bible is a collection of human responses to what were felt to be encounters with God in the history of Israel and in the dreams, visions and oracles of the prophets. Its various documents are mixtures of insight and prejudice, moving poetic evocations of transcendence and ugly expressions of human vindictiveness and petty-mindedness.

Overall, however, the Bible shows a series of developing insights into the nature of God as one creator of perfect beauty and perfection, who has a moral goal for the human world, and who relates to human lives with a mixture of categorical moral demand, forgiving compassion and the promise of ultimate hope for human fulfillment. It is one of the fullest and most complete accounts of the development of a human religious tradition over many centuries. It shows how contemporary religious believers have come to be where they are, and its general trajectory of thought suggests further directions of spiritual development.

We can speak of the Bible as inspired, in that we can see God at work influencing and guiding the minds of biblical historians, lawyers, priests, poets and prophets, so as to lead them to a cumulative tradition of insights into the nature and purpose of God, the ultimate spiritual reality. For Christians who believe this, the Bible is not the words of God, somehow by-passing the minds of men and women and dictating words direct from the divine mind. It is a unique witness to the gradually perceived purposes of God, which culminate in the prophetic teaching and life of Jesus, seen by Christians as a decisive and normative disclosure of the nature and purposes of supreme spirit.

Transcendent spiritual reality is spoken of in the Bible as a personal God, as appearing, calling, liberating, judging, forgiving, comforting, renewing, guiding and blessing. God is seen as relating actively with humans throughout their individual and social histories. This is a record of very varied discernments of a supreme spiritual transcendence and goodness which is not just a passive and impersonal ideal. It is apprehended as active in a personal way in the events of human lives. Such apprehensions are always perceived through the lens of human minds and thoughts. How prophets have seen God acting is partly a function of how they themselves relate to apprehensions of supreme goodness. In that sense the Bible is the record of one long tradition of human discernments of the divine.

For Christians, those discernments culminate in Jesus Christ. Many New Testament letters were written within a decade or so of the death of Jesus, and they give a vibrant account of the beliefs of the earliest disciples, who had either known Jesus personally or had been able to talk to those who remembered what Jesus had said and done. The letters and the Acts of the Apostles record the experience of the Holy Spirit in the early Church, bringing new life and hope, founded on the belief that Christ was risen and glorified, to the disciples. We trust their accounts if we accept that their new and living faith was indeed an authentic experience of God, which had come to them through the person of Jesus.

The Gospels are early records that contain remembered words and deeds of Jesus, and that witness to his death and resurrection. Many of those disciples were prepared to suffer and die for their beliefs, so it is entirely reasonable to trust their testimony to his teachings, death by crucifixion and appearances after death. Beginning from this point, it is Christ who must provide the key to the interpretation of the whole Bible. For Christians see the Old Testament as a gradual preparation for the decisive revelation of God in the person of Jesus, and its various texts must be interpreted in the light of Christ.

Even then, we must be aware that our personal discernment of Christ is imperfect, and so the spiritual task of reading the Bible sensitively and positively will never end. There is always more to learn, for the mystery of Christ will never be completely plumbed by any human agency of thought. Nevertheless, in our continual task of seeking greater understanding, the Bible is an essential guide to spiritual discernment, because it is in fact our only written guide to developing and recording the human discernment of the nature and purpose of God in Christ. In that sense, the Bible has final authority for Christians. But we should always be keenly aware that our own personal interpretation of the Bible will never be inerrant or completely adequate. God is revealed in and through the Bible, but our interpretation of the Bible, or even the one we learn from our friends, may leave much to be desired. That is why it is important to know about how the many diverse Christian churches, in many lands and at many different times, have interpreted the Bible for their own ages and cultures. That will help to put our own views in historical perspective, save us from undue arrogance and certainty, and give us a much broader understanding of the richness of the Christian gospel, which speaks in many forms to people of every age.

Is the Bible Inerrant?

The Bible, regarded as a set of literal truths that are to be accepted just as they stand, says some very unpleasant things indeed. It says some things that are plainly and indisputably false, and some things that most people would regard as immoral. I will be talking about these in some detail later.

It will be a great help in reading the Bible as a spiritual text if we can admit that there are some errors and some limitations of perspective in it, that have been produced by the inability of the human writers to grasp the fullness of the love and mercy of the God revealed in Christ. Those errors and limitations do not undermine the witness of the Bible, taken as a whole and in the light of the life of Jesus, to the unlimited loving nature and purpose of God. Indeed, they can be a positive help in seeing how humans can grow, and must continue to grow, in understanding of God, how our understanding of God is never complete and final, and how God can use even the weak minds and hearts of men and women to convey a truth which is sufficient to unite us to God for ever.

We can very quickly see that the Bible is not inerrant, if we compare the accounts in different Gospels of Mary Magdalene and another woman or women coming to Jesus' tomb on the morning of the resurrection. Matthew's Gospel records that two women saw an angel descend from heaven, roll back the stone covering the entrance, and speak to the women. But the other three Gospels say that when Mary Magdalene went to the tomb, either alone (John), or with two other women (Mark), or with a whole group of women (Luke), they found that the stone had already been rolled away. They saw no angel descend from heaven, though Mark says that one angel was inside the tomb, Luke says that two were, and John says that two angels appeared later to Mary Magdalene. Then Matthew, Luke and John state that the women told the other disciples what they had seen, though Mark records that 'they said nothing to anyone, for they were afraid' (Mark 16.8).

I have chosen this event because the resurrection is of the very first importance to Christians. It is not just some peripheral and insignificant event; it is the very foundation of Christian faith. And the point is that the different Gospel accounts cannot all be correct. At least three of the accounts are indisputably false in some particular details. Whether you are a Christian or not, that is a fact you cannot escape. And of course if you are seriously concerned about the truth, you should not try to escape it. The conclusion is unavoidable: some Gospel accounts of the empty tomb are not literally accurate.

The only question is, what are we going to do about it? One course is to reject all the accounts as not trustworthy, and say that they are just made up long after the event. There was no empty tomb, and no vision of angels, at all. These are legends made up to support the reality of the resurrection appearances of Jesus. The theologian Rudolf Bultmann took this view, so it is not necessarily an anti-Christian view. But it does mean that there are legends, fictional stories, made up to make some sort of religious point, in the Bible.

However, there is another possibility. Human memories are notoriously unreliable, and second-hand accounts of events that someone else saw get embroidered and exaggerated very easily. If you ask a group of people who saw some event twenty years ago exactly what they saw, you will get quite a lot of variations in what they say. In fact, if you got exact agreement, you would immediately think that they had colluded in order to get their story straight. Small errors of memory are an indicator that there was a significant experience they all had, not a disproof that there was any such experience.

So a reasonably impartial historian might say that the different Gospels preserve different oral traditions that have developed in different ways, but may well preserve the personal testimonies of some women who recall having seen an empty tomb and having had a visionary experience of angelic presences.

That interpretation is, I think, a highly probable one. But there remains a major difficulty for many. The fact is that bodies do not normally disappear from tombs, and it is not at all certain that angels exist. These are extraordinary, miraculous events. Jesus' body simply disappeared, and there was a divine vision and a divine voice of some sort. If you are sure that such miracles cannot or do not occur, you will not accept the biblical account. On the other hand, if you think God could transform Jesus' physical body into a spiritual body, and that God could cause visions to occur, the literal accounts of the empty tomb will remain very striking.

Can We Believe in Biblical Miracles?

How can we rationally decide whether or not miracles occur? A miracle is an extraordinary event, caused by God, which reveals the divine presence and purpose in a special way. A believer in God is committed to thinking that God, a purely spiritual power, is the cause of all things. So it is certainly possible that extraordinary events may occur which have a partly non-physical cause. Moreover, if there is a God with a purpose for the universe with which God wishes humans to co-operate, it is highly probable that God will bring humans to know what that purpose is, and how they are to co-operate with it. So it is probable that there will be extraordinary revelatory events. The prophetic visions and oracles of the prophetic tradition are such events. The Bible also records acts of liberation like the exodus, which have become definitive for development of the biblical idea of God. It is reasonable for a believer in God to think that such 'miraculous' events, awe-inspiring and not wholly accountable for in purely physical terms, are likely to occur. They will often occur through the mediation of prophets and those who are close to God. So it is especially likely that they will occur around the person of Jesus, who is the human embodiment of God.

All these considerations lead one to think that the miracles recorded in the Gospels may well have occurred, and are even rather likely to have occurred. On the other hand, we cannot just accept any claim to the occurrence of a miracle. We know that there is much deceit in spiritual matters. We know that human accounts of extraordinary events and people become embroidered with additional details, so that the lives of the saints are quickly surrounded with legendary elements. We know that sometimes metaphors get literalised, and that illustrative parables can be turned into allegedly historical accounts by pious imaginations. So we have good reason to think that many alleged miracles are largely products of human piety and imagination.

Since we have accepted that the biblical accounts are not inerrantly true, we might expect that, while miracles will occur in the life of Jesus, there may be elements of hyperbole and literalization in written and remembered accounts of them. This suggests that it is quite reasonable to be rather agnostic about the literal truth of many recorded miracles, but to accept that God was at work in extraordinary ways in Jesus' life, so that there is an important core of truth in the Gospel miracle stories.

There is an area of legitimate and inevitable uncertainty about the interpretation of the biblical narratives. I am not proposing to give the one correct interpretation. What the Gospel records show is that early Christians believed Jesus to be a person in and through whom God acted in extraordinary and spiritually profound ways. This belief was expressed partly in stories of miracles surrounding the life of Jesus. That belief is important to Christian faith. But I do not think it is necessary to accept that the miracles occurred just as they are literally described in the Gospels.

I suggest that there is a range of acceptable opinions, from fully literal acceptance to the view that these are partly legendary accounts of the sort we often find in traditional stories of holy men and women. The view we take will depend upon our more general belief about the way in which God acts in the world. It seems possible that God could act in extraordinary ways occasionally without disrupting the general order of nature, and this thought will encourage those who take the miracle stories literally. On the other hand, we may ask why God does not act in these ways more often, or why the point of some miracles seems so trivial, or why miracles seem so rare today. And once we have agreed that the Bible as a whole is not inerrant, we may accept that over the years humans are very prone to exaggerate the unusualness of events they have witnessed – medieval monasteries were filled with improbable things like pieces of the true cross or even, in the case of Reading Abbey, in England, a bottle of Mary's milk and the foreskin of Jesus.

So a certain amount of skepticism is not unreasonable about these matters. Literalists and skeptics will just have to live together, agreeing that the important thing is that the records we have express the spiritual claim that in Jesus God was disclosed in new and liberating ways.

I think it is only fair to state my own view, since though it is not one I would impose on others I believe it is well within the limits of reasonable Christian belief. My view, then, is that it is highly probable that Jesus performed extraordinary acts of healing. That is an important part of his message that God wills to heal and to save. I doubt if the healings were quite as instantaneous and total as some accounts claim, and I do not believe he exorcised demons. That is because I do not believe in demons, and think that these are exaggerated accounts of healings of mental illness, put in terms of what were then widely accepted, but false, beliefs about the causes of mental illness.

I doubt if the natural miracles, like turning water into wine – which are few in number (nine at most out of a recorded 35) – occurred, partly because they mostly seem like theological points (the water of the law turned into the new wine of the Spirit) turned into historical events, and partly because they conflict with Jesus' recorded refusal to produce any miraculous signs of his lordship (Mark 8.12: 'No sign will be given to this generation').

I doubt if the virgin birth occurred, since some texts seem to deny it (the Baptist did not know who Jesus was – 'I myself did not know him,' John 1.33 – which is odd if he really was his cousin, and Jesus' mother and brothers at one time tried to restrain him when people said he was mad – Mark 3.21 and 31 – which is odd if she knew his birth was unique, and if she had no other children), and it seems to rest on the misunderstanding that if Jesus was the 'Son of God' he could have no human father. However, being 'Son of God' is not a physical relationship, and so the incarnation of God in the person of Jesus is quite compatible with Jesus having a human father and mother.

I realise that in saying this I am distancing myself from ancient Church tradition, which very quickly developed devotion to the Virgin Mary as an important spiritual resource. Yet talk in the ancient creeds of God as 'Father', of Jesus as 'Son', and of Jesus as 'ascending into heaven' and 'sitting at God's right hand', is metaphorical, not literal. So it is not hard to see talk of 'the Blessed Virgin' as a metaphorical expression of Mary's innocence, purity and total devotion to God, and to revere her as the uniquely chosen vessel for the birth of God incarnate.

Thus I think Christians could regard belief in the 'virgin birth' as having the status of a very early tradition, recorded in two Gospels, Matthew and Luke. But it is recorded in a story-like context, including stories of the wise men, shepherds and angels which many biblical scholars regard as unlikely to be literal. It is not, after all, theologically very important that Jesus had no human father. It has even been harmful in suggesting, quite falsely, to some that there is something impure about sexual congress, or that Jesus is the Son of God in some sort of physical sense, rather than that he is the incarnation of the Eternal Word. For these reasons, while I value devotion to Mary mother of God, I think the time has come to permit diversity of opinion in the Church as to whether the virginal conception of Jesus was a literal fact.

On the other hand, I believe the resurrection appearances did occur, since otherwise the Christian faith could hardly have arisen, and so the resurrection has an importance that the virgin birth does not. But some details, like Matthew's story of the dead rising from their tombs and walking around Jerusalem, seem to me legendary, if only because the dead are not confined to tombs after death.

What about the empty tomb and the angels? Since I believe that all humans will be resurrected in spiritual, not physical, bodies (I Cor. 15.44), I think that Jesus was resurrected in a spiritual body. In that sense, it would not matter if his physical body disappeared or just decayed in the normal way. Yet the Gospels suggest that Jesus was able to manifest for short periods of time in a fully physical way (he ate fish, for instance – Luke 24.43 – and he bore the marks of the nails in his hands and side – John 20.25). In that case it would have been confusing if his physical body was still to be found in a tomb. I therefore find it quite believable that the physical body of Jesus in the tomb was instantaneously transfigured into a spiritual body, and left the tomb empty.

As for angels, it is undeniable that each of the Gospel accounts is different in detail, but all of them mention figures in white who declare that Jesus had risen. It is entirely intelligible that there should be created beings other than humans, and immaterial beings (which we may call angels) could well be among them. There are many accounts throughout the world of visions of spirits or non-human entities, and of voices or thoughts which seem to come from outside oneself. On the other hand, there are undoubtedly many hallucinations and delusions in human experience, and the medieval ranking of hierarchies of angels sometimes smacks of imaginative fantasizing of a rather uncontrolled kind.

A decision about the genuineness of such visions and auditions will depend on two main factors. Does belief in visionary experiences form part of an intelligible and coherent pattern of beliefs about the world? And is there any parallel to such experiences at the present time? Some will feel that angels play no causal role in our explanations of the world, and that claims to have such visions are too closely associated with mental illness to be taken seriously. But others will think that, given the existence of God, one might expect some visionary experiences which will be genuine manifestations of God, and which may take various finite forms. And they may feel that not all claims to visionary experience by apparently sane and intelligent people can be discounted.

Reasonable opinions may be expected to differ. The important point is the disclosure of divine nature and purpose in rare and astonishing human experiences. This may involve genuine apparitions and visions, or accounts of such apparitions may be literary ways of recording such moments of disclosure. My own inclination is to accept the authenticity of 'visions of angels', though with a tinge of uncertainty about what exactly their content was.

What I mean is that angels may not exist as specific and distinct individuals, for they may be finite forms of manifestations of the divine. That is, after all, how they are sometimes portrayed in the Old Testament, where there is often little distinction between an 'angel of the Lord' and the Lord in person (see Gen. 32.30, where Jacob wrestles with a man, and says, 'I have seen God face to face'). In other words, I accept the veracity of some strange and momentous human experiences of the divine, which may appear in various forms. But there are elements of the biblical accounts that I doubt or am agnostic about, because they seem to conflict too radically with our present knowledge of natural processes, because various biblical accounts differ among themselves, and because we know that humans have a tendency to exaggerate and embroider events that have been important to them.

I have said that 'I doubt' rather than 'I disbelieve', because I am simply not sure that all the New Testament miracles occurred exactly as they are recorded, and I do not think that the occurrence of all of them is important to accepting Jesus as Messiah. But I do not doubt that they could have occurred, and so I prefer to be agnostic. To me the texts we have in the Gospels suggest that Jesus was perceived to be a man of extraordinary spiritual power, who did extraordinary things. Even so, the narratives of his life may show the same sort of hyperbolic exaggeration that we find in the hagiographies of many saints.

What is important for Christians, I think, is to believe that God did act to reveal and liberate in Jesus. Gospel accounts of these acts are shaped so that they might evoke in their hearers or readers the sort of disclosure that originally occurred to the disciples through Jesus. The accounts have been reformulated in the light of subsequent Christian experiences in the infant Church. So for readers now the important task is to bring out the point of the miracle stories – and that point is to evoke disclosures of God and to see Jesus as the focal point of a new and amazing act of God in human history. This can be done even though the Scripture is not inerrant.

God does not provide one and only one consistent account of what actually happened in history, which cannot contain any errors of fact. In particular, biblical accounts of what Jesus did and said are based on more or less ordinary human memories, recorded, composed and interpreted to evoke in readers a sense of the presence of God in Jesus. That sense still has the power to transform our understanding of our world, and to bring to us the power of new life in the Spirit. That is the purpose of the biblical accounts, and that is the central clue to understanding what the Bible truly is – not a literally inerrant history book, but a means of evoking a new spiritual perception of and a new way of living in the world.

Diversity in the Bible

There is a profound significance in the fact that in the four Gospels the Bible contains four different accounts of the same events that differ in detail. Each Gospel relates events from a unique viewpoint, placing them in different contexts of interpretation, even in different orders, and emphasizing different insights into the significance of the events. In the case of the resurrection narratives, Matthew gives the most dramatic account, with an angel rolling away the stone and astounding the guards, and with other bodies of the dead walking around Jerusalem. Mark's account is rather terse, and ends with the women keeping their experience to themselves. Luke gives a more literary version, with references to past words of Jesus. And John alone develops a story about Mary Magdalene seeing Jesus himself in the garden.

These differences reflect different interpretations of Jesus in each Gospel. Why should God reveal himself in this indirect way, through the collected memories and the personal interpretations, in different styles and narratives, of four different editors? One thing seems clear: these cannot be the words of God himself. They are the words of different persons, responding to what they know of traditions about Jesus. Those traditions themselves developed as they were passed on in various groups of disciples from original memories. The Bible contains human responses to revelations of God which have been experienced and interpreted and developed and reflected upon in different ways by different individuals and groups of disciples. In other words, there is no biblical revelation which is not already saturated with experience from a personal point of view, with interpretation and with many years of reflection included within it.

There seem to be six main stages in the genesis of the Gospel records as we have them. First, there are the original divinely caused events, often sayings or acts of Jesus. Second, there are the original observations of these events, usually by small groups of people. Third are the memories of these observations, which seem subject to many of the normal vagaries of human memory. Fourth is the oral tradition which recounted and passed on these memories, and often included reflection or comment upon them. At this stage, many elements may have been added or elaborated. Fifth is the editing of various traditions into a narrative text, which expresses the characteristic interests and concerns of an editor. And sixth is the inclusion of the text into a canon of Scripture – a task performed by a committee, but perhaps reflecting some sort of consensus about the general reliability and spiritual importance of various texts.

There is a seventh stage, too, which is the later interpretation of the Scripture in a specific religious society. The Scripture might be translated in various ways, and different societies will interpret it in different ways – for example, whether people believe there is an intermediate state of Purgatory after death or not depends on differing interpretations of a range of biblical texts. Diversity again seems to be inevitable, and that may lead one to think that God must in some sense intend it. That is, Scripture invites a range of differing interpretations. This invitation is canonically enshrined in the four different Gospels, and is apparent in the many differing churches which exist in the Christian world.

The strange fact is that the more one church insists that it alone has the one true interpretation of Scripture, the more it evokes opposition from others who disagree. The most reasonable course is to accept the permissibility of a variety of interpretations. Of course they cannot all be correct. But there is no decisive way of certifying one as correct, and it seems to be more a matter of plausibility and spiritual efficacy than of certifiable truth.

We can put this fact of diversity in a positive way if we accept that it points to an inevitable partiality and limitedness in our own view, that needs complementing or even correcting by other views. It is a bit like the interpretation of a great literary work. Such a work invites diverse interpretations, bringing various sorts of insights. Some may be utterly implausible – if we think *Hamlet* is a comedy, for example, that is pretty implausible. But we would be glad that new voices can throw new light on literary works. We will have our own view, though it will be better if it is aware of other views and takes them into account. But we would be wrong to say that ours is the 'correct' view. What we are doing is bringing our personality and cultural tradition into conversation with a complex set of texts, which themselves contain many viewpoints. The uniqueness of our viewpoint is as important as our knowledge of other viewpoints. And of course some literary commentators are widely acknowledged to be more knowledgeable or insightful or exciting than others. In literature we do not look for the one true view. We look for creative and imaginative approaches which can deepen and enlarge our own understanding of human life, and enable us to see things in new and illuminating ways.

But isn't the Bible about truth rather than about literary appreciation?

Consider the question, 'What is the truth about Henry VIII?' There are some facts about Henry, there is no doubt about that. But many of those facts have not been observed by anyone, or they have been observed by people who later remember them differently. He broke with the Roman Catholic Church, that is a fact. But why? What was he trying to do? What were his own most basic beliefs and aims? Those things we cannot know for certain, since we only have later accounts from those who loved or hated him, and they interpret his actions very differently. We want to know what motivated him, what the meaning of his life was, why he acted as he did. Those things are seen differently, largely depending upon what our own attitudes and ideals are. The subjectivity of the observer cannot be eliminated. Indeed, it seems that the ideally dispassionate approach that the natural sciences require would be out of place in trying to understand another person. That is why a good novel or play will bring out many shifting facets of human character, but will still leave the innermost springs of human feelings, attitude and intentions ambiguous or hidden, even from the agent who has them.

What we seek in literature is an imaginative sensitivity to the complexity of other persons and the way they see their world. Their inner reality remains hidden, and what we see of it depends on the way we approach it and the way in which it is expressed by a judicious selection of episodes from their lives, presented in a way that is intended to convey some specific points.

So it is with the Bible. The Bible is, overall, a narrative of the history of God, seen from a number of perspectives that respond to God in many different ways over many centuries. In the Christian Bible there are histories, law-codes, proverbs, hymns, stories, prophecies, records of visions, letters and the four Gospels. The books of the Hebrew Bible have been used by the Jews to inspire and sustain a rich tradition of debate, discussion and imaginative reinterpretation (found in parts of the Talmud). The books of the Hebrew Bible remain important to Christians, though Christians no longer have a tradition of Rabbinic interpretation, and reinterpret the books in the light of what they regard as a supreme revelation of God in Jesus the Messiah, or Christ.

The Gospels are edited collections of memories of Jesus, seen by Christians as a decisive disclosure of God, bringing the whole Jewish tradition to a sort of culminating revelation. The Gospels are already theological works, since each presents a distinctive interpretation of the meaning of Jesus' life and words. They do so in narrative form, the interpretation being largely given by the selection and juxtaposition of the materials. The other main part of the New Testament is a number of letters written to very early churches (often pre-dating the Gospels). These letters are obviously not the actual dictated words of God, addressed to humanity in general. They are written to specific groups in response to specific problems, and from various points of view. They are interpretations of the 'basic gospel' of Jesus' death 'for our sins', his resurrection, and his final appearing in glory. They are regarded as 'inspired' because they came to be regarded as profound insights into the meaning of Jesus' life, written very early in the history of the Church by leading teachers in the Church, and accepted as an authoritative basis of Christian discipleship.

They are authoritative in much the same sense that the teachings of Augustine or Aquinas or the Pope may be authoritative, though they possess the advantage that they are nearer the source of Christian faith in time – although it is true that later reflection on past events in the light of subsequent history can also bring out meanings that were not perceived at first. If we think that God was over many centuries guiding the prophets of the Hebrew tradition to fuller insights into the divine nature and purpose, then the prophetic message of Jesus, and the insights that his life, death and resurrection prompted among his disciples, will be of crucial significance in religious history. It will be wholly reasonable to think that God inspired the New Testament authors and editors in such a way that a new paradigm revelation was definitively recorded and witnessed to in their writings.

Not everything they say is inerrant. But it is reasonable to believe that the main outlines are definitive for all future developments in Christian thought and practice, and it is by God's will that they are preserved in Scripture. Each part of the letters has something valuable to express – even if sometimes, as with parts of the Old Testament, it may express how limited even the most faithful human perceptions are.

The existence of the New Testament letters confirms a view of divine revelation as God's co-operative guidance of many diverse human minds, as they reflect on experiences of God that have occurred around the person of Jesus or in the communities founded in his name. They are the authoritative founding documents of the Church. But we still need to read them with discernment, distinguishing their central important truths (what Jesus' death, resurrection and glorification means for our human world and for the cosmos) from cultural or psychological conventions or the very limited scientific knowledge of their day, and re-interpreting their insights in the very different circumstances in which we may now live.

What Does Inspiration Mean?

Christians usually believe that the Bible is inspired by the Spirit of God. The biblical view of inspiration is quite different from the view that some other religions take. Biblical inspiration cannot be divine dictation, as it is said to be in the Jewish Torah, the Muslim Qur'an or the Indian Veda. What then is it? I have suggested that we might best see it as a sort of divine guidance, a raising of the mind and heart to a greater sensitivity to divine presence and purpose, with an increase in the ability to express in memorable ways the insights such sensitivity brings. Such influence does not, as has been demonstrated, eliminate all errors or defects of memory. It does not overrule the unique personal styles and interests of human persons. But it does shape them to a deeper insight and more meaningful form of expression.

This is a fairly common sense of 'inspiration' in human life. The speech of an orator may be called 'inspired' when it gives a new insight or produces courage and devotion in its hearers. This everyday sense of inspiration need not have God as its source. It may be that orators like Adolf Hitler were inspired, but not by God. Biblical inspiration is distinctive because Christians believe it is caused by God, and in some fashion it conveys what God wishes to convey. Through his inspiring of human minds, God wishes to convey something of importance for human fulfillment and salvation.

In the case of the empty tomb, we may think that God did act directly and miraculously to transform Jesus' physical body into a spiritual body, and perhaps to cause an angelic vision to occur – though some Christians would think that such events are not important to belief in the resurrection, and may not have literally occurred. There follows a long and complex process of inspiration. Even if such events occurred, God must ensure that someone observed the tomb and the vision, or there would be no revelation at all. God must ensure that the observers do not completely forget or misinterpret what they have seen – though there is apparently room for memory, vagueness and literary elaboration. God must ensure that such memories get passed on in an oral tradition – though again there will be differing traditions, so that it is the general or core elements that are preserved rather than the details. God must ensure that the traditions are incorporated into a canonical or authoritative body of teaching (a Scripture) – a Scripture that will include memory differences and diverse interpretations of their meaning or spiritual significance.

I think the most plausible account of this long and complex process of inspiration is that God does not act unilaterally to put thoughts or words into people's minds. Rather, God co-operates with human minds, influencing memories and thoughts but not overruling them or taking them over like an alien mental controller.

Once we have accepted that there are differing accounts in Scripture, and that not all of them are strictly accurate, it will be reasonable to allow more radical accounts, which see more elaborations and legendary accretions in Scripture, to live alongside more conservative accounts, which are happy to accept that empty tombs and visions can and are likely to occur. We will not be automatically committed to more radical views. That may depend upon more general factors like whether we think physical miracles occur, and what the physical limits on such miraculous events may be. It will be natural for us to accept what seems more likely to us, given our general evaluation of probabilities, and our sense of what physical events are required for full belief in the resurrection of Jesus. I would expect differences of judgment on such issues among those who accept the fact of Jesus' resurrection, and I would not be inclined to draw a hard and clear line that defines what beliefs are strictly required of a Christian in these areas.

The effect of such divine influence will partly depend on the receptivity of the human mind to it. If that is so, there may be certain blocks or deficiencies of vision that impede a full understanding of what God wishes to communicate. We might expect to find not only an expression of personal insights and concerns, but also some failures to understand God's nature and purposes, because such fuller understanding would be completely alien to the mind of the observer or writer.

That is one reason why diversity might be important. The deficiency or 'one-sidedness' of some accounts might be counter-balanced by complementary insights in other accounts. In the case of the Gospels, the concentration on Jesus' humanity in Mark is complemented by an emphasis on Jesus' divinity in John. Read separately, these Gospels give very different views of Jesus' relation to God. Taken together, they do not provide one wholly harmonious account. They give two perspectives on Jesus, and invite the hearer to form a personal perspective, given that such a diversity of interpretations is natural and proper to human life.

The Bible, then, contains some errors, and also contains limitations of insight and understanding. It is a human document, or rather a set of documents compiled over hundreds of years by very different writers at very different stages of history, from the Bronze Age to the Classical era. But Christians take it as inspired by God, in the sense that, taken as a whole and read sensitively, it conveys the message of salvation and of God's nature and purposes that God has wished to see communicated through this religious tradition. God has overseen that process of communication, but has not overruled the diverse and developing human perspectives that have gone to form it over a long period of time.

This could be called a 'co-operative guidance' model of inspiration. God leads some humans, living within one social tradition with a long history, gradually towards greater insight into the divine purpose. But some perspectives need correcting or placing within a wider context, and none are guaranteed to be immune from misuse or misinterpretation.

The question that all those with a strong sense of biblical authority ask is: if so many parts of the Bible are in error, or reflect human responses to divine actions, how can I trust any of it or suppose that it relates what God's purposes truly are?

This is not a question that would seem reasonable with regard to any other literary or scientific or historical text. We might trust a historical account of the Battle of Waterloo, while expecting that some details may be inaccurate or expressed in a partisan way.

We know that people make mistakes and have limited perspectives. That does not stop us trusting what they say on matters they have researched carefully. A Dostoevsky novel may give great insights into human life, without its views being wholly acceptable. A scientific treatise by a reputable expert may turn out to be mistaken, but we would be well advised to accept it as the best account we have on a given subject, and it would be silly to think that it is entirely mistaken from start to finish.

So why should we expect a religious text to be exempt from such common human errors? What distinguishes the Bible is that it is about the acts of God in history – acts of saving from disaster, or inspiring poets and artists, or causing visions, auditions and miracles to occur. We may say that we would not know how God has acted unless these accounts of them are preserved from all error. That is like saying we would not know who won the Battle of Waterloo unless some historian was preserved from error. That is both false and unrealistic. Some historical claims are so well attested, on such reliable authority, that we do not doubt them, even if we cannot test them ourselves. We do not need infallibility; we need trustworthy witnesses of well-attested events.

When events are recorded in the Bible, that does not prove that they actually happened. It would not help to say that the Bible is inerrant, for we cannot know that until we know if the events it records happened. What, then, makes the biblical accounts of Jesus believable? In the first place, the fact that reliable witnesses, who have much to lose by their claims, testify that they have personally witnessed the life of Jesus over a fairly long period of time, that he appeared to them to have immense wisdom and authority, and that they saw him die and appear after death. In the second place, a general belief that there is a God will raise the probability that God has decisively revealed the divine nature and purpose in an extraordinary way. In the third place, the Old Testament prophets looked forward to a decisive disclosure of God in a Jewish Messianic figure, and Jesus is claimed to be that figure. In the fourth place, these accounts have been used to form the devotional life of a church, and they have conveyed a sense of Jesus as a living and transforming spiritual presence to thousands of devotees who meditated on them. They speak of God revealed in the person of Jesus, and they convey such a revelation to their hearers on many occasions.

So we start with the Gospel accounts of the life of Jesus. These have been collected and edited from the oral traditions of different groups of disciples, and they are based on memories of those who knew Jesus personally. We have every reason to think that they are broadly accurate, though they will probably contain some obscure or inaccurately remembered or embroidered material, and quite a lot of personal selection and interpretation, especially by the editor.

The accounts have been written down for a purpose, and that is to present Jesus as a living mediator of God. They are not just biographies. They are like collections of mini-sermons to bring readers into the presence of their Lord. They have a devotional purpose, and we misread them if we do not see that. But devotion takes many forms, depending on our own ideals and values, and so the four Gospels express different devotional attitudes. The existence of four Gospels shows that all those attitudes are appropriate for Christian disciples.

The Gospels are inspired – that is, the whole process of remembering, selecting, writing down and inclusion in the Bible is guided, Christians believe, by the Spirit. Human memories and perspectives remain, but God uses them to create new insights into God's nature and purposes, and to shape our minds on the mind of Christ.

In reading Gospel passages, we must seek such insights from God. But we should also be aware of our own limited understanding, and of the fact that there may be great limitations in the written texts, as the disciples, the churches that preserved their memories, and the editors who wrote them down, put some of their own prejudices and hang-ups into the text.

The Bible is not primarily a set of true propositions to which we are asked to give theoretical assent, even though many fairly straightforward truth-claims are made in the Bible. It is primarily the sacred text of a religious community, a community that relates to God, the primal reality, in worship and reverence. A sacred text is not information about otherwise unknown facts. It is like a sacrament, an outward and visible sign of an inward and spiritual meaning. Its information content is often indirect and mysterious, metaphorical and allusive. Moreover, it must be taken holistically and in a context of worship. Individual parts cannot be taken out of context, for their meaning depends upon the wider set of texts of which they are part. And the whole set of texts, the Bible itself, is properly read as part of an act of divine worship, of glorifying God.

To be a biblical Christian is not primarily to accept the truth of lots of unusual facts. It is to respond passionately to a God who reveals the divine reality through events of personal significance, but in a way that can only be rightly discerned, believers would say, by minds and hearts open to transcendence. Reading the Bible in the light of faith in the unlimited love of God shown in Jesus Christ is one way of allowing God to reveal the divine presence to us. Such a revelation cannot be identified with simply accepting that whatever the Bible says is true. The text must be used in such a way that it allows God to address us personally, as we read it in the context of the Church's worship and of the Christ-illumined key to interpreting each part of the Bible.

13

Breaking Out of Literalism

The Uniqueness of Jesus

What God wills for the universe, and for the earth in particular, is the existence of a community of persons who will bring the potentialities of the material world to new and fruitful actualisations, who will be guardians of the earth and fellow-workers in realising the creative purposes of God. Such a community is a community that will rejoice in the loving presence and creative power of God, that will flourish under the rule of God, a community where God is king. It could be called the kingdom of God. One of the best-attested facts about Jesus is that he devoted his life to proclaiming that 'the time is fulfilled, and the kingdom of God is at hand' (Mark 1: 15). One of the best-attested facts about the early Christians is that they believed Jesus to be the king, the Messiah (deliverer and ruler), who was to found this kingdom.

An awkward fact about assessing the place of Jesus in the religious history of humanity is that he is not represented primarily as a prophet or great spiritual teacher. He resists complete assimilation into the set of God-enlightened or God-inspired men and women who have deepened the human sense of God and the divine purpose for creation. What is unique about him is that he is claimed to have a quite specific role in the fulfillment of God's purpose for the earth. He is proclaimed by his disciples to be Lord in the liberated community of the divine love. Such a claim is a stumbling block for any attempt to see Jesus as one religious teacher among others.

It is natural and right to see a God of universal love as working everywhere to reveal something of the divine nature and purpose. This leads one to look at all human cultures for signs of such revelation. It is not hard to find such signs. In the prophets of Israel one can discern a growing insight into the justice and mercy of God. In the Qur'an there is an insistence upon the absolute uniqueness and sovereignty of God. In the

Upanishads one is directed to look to 'the cave within the heart' to find the presence of that being of wisdom and bliss that is the one truly Real. In the teaching of the Buddha there is outlined a path to that wisdom, compassion and bliss that delivers from evil and suffering. In Confucian teaching, the 'Way of Heaven' is a way of justice, order and the harmony of all things. Even in modern humanist, anti-religious cultures, the concern for human welfare, freedom and equality can be seen by theists as prompted by the Spirit of God in an ambiguous and hatred-obsessed world.

If one was looking for a distinctive insight given by Christianity, it might lie in the emphasis laid upon the forgiving and self-giving love of God, which seeks to save all who are lost, 'not wishing that any should perish, but that all should reach repentance' (2 Peter 3: 9). But there is something else that is distinctive about Christianity. It does not just teach that God is love as a general truth that might be confirmed in general human experience. It seems to be essential to Christian faith to claim that Jesus is the liberator, the Christ, who establishes the kingdom of God. At this point in human history, the followers of Jesus claimed, the foundations of the kingdom were laid, and God acted decisively in and through the person of Jesus to found the kingdom in history.

That claim is an awkward one, because it asserts a sort of uniqueness for Jesus that seems to conflict with the expectation that God will act in the same sort of way everywhere. One of the things many people have tried to learn in the modern world is that old assumptions about the inherent superiority of our own beliefs and practices need to be given up, as we understand more about other cultures. It seems much more tolerant to see our religion as one among others, and to see Jesus as one teacher or religious figure among others, rather than to assert that God acts uniquely in him. Why can we not see the way of Jesus as one way to God among many?

There is an important sense in which even (or especially) wholly orthodox Christians can and should do so. There are indeed many ways to God. God does act in all cultures to show something of the divine nature and purpose. The way we understand our own beliefs is very limited and fallible. These are important facts, which religious believers sometimes forget, largely because we are still prey to that greed, hatred and ignorance that Buddhists discern so accurately. Greed leads to the desire for power, which makes us see our religion as 'inerrantly true', whereas all others are to be mocked or suppressed. Hatred leads us to see members of other faiths as blasphemers or idolaters. Ignorance leads us to reject the beliefs of others when we do not even understand them properly. Since religion is bound up with human nature as it is, it will never be free of these tendencies. It is certainly important to try to counteract them, to treat the beliefs of others with respect, and to learn from them.

Nevertheless, it is not possible to believe everything at the same time. Disagreement is part of religion, too, and it is wrong to pretend that every belief can be equally true. What we have to learn is that divine revelation is received by fallible human beings, and if we are fallible, any of our beliefs may need correction. So we may have to disagree with others, or even with our past selves, to discover where this correction might be needed, though we should do so with respect wherever that is possible. There are many disagreements in religious belief. Some believe in reincarnation, whereas others think we are only born once on earth. Some think God is a personal agent, whereas others think the supreme reality does not act in the world. Some think the soul is immortal, while others think that there is no life beyond death. It is not possible for all these beliefs to be correct. So while we can certainly say that God is at work in all human cultures, we cannot say that all human beliefs about God's nature and purpose are more or less equally acceptable.

When we come to consider Christian claims about Jesus, we find that they are not just claims about whether some general teaching is more or less true. They are also claims about Jesus himself, claims that he really was in some sense the founder of the kingdom of God on earth. It looks as though Jesus was either mistaken about his central message, the coming of the kingdom, and the disciples were mistaken about his role in it as liberator and ruler of Israel, or he really does have a historically unique role to play in human history.

The Literalist Fallacy

It is quite possible to interpret Jesus as a Galilean exorcist, healer and preacher, who taught that God's kingdom was about to come, putting an end to the world as it was then known, and who died in an attempt to force God to bring history to a close. That was how Albert Schweitzer, a great biblical scholar, saw it in his book, *The Quest for the Historical Jesus*. But on that view Jesus was wrong in his central teaching. He must pass into history as one more failed preacher of the end of the world. It is hard to see such a man as one who should be taken as a supreme religious authority. It would be impossible for the Christian Church to take such a man to be the very incarnation of God.

There is another way to see the story of Jesus, however. Proponents of the alternative story might think that Schweitzer's view was conditioned by two main presuppositions neither of which is obviously true. First, Schweitzer assumes that the miracle stories were all grossly exaggerated, especially the story of Jesus' resurrection. Schweitzer assumed that God does not act in the universe in specific ways, so a naturalistic account has to be given of the life of Jesus. He could be an exorcist, healer and preacher. He could even be a Messianic claimant, hoping that God would miraculously deliver Israel from the power of the Roman Empire. But he could not be a man in whom the wisdom and power of God was plainly manifest, who founded a Church to spread throughout the earth, and who was really raised from death to appear alive to his disciples. Schweitzer's first presupposition is that God does not act in historically unique ways for human salvation, and so could not have acted uniquely in Jesus. If, however, one accepts the possibility of divine action, it becomes plausible to think that God might have acted miraculously through Jesus (i.e. in ways transcending the natural powers of objects) to realise an important purpose on earth. Jesus may really have been raised to life after his death. Then it would not be enough to call him a healer and preacher. Jesus would be unique in human history, the only person who returned to the earth from the world of the dead.

Schweitzer's second presupposition is that religious beliefs are almost always to be taken literally. If Adam and Eve took forbidden fruit in Eden, then there was a tree in some garden, and they physically ate its fruit. If Jesus preached the end of the age and Judgment, that means that angels will visibly appear in the sky blowing trumpets and all the dead will be raised out of their tombs. If Jesus preached hell for those who reject God, that means that their bodies will burn for ever if they have never heard the name of Jesus. If Jesus taught that he would soon return in glory, that means that a young Jewish man would collect his disciples into the air sometime not later than around 100 CE.

It is not hard to see why Schweitzer thought all these beliefs were false. Quite simply, Jesus did not return on time. This sort of literalism is fatal to Christian belief, because Jesus was not literally the Messiah, the deliverer and ruler of Israel. That is why Jews reject the Messianic claims of Jesus.

He did not bring the twelve tribes back to Jerusalem in triumph and drive out the Roman occupation forces. For Jews, it is obvious that the Messiah has not yet come. To make the claim that Jesus is the Messiah plausible Christians have to reinterpret the idea of the Messiah in a non-literal way. This is what they did, seeing Jesus not as a political deliverer of the nation of Israel, but as the spiritual deliverer and ruler of a new community of divine love, the Church, which would have its origin in history but would be fulfilled beyond historical time, at the consummation of all things. From the first, Christians adopted a non-literal – that is, a spiritual – interpretation of Jesus' Messianic role. It is because Schweitzer did not recognise this fact that he regarded Jesus as a failed prophet of the end of the world.

Total literalism, besides being fatal to Christianity, is in any case a complete misunderstanding of many of the spiritual truths the Christian faith teaches. I have already tried to show how the Genesis accounts of creation should be taken non-literally[1] if one is to understand the enduring spiritual truths they teach. The same goes for the teachings about the 'end of the world' and the coming of the kingdom of God that form the heart of Jesus' message. I shall give a short interpretation of these teachings later, in chapter 15. Two thousand years ago it was possible to take these teachings literally. Given the worldview of that age, many people probably accepted that the earth had only existed for a few thousand years, and that it might well end in a cosmic cataclysm in the near future. Within that worldview, part of the Christian message was that the end of the earth would not be the end of human existence, and it was not something to be feared. Whenever it happened, God would liberate those who trusted in the divine promises into a fuller life in a new creation. The kingdom established by Jesus would not be destroyed, but would achieve its full realisation with the ending of suffering and evil that the end of the earth would bring.

So in what is generally thought to be the earliest New Testament document, the first letter to Christians at Thessalonica, Paul exhorts the believers 'to wait for his Son from heaven, whom he raised from the dead, Jesus who delivers us from the wrath to come' (1 Thessalonians 1: 10). The 'wrath to come' is the envisaged ending of the earth in fire, which will be destruction and judgment to all who are evil, since it will put an end to

1 See Chapter 3, 'Sacred Cosmology: the Genesis Creation Narratives', in *God, Faith, and the New Millennium*

the present world order. Paul's message is that God delivers from destruction and gives eternal life in a new creation. This promise was given in the life of Jesus, who was raised from death and continued to exist in a different, glorified form with God. The end of the earth, Paul taught, would also be the birth of a new creation, and its form would be the form of the transfigured humanity that the apostles saw in the risen Jesus.

The spiritual truth of this teaching is distinct from its literal interpretation, and already within the New Testament a different, literal world view begins to emerge. In the Letter to the Romans, Paul writes that 'a hardening has come upon part of Israel, until the full number of the Gentiles come in, and so all Israel will be saved' (Romans 11:25). As the Christian message began to spread in the Gentile world, it became clear that an early end of the earth would leave the vast majority of humans without the chance to hear about God's redeeming love. Soon, Christians began to pray that the earth would not end soon, so that the message of divine love could spread throughout the globe. The second letter of Peter makes the point explicit: 'with the Lord one day is as a thousand years, and a thousand years as one day' (2 Peter 3: 8). Christ will come again – that is, there will be a fulfillment of the kingdom, in which peace and justice reign and suffering and evil are destroyed for ever. In that kingdom, Jesus will be clearly revealed as the man in and through whom God acted in human history to deliver humans from selfish desire and make them 'partakers of the divine nature' (2 Peter 1: 4). But the time of that 'coming again' is in God's hands, and it will only be when the 'full number' of those who are to hear the gospel is complete.

Since the sixteenth century, our view of the universe has expanded enormously, and we now know that the end of the earth will not by any means be the end of the universe. It will only be a small blip in cosmic history. So for us a literal interpretation of the biblical accounts of creation and the end of all things is ruled out. It is important to see, then, that the literal account was never essential to understanding the deep spiritual truth of these biblical stories. Totalliteralism has now become the greatest obstacle there is to understanding the truth of Christianity.

The Sacred Cosmology of Christianity

Of course, there must be some literal truths in Christian teaching, or it would have no content. Jesus must have existed and been very much the sort of person the Gospels say he was. God must really exist and there must be a continuance of human life beyond death. But such truths are typically expressed by the use of highly symbolic imagery, especially when they deal with events (like the origin of the universe) so remote in history that no one can remember them, or (like the resurrection of the dead) so far beyond present human experience that we can hardly imagine what they will be like. The accounts of Jesus' life in the Gospels are not in this category, as the events were well within the memory of many people then living. Even then, those accounts would have been written so as to express specific spiritual meanings and insights that probably would not have existed at the time the remembered events occurred.

When it comes to questions of an overall view of the nature of the cosmos, it will not be surprising if the central spiritual teaching needs to be completely disentangled from contemporaneous beliefs about how the universe began or will end. We will naturally place the spiritual truths of the Christian message into the evolutionary form of our modern world-view. That worldview may turn out to be mistaken or quite inadequate at some future time, and yet we may be sure that the spiritual message will remain intact. I would think, however, that the general evolutionary view is so well established that it will not be completely overturned, even though, it may be drastically modified. It might be as well to be agnostic about some of the finer points of modern scientific theory, but the overall view does seem fairly definitive. As I have argued, that general view actually helps to give a more plausible account of Christian faith, in many ways. But that will only be true if one has a firm grasp of the spiritual, non-literal sense of much scriptural narrative. It is because Schweitzer chose not to recognise that fact that he could regard early Christian teaching as false prediction, rather than as a profound teaching about God's kenotic, unitive and redemptive love, conveyed in symbolic forms.

So, for example, when Jesus teaches about hell, he is warning of the course of self-destruction upon which people embark when they choose lives of selfish desire. The fires of hell are the fires of unquenched desire, and the outer darkness is the separation from God that love of self inevitably produces. Selfish desire does bring suffering and destruction. In that sense hell is real, but it is not a literal fire from which there is no escape.

On the contrary, the whole point of Jesus' teaching is that people should repent – turn from selfish desire – and accept God's free gift of eternal life. When he speaks of 'the coming of the Son of Man in glory', he is speaking of the emergence of a truly personal community, filled with the joy of God's presence, when all evil and suffering has been overcome, That community will only emerge fully at the end of time, but within the lifetimes of those who heard him teach it can already be seen as a spiritual reality in time.

In other words, Jesus was not prophesying that the world would physically come to an end within a few decades at most. If he had been, Christianity should have died out, as a falsified millenarian sect, almost at once. Jesus was intending to found a new Israel, a 'kingdom not of this world' (John 18: 36), a community in which he would be permanently present as ruler. In his person, that kingdom was already present, for he is one who unites human and divine in himself. His humanity is freed from selfish desire, and is the vehicle of the rule of the divine Spirit. Knowing himself to be uniquely one with God, at once fulfilling and transcending Jewish Messianic hopes, he gathers a group of disciples, formed around 'the Twelve', leaders of the new Israel. He proclaims the birth of a new Spirit-led community, and prepares to send it throughout the world, where it will be the 'body of Christ', the community through which all things can be liberated from self and ruled by the Spirit of God. He promises his presence with that community, and teaches that there will be a consummation of all things, in which he (the cosmic reality of Christ, embodied in what will then be the glorified and transfigured humanity of Jesus) will be known in his true form.

This is, of course, one version of the picture of Christ that is held by the orthodox Christian churches. It is not some sort of radical new interpretation that exposes the orthodox tradition as a fraud or invented myth. Yet it is radical in at least two ways. It places the orthodox Christian story squarely within the modern scientific evolutionary worldview. This is clearly different from the worldview of biblical times, and yet the surprising thing is that, at least in my view, it gives even deeper meaning to the orthodox story.

It also insists on a non-literal interpretation of the 'sacred cosmology' of the Christian faith, the religious imagery of creation, fall, atonement, heaven and hell, the return of Christ and the Last Judgment. Many Christians will find this radical, because unfortunately total literalism has become so widespread in recent times. Such literalism is doomed, however, not only because science has shown that the universe is much bigger than literalist accounts suppose, but also because it misses the spiritual depth of Christian teaching about the cosmic purpose of God.

Albert Schweitzer thought that Jesus preached that the world would end in cataclysmic judgment within a few years, in which case Jesus was, to put it bluntly, just another crank. Suppose, however, that Jesus was a profound spiritual teacher, who taught in 'mysteries' and parables of a new reality, the community of the Spirit of God. In this community, humanity and divinity would be united, and all things would be reconciled in the cosmic Word. Jesus himself founded this community, which would be patterned on his life, and would indeed express the life of the cosmic Word that is one with his humanity, with the vocation to unite the estranged world to God.

The fact is that Christianity requires one to make a decision, not just about the truth of some general spiritual teaching, but about the person and role of Jesus of Nazareth. The Christian Church claims that he was indeed the inaugurator of the kingdom of God, a new spiritual reality existing, however ambiguously, in history, and to be fulfilled beyond history. If this claim is justified, then the belief that Jesus was the earthly incarnation of the cosmic Christ will not be a myth, almost comically exaggerating the importance of an obscure Galilean prophet. It will be a fact that marks Jesus out as unique in world history, since he is the human person in whom God acts to establish a community in which the divine purpose for this planet is to be declared, and through which it can be at least partly fulfilled.

This may seem like asking too much of the Christian Church. Surely it is not that much better than other religious communities? And is it not rather arrogant to claim that God's purpose is to be fulfilled through just this one religious community, rather than through many communities throughout the world? At this point the problem the Church has is very like the problem Jews have, about being a people 'chosen' by God. Both Jews and Christians have at times thought this 'chosen-ness' gave them some inherent superiority. But in their wiser moments, they have both seen that they are not chosen for their virtue or wisdom. The apostles were neither wise nor virtuous. They often seem particularly obtuse, power-hungry and fearful. It is better to see the Church as a community of forgiven sinners than as a society of perfect saints. The Church will not be 'better' than other social groups, and it should not base its claims to truth on such a fragile base.

One claim that is central to Christianity is that Jesus is a servant-Lord. By his direct command, his followers are to serve the world as he did, not dominate it (John 13: 14 and 15). So the only claim the Christian Church should make about itself is that God has called it, through Jesus, to serve the needs of the earth and work for the establishing of a global society of justice and mercy. There are many other communities in which God might be known and served, and Christians should cooperate with them in working for the welfare of the world. Christians should rejoice with them in the knowledge and service of the creator, and learn from them what God has revealed in their distinctive paths. Christians should not claim that God only works to fulfill the divine purpose through the Church, or even some favoured part of the universal Church.

The distinctive path of Christianity is that it should form a community in which self-giving divine love can be mediated for the welfare of the earth, and in which human lives can be liberated from selfish desire, empowered by the divine Spirit and fulfilled by being made sharers in the divine nature. Of course, Christians believe that when God's kingdom fully comes, it will be the fulfillment of what is so ambiguously and fitfully present in the Church – just as Buddhists believe that the final human goal is nirvana, and Muslims believe that it will be the resurrection to paradise of which the Qur'an speaks. Perhaps the final human goal is not less than, but so much more than all that our religious images convey that many different images will find their fulfillment there, in unimaginable ways. For the present, it is surely enough for Christians simply to witness to the love of God, which has been made known to them through the person of Jesus, whom they believe to be the Christ, the liberator and ruler of a community chosen to be a vehicle of divine love on this planet. That is the calling of the Church, and that is the criterion by which the 'true Church' should be judged.

14

Morality and the Bible

The Problem of Obsolete Moral Rules in the Old Testament

Religious morality is based on the belief that human life has moral significance, and that it is possible to overcome selfish egoism and attain a state or achieve a positive conscious relationship to a being of wisdom, compassion and bliss. This sounds the opposite of dangerous. But some people think that there is something dangerous about religious morality. That is because they think religious morality is based on unthinking acceptance of the rules of some holy book like the Bible. It might be bad enough to accept moral rules unthinkingly. But even worse if many of the moral rules in the Bible now seem to be cruel and reactionary. In the Old Testament, in particular, people can be stoned to death for adultery, for worshipping the wrong gods, even for disobedience to their parents. There do seem to be lots of what we would now call primitive moral ideas. Perhaps the worst of all can be found in Deuteronomy 20:16. It is called 'the Ban', and it reads: 'As for the towns of these peoples that the Lord your God is giving you as an inheritance, you must not let anything that breathes remain alive. You shall annihilate them – the Hittites and the Amorites, the Canaanites and the Perizzites, the Hivites and the Jebusites.' This applies only to Canaanite towns that make war against the Israelites, and do not submit peacefully. Even so, it is a pretty horrific scenario.

Reasons given for this command include the fact that no slaves or booty should be taken for personal use, and that the Israelites should not assimilate to the customs of the Canaanite cities. But the fact remains that this is a savage attitude to war that few would accept today.

And that is the point. Moral attitudes have changed over the last three millennia, and sometimes they have changed for the better. If you leave God out of it altogether, and look at human attitudes to warfare, we can see developing over time a set of rules for limiting conduct in war. Such rules include a degree of protection for the innocent, regulations about the fair treatment of prisoners, and the prohibition of torture and needless cruelty.

As a matter of fact, the general rules for war in the Torah require that there should be no pre-emptive strikes, that women, children and animals should not be killed, and that fruit trees should not be destroyed. Later rabbinic commentary elaborated these rules to make it clear that loss of life should be minimised and that the environment should be safeguarded. However, the later history of Israel and its final ejection from its territories in 132 CE rendered most rules for warfare within Canaan obsolete. A central moral value for modern Jews is *shalom* – peace, wholeness and harmony. So for most Jews these rules for war are wholly obsolete, and cannot be used to undermine the prophetic obligation to work positively for peace and justice in society.

Modern rules for the conduct of war owe much to scholarly developments of biblical thought, and in particular to the Catholic 'just war' tradition, which developed principles governing Christian participation in war. In the thirteenth century Thomas Aquinas held that a justifiable war must be declared by a sovereign, must have a just cause (usually self-defense), and must have a realistic prospect of advancing good or avoiding evil. In the sixteenth century the legal theorist Vitoria added that war must be waged by proper means, that it must be discriminate (not, for instance, killing combatants) and proportionate (using minimal force achieve a good end).

These rules are, like all moral principles, hotly debated, and it is not clear that they can be applied in conditions of modern warfare, where weapons of mass destruction have been used. But they illustrate the way in which religious institutions have devoted much thought to the question of the moral justification for killing, and have not simply quoted texts from the Bible. Indeed the whole tradition of Christian moral theology is based on rational reflection on the basic doctrines of creation and of rather general moral guidelines discerned in the life and often extremely cryptic teachings of Jesus. Biblical texts are usually quoted in support of particular arguments, but they are rarely decisive, and they are never the basis of moral debate.

Modern warfare is a terrible thing, and hardly anything more cruel or indiscriminately deadly than the saturation of cities with napalm gas or firebombs can be imagined. Cruelty and indiscriminate killing has not disappeared from the military practices of the most 'civilised' countries in the world.

Even so, the complete destruction of 'anything that breathes' is a pretty extreme practice. Such wholesale massacres do occur – they occurred in former Yugoslavia in the twentieth century, and they occurred in Soviet Russia, China and North Korea. But we hope that they are exceptions, to be condemned by the international community, not morally appropriate acts.

We hope that moral attitudes to war have developed in a more humane direction since the times when it was thought acceptable to slaughter whole city populations if they resisted military takeover. Such a humane development can undoubtedly be traced in the Bible. By the sixth century BCE, prophet Ezekiel taught that each person should be punished only for their own sin – which rules out indiscriminate slaughter. And the Old Testament records many occasions when groups of Canaanites were not by any means destroyed. Hittites and Canaanites play an important part in the life of Israel: Tamar and Rahab, ancestors of Jesus, were Canaanites; Ruth, another ancestor, was a Moabitess; and Bathsheba, wife of King David, was married to Uriah the Hittite.

Most biblical scholars think that 'the Ban' was written long after the entry of the Israelites into Canaan, after the exile in Babylon, and that it was an imaginary version of the conquest of the land, extolling the irresistible power of the Israelites. It never actually happened like that, and such a rule was never put into practice, historically.

Even so, it is a bit of bloodthirsty imagination, and it could conceivably be taken to show that if God orders it, any moral monstrosity may become possible. It could, but no sane Jew would read it that way. The fact is that by the time the Ban was written down it was already obsolete. It never was an actual rule for the Jewish conduct of war, and it was already countermanded by other commands of the Torah, such as the famous 'an eye for an eye' command, which limits the amount of retribution to something proportionate to some committed offence – and, of course, that rule was in turn countermanded by later developments, for Christians most obviously by Jesus' teaching in the Sermon on the Mount.

So the Ban is a horrible rule, but most scholars believe it was never put into practice, and was obsolete even before it was written down. It would be slander to suggest that any Jew has ever seriously considered massacre to be ordered by God in any actual historical situation since the writing down of the Law.

A serious reading of the Bible makes it clear that perceptions of what God requires have developed in some respects over the centuries. In fact, saying, that 'God requires X' is more or less equivalent to saying, 'I believe it is morally right.' It used to be thought, by many people that it was morally right to massacre all one's enemies in battle. But as people reflected on what morality requires they generally came to think that there should be some limits on the treatment of defeated enemies and their kin.

At least, it might be said, the Israelites were asking the question of what morality requires in war, and were not just saying that victors can do anything they feel like, or that moral issues are not at all relevant in war. They did not accept the concept of total war. So the correct attitude to this biblical rule is, 'People used to think that it was right to massacre those who are defeated in battle, in certain circumstances (during the conquest of Canaan, when the Canaanites went to battle with the Israelites). But those circumstances cannot ever apply again, and consequently it will never again be right to massacre enemies.'

Three Attitudes to Ancient Biblical Texts

There are three basic religious attitudes that can be taken to biblical rule and others like it in the Old Testament. The first is that they are examples of primitive moral attitudes, projected onto an imagined past, which were very rarely if ever put into practice, and are now totally obsolete. That is what an anthropologist might say, and in this respect the Bible parallels the sort of moral development that has taken place in most human societies. We might well say that the Bible shows a process of continuing moral reflection that is far in advance of the other human societies of the time. But nobody in their right mind would think of applying any of these ancient moral codes to society in the present day.

The second is that God really did give such a command, but only to people who were morally primitive and in the unique circumstance of the conquest of Canaan. The command is now obsolete, and must be seen in the context of a long subsequent history of rabbinic commentary and reflection. Such reflection has added many principles limiting the destructiveness and the conduct of war, and has emphasised the importance of having a goal of harmony and peace. This is what a conservative Christian might say, and it has the consequence that such rules do not give direct moral guidance now. It follows that even for the most conservative Christian, moral rules found in the Bible should not be taken out of context without bringing them into line with the more important rules of the Torah – such as 'love your neighbour as yourself' (Leviticus 19: 18) – and without paying careful attention to the long tradition of rabbinic legal commentary and interpretation.

The third general religious attitude is that even the Ban expresses some perception of the divine will – in this case, a will for total devotion to God, and for the renunciation of all private gain from battle. But it was a very limited perception which involved a distorted view of what God really requires (which is love of, or at least respect for, enemies). As such, it was corrected by developing perceptions of God's will by later prophets of Israel.

This is the interpretation I prefer, and it entails that there is a developing understanding of God, a very useful record of which can be found in the Old Testament. At first God was taken to be a tribal war God (the God of Hosts, or armies) leading Israel to victory, and being one among many other gods – 'a great King above all gods' (Psalm 95: 3). But by the time of the major prophets, in the eighth century BCE, God was seen to be the only true God, the creator of all things, whose will is for universal justice. It is the fully developed view that is important, not the primitive beginnings of the prophetic knowledge of God.

Whichever of these interpretations you take, nobody holds that commands such as that recorded in the Ban are to be applied at the present time. The main lesson is that you must read the particular rules of the Bible, especially of the Old Testament, in the light of later more developed moral views found within the Bible itself, which often render them obsolete or transform their interpretation.

Biblical Language about God

The Hebrew Bible presents the story of how God's acts are intertwined with human hatred, greed and arrogant pride, and how God repeatedly raises up leaders and prophets to turn the people back towards a love of justice. That story, spanning millennia, contains many diverse perceptions of what God is and of how God acts. It is a story of developing perception of the will of God. It contains many primitive and imperfect perceptions, but these are counterbalanced and in the end transformed by the deeper perceptions of the great prophets.

The biblical viewpoint is that the world is corrupted by sin – by greed, hatred, arrogance and hypocrisy. The wars and massacres that litter human history are the results of a massive turning away from God and from devotion to goodness. The 'judgments of God' are the ways in which human egoism is destructive in the end. The wages of sin is death – the death of the soul, the death of goodness, the death of all true happiness and fulfillment.

It is possible to interpret the Bible very literally, and to suppose that the biblical God is an invisible person who punishes things he does not like by sending earthquakes and floods, and who gives long lists of fairly arbitrary commands that his worshippers are just to accept without question. But such a literal reading is untrue to the long tradition of Jewish Christian theological reflection. Jewish and Christian theologians are agreed that the Bible speaks in vivid metaphors about God that are not to be taken as literal descriptions. When God is said to enjoy the smell of a good sacrifice, we are not supposed to think that God has nostrils, and literally likes breathing in the smell of roasting meat. God has no body and no bodily sense-organs. What is expressed in such pictures is that God is pleased when humans show their commitment to reverence of supreme goodness and beauty (when they do so sincerely) by offering something of value to God – which symbolises the offering of their own lives to the service of goodness.

Even then, we are not to think of God as being cheered up when he is depressed, or of God being pleased when humans grovel and utter all sorts of obsequious and flattering sentiments. We have to get rid of all anthropomorphism, and recognise that metaphorical talk about God is a way of saying what humans should do and how they should see their lives in the context of a supreme reality of ultimate goodness. When we say that 'God is pleased', we are expressing the fact that we fulfill the purpose of our lives when we orient them to supreme goodness and seek to let such goodness be expressed through us.

This is not some modern, trendy reworking of the idea of God. It is written into the texts themselves, and is the unanimous teaching of major theologians such as Augustine and Aquinas (in Christianity), Maimonides (in Judaism) and Al Gazzali (in Islam). Thus Aquinas said that there is never any change in God at all. God is changeless in perfection. When we speak of God being pleased or angry, we are really speaking about changes in human life and attitudes, changes perhaps in how we see God, but not in how God is.

The prohibition of making any carved images of God is an expression of this teaching that nothing in all finite creation is like God. For the Jewish tradition, God cannot be adequately represented by any finite form, and so in the Holiest place in the Temple there was no statue of God. God remains the Unknowable, beyond human understanding. God is certainly not a person who has tantrums like a human tyrant. For God is one 'with whom there is no variation or shadow due change' (James 1: 17).

So in the Bible the idea of God develops as a way of affirming that the world has a fundamental moral order. The 'wrath of God' is a way of talking about the self-destructiveness of evil. The 'love of God' is a way of talking about the fulfillment of human life in positive relationship to a Supreme Good. That Supreme Good exists, and it is the foundation of the whole cosmos. But we can speak of it only by speaking of how human beings relate to it, indirectly and by means of metaphor.

Part of the message of the book of Job is that we must not think of God too anthropomorphically, as a person who distributes rewards and punishments in accordance with human virtue and vice. And it is more characteristic of Jewish biblical meditation continually to question God than to blindly accept whatever God says. Very often, the beginning of wisdom in religion is to learn to distinguish between literal description and metaphor, and then to learn that metaphors in religion have the function of guiding human feelings and behaviour, aspirations and hopes.

Jewish Attitudes to Biblical Laws

An orthodox Jew will certainly accept that God gave the Law to Moses. But how that Law is to be interpreted and applied is very much a matter for discussion. For Jews, the Torah is not a list of rules that anyone can read and apply literally in modern life. The Torah needs to be interpreted by rabbinic reflection and debate. So, by the time the Talmud was written down (in the third century CE) all the laws concerning polygamy, stoning to death and the conduct of war had long rendered obsolete. Religious law, like any *body* of laws, develops and is interpreted by lawyers or religious scholars. The specific laws of the Old Testament and the Talmud are precedents that can be amended, amplified or reinterpreted as new occasions arise. In Judaism, the Law is a living tradition, and professional lawyers, the rabbis, have the job of applying old rules to new cases – or of deciding that the old rules do not apply any more. Orthodox Jews have no difficulty in saying that there are rules in the Old Testament that we would now regard as morally primitive. But, they might well say, the fact we now see them as morally primitive is largely due to the prophetic tradition of seeking to discover the divine will more fully in the light of experience and deeper understanding of what God requires.

Jews can cheerfully say that there are many obsolete and primitive moral rules in the Hebrew Bible. This is because the Hebrew Bible is a very good record of the developing moral perceptions of the Jewish people. This record parallels that of most ancient cultures, but there is little doubt that the idea of one creator God concerned for justice and for the flourishing of creation originated with the prophets of ancient Judaism. There is a crucial emphasis on justice and mercy, on concern for widows, the old, the poor, resident foreigners and the oppressed, and on the duties of open-handed giving and taking responsibility for the disadvantaged. The land is to be cultivated responsibly, and not despoiled. All debts are to be released, property returned to its original owners, and slaves freed, every fifty years. By the time of Jesus, rabbinic interpreters of the Law regarded many of the older rules – for instance, concerning the right of private retribution polygamy – as obsolete, and offered various interpretations of the remaining food laws, laws of religious ritual, and laws enjoining charity and care for dependants and the poor. After the destruction of the Temple in 70 CE, most of the ritual laws and laws referring to the 'promised land' also became obsolete. So the Torah is now partly a set of rules, such as food and Sabbath laws, that set Jews apart as a people called to witness to the sovereignty of God, and partly a set of moral exhortations to social responsibility, kindness, justice and mercy. It is only when the religious Law is seen as a holistic set of living, changing, dynamic principles underlying the life of a specific community that specific biblical rules can be placed in their proper historical context.

It would be quite wrong to think that Jews then or Jews now would simply point to rules in the Hebrew Bible and say, 'We must do this.' Such an attitude would be regarded by them as unprofessional and ignorant. What has to take place is long and detailed discussion of how the underlying principles of the Torah are to be applied. Knowledge of a variety of different historical interpretations, and knowledge of previous rabbinical precedents, is always a part of this process. To fail to see this is simply to fail to see what living Judaism is.

The Sermon on the Mount

Christian thinking on biblical morality is deeply affected by the fact that Christians have given up the Torah, as a complete system of God-given rules all of which they have to obey. In the first Christian generation, largely because of the large number of Gentile converts to the new faith, Christians abandoned the food laws and the laws of religious observance and ritual purity that had existed to set Jews apart as a covenant people. They also set aside specific laws about slavery and property and family (which allowed limited slavery and polygamy), thus regarding the vast majority of Old Testament rules as obsolete.

As the apostle Paul said, 'Christ is the end of the Law' (Romans 10:4), and he wrote that the whole Law is summed up in loving your neighbour as yourself (Galatians 5:14). The moral ideal, for Christians, is to be found not in a written text ('the letter kills, but the Spirit gives life', wrote Paul in Corinthians 3:6), but in the dynamic person of Jesus, who is the living and personal Word of God. So it is to the teachings and the life of Jesus that Christians look to find their moral inspiration.

Christianity is not a religion of a written law, but a religion of grace, of God's love given unconditionally in a human person, the person of Jesus. So for Christians, morality finds its culmination in the life and teaching of Jesus, and there can be no question that every moral rule in the Bible is transformed when it is seen in the light of the self-giving love of Jesus.

Jesus had a very humane attitude to religious and moral laws. He strongly criticised the legalism of some Pharisees, who seemed to be more concerned with rigorous adherence to rules than with care for human well-being. When he healed on the Sabbath, when his disciples ate corn on the Sabbath, when he touched lepers and corpses, and when he ignored traditional rules of washing and fasting, he pointed out that the 'weightier matters of the law', loving-kindness and care for others, were more important than observance of minor regulations that were in any case capable of various interpretations.

Matthew records the main teaching of Jesus about morality in the so-called Sermon on the Mount (Matthew chapters 5–7). In that teaching, Jesus denies that he is abandoning the Torah, but he does take it upon himself to reinterpret it in quite a radical way. So in the five 'Great Antitheses' (Matthew 5:21–48), Jesus says, 'You have heard ... but I say to you ... It is not just killing that is wrong, but anger. It is not just adultery that is wrong, but seeing others solely as objects of sexual desire. It is not just breaking an oath that is wrong, but all untruth. You should not just confine justice to exacting a fair penalty, you should be ready to forgive evil. You should not love your neighbour and hate your enemy, you should love your enemy also.'

In this series of astonishing statements – so astonishing that it seems highly probable that they must go back to an outstanding moral teacher, and there is good reason to think this was Jesus himself – the religious Law is not abandoned. But it is interpreted in such a way that most of its specific commands are rendered obsolete. The Law, Jesus teaches, is not to be simply cast aside as worthless. But it is to be fulfilled and transcended by a more inward, more universal and more demanding morality. Not just outer acts of killing, adultery and oath-breaking, but inner attitudes of anger, lust and untruthfulness, are condemned. Concern to limit punishment is extended to throw doubt on the appropriateness of any retributive punishment. And the limitation of love to neighbours is extended to all people without exception, including enemies.

The fulfillment of the Law is seen to be unrestricted love and concern for the welfare of others. And such concern is to be a matter of the heart, not just of external observance. It is not surprising that when Jesus was asked what the most important laws were, he picked out two (neither of them, incidentally, in the Ten Commandments) – the love of God and love of your neighbour as yourself (Matthew 22: 36–40). Those are the laws by which all others are to be interpreted or, where needed, rendered obsolete.

If Christians take the Sermon on the Mount seriously, they have to see the Torah as pointing towards, and being fulfilled in, the teaching that universal unrestricted love is the key principle. Luke's parables of the Good Samaritan and prodigal Son illustrate this point vividly by stressing that vindictiveness and resentment have no place in love, and that no one is excluded from the universality of love.

In view of the clear teaching of Jesus, it is a gross misunderstanding of Christian morality to say that Christians have to obey a lot of primitive moral rules just because they are to be found in the pages of the Bible. For

Christians, the key to teaching is to be found in Jesus' Sermon on the Mount, and all other moral rules in the Bible have to be judged by how far they meet the standards of that sermon.

Was Jesus Morally Perfect?

Most Christians would agree that the standards of the Sermon on the Mount are illustrated in the life of Jesus himself, who shows the divine love as fully as it can be shown in human form. Nevertheless, there are those who find the life of Jesus himself less than morally perfect. Writers such as the philosopher Bertrand Russell (in his short essay, *Why I am Not a Christian*) accuse Jesus of moral imperfection by pointing to the cleansing of the Temple, which seems to have been an intolerant and violent act. They point out that Jesus called the Pharisees and lawyers 'whited sepulchres', hypocrites and blind guides, which seems rather uncharitable. He spoke a lot about the flames of hell and the danger of judgment, which seems very judgmental. And he cursed a poor fig tree, which had done nothing wrong, but just failed to produce figs – out of season, too. Was he really such a saint, after all?

Was Jesus a violent, intolerant, judgmental and character? All we know about Jesus comes from the four Gospels, and they certainly intended to represent Jesus as 'without sin', so it would be very surprising if they had unintentionally portrayed him as quite an unpleasant character. He healed, he forgave sins, he mixed with socially borderline people, in parables and stories he taught the necessity of unlimited self-giving love, he claimed to bring people into a closer relationship with God, and he accepted a violent death rather than betray his commitment to God. That is quite a good start.

But was he violent? He did not foment revolution against the military occupying power of the Roman empire or against Herod the puppet-king. He taught that you should turn the other cheek, and that the meek were blessed. He resisted the attempts of the common people to proclaim him king. So how could anyone think he was violent? Well, he took a whip, says John's Gospel, and drove the money changers from the Temple precincts. He drove out cattle and overturned tables. It does not say, however, that anyone was hurt. This was certainly decisive action against commercial activities in God's Temple. Are we to suppose that it is always wrong to use moderate force to eject undesirables from our property?

This account shows that Jesus was not always 'meek and mild', passively putting up with anything. He could take decisive action to remedy what he saw as sacrilege in his Father's house. I cannot see anything unacceptably violent about that. It seems to me to show courage and resolution, without actually physically harming anyone

Was he intolerant? He did criticise the lawyers and Pharisees in strong language. But again, may they not have deserved it? It is noteworthy that Jesus did not insult the poor or the marginalised. He insulted the privileged, the religious leaders, those who claimed to possess the authority of God, but who were actually arrogant and self-satisfied. If what they were doing was wrong and deceitful, was it not appropriate to criticise them? It is a very strange notion of moral goodness that does not allow you to criticise hypocrites and deceivers who pervert religion and morality. Again, no violence was used, and there was no danger of anyone being ostracised or harmed by Jesus' attacks. He was a social outsider, mocking the rich and powerful and exposing their deceits. I think that was morally justifiable – and probably good fun, too, for those poor people who heard him.

All right, then, what about hell and judgment? The simple answer is that if there is hell and judgment, then we could hardly expect Jesus not to mention the fact. He undoubtedly called for repentance, and offered eternal life to all who turned to God, so he was not telling people that they were going to hell whether they liked it or not. He was telling people that they need not go to hell, and offering them a free pardon. He made it quite clear that he made this offer to all, and especially to those who were sinners and not morally upstanding citizens. That is hardly being judgmental. It is just about as merciful as you can get.

It may be held that belief in hell is in itself harmful. I have dealt with that question in the previous chapter.[1] If there is divine judgment, the fact will have to be mentioned, whether it is harmful or not. It should be remembered that the whole point of the Christian gospel is to avoid hell and to forgive guilt. It is not to tell people that they are going to hell. It is to tell them how to avoid hell. It is to warn them of the seriousness of judgment on their actions, and to promise that God in Christ has taken that judgment on himself. Some people may find that odd, but it is hardly harmful.

1 See Chapter 5, 'Life after death', in *Is Religion Dangerous?*

Finally, what about the fig tree? Nobody was harmed in this episode. If it happened, it was most likely a parable to warn the disciples that if their lives were not fruitful, they would be in danger of destruction, or to warn Israel of destruction if it failed to reform its ways. The story may have been a literalisation of an actual parable (found in Luke), which had been transformed in the telling. Either way, it does not show that Jesus was cruel to any conscious being.

My conclusion is that there are no serious objections to moral perfection of Jesus. And, most importantly, the main lesson is that we should interpret the life of Jesus in the light of the whole Bible, and of the main events and teachings in it – the Sermon on the Mount, the parables of forgiveness, and eternal life, and Jesus' death on the cross. Jesus was a man of healing power, forgiving love, identification with the outcast – and also, these points show, of courage in seeking purity of faith, relentless criticism of the arrogant and hypocritical in religion, and a deep concern for the ultimate welfare of all people.

This does seem to me to be a standard of what a human life should be. But above all, Jesus' life was a life of prayer, of constant and undivided attention to his heavenly Father, and of dedication to his Father's will. It is in that deep centredness in prayer that the secret of moral life is to be found. It is from that resource that the divine love can flood into a world of suffering and hatred. It is there that the joy of eternity can assuage the hurts and inevitable frustrations of time.

Religious law and its interpretation

Christian moral standards should be quite clear. They are based on understanding of the life and teaching of Jesus, and have replaced a set of religious laws with the Gospel records of the person of Jesus.

Christianity is not a religion of revealed divine law at all, and so it is particularly inappropriate to think that it is possible to solve moral problems just by quoting ancient biblical laws. Of course it is possible to find people who do precisely that. In April 2006 the members of the Westboro Baptist Church, Topeka, Kansas, demonstrated at the funerals of American soldiers killed in Iraq with placards reading, 'Thank God for Dead Soldiers' and 'God Hates Fags'. Their pastor justified the action by saying that soldiers who defended a 'fag nation' (in other words, America) deserved no respect.

This sounds rather worrying. But it turns out that the church in question consists of seventy-six members of the pastor's extended family. The only appropriate comment one can make is that irrational prejudice does exist, and that nobody can stop an unbalanced individual from starting his own church, stocking it with his own family, and using it to publicise his own shockingly corrupt views. Perhaps he is even now organising a world tour to find any remaining Amalekites and stone them to death, as the Old Testament recommends. With luck, he may be away for a very long time.

The attitudes of the vast majority of Christians are very different from this, and to take such weird cases as typical of religion is like taking the British National Party to be representative of the Conservative Party. Of course there are religious people who are prejudiced, ignorant, repressed, obsessive, neurotic, unbalanced or completely mad. But to form a dispassionate assessment of religion requires that we pay more attention to the sane, intelligent and morally committed members of major religious communities. If we do that, we shall find that the history of Christian moral thought does not consist in quoting biblical texts out of context. It appeals to the person and teaching of Christ as the criterion by which to judge all biblical teachings. This is not a matter of obeying written rules without question. It calls for sensitive judgment, for a balanced interpretation of the person of Jesus, and for a good deal of personal decision-making in applying basic moral principles to particular situations. In other words, Christian moral reasoning is precisely that – reasoned argument about what is best for loving one's neighbour as oneself, in the light of the life of Jesus, who is the supreme exemplar of self-giving love.

This is true of Christianity. But religions of law, of the Torah and *Shari'a,* also require reasoned argument to interpret the law in new situations. The commands and prohibitions of the law are very rarely taken literally, and various traditions of interpretation exist, allowing a great deal of room for creative moral decision-making. There is bound to be disagreement about moral decisions, but we should at least recognise that decisions are being made, arguments deployed and reasons given.

It is not the case, in any instructed religious community that ancient commands are just being blindly and unquestioningly obeyed. Most religious moralities do not depend on blind obedience to some ancient written text. Much more important are the interpretations and applications of moral principles that are sometimes only implicit in the scriptures, and that often need to be formulated in new ways in new situations. Critics may still disagree with some of the conclusions of religious ethicists. But at least they should realise that they are disagreeing with complex processes of moral reasoning, informed both by scripture and by a continually developing understanding of human nature and the natural world.

Even though there are religious sects that may apply the rules of archaic texts literally to modern conditions, such sects are not representative of the great world religious traditions. In the case of those great traditions, their methods of moral reasoning are so widely recognised that religious leaders are routinely consulted on moral matters by many major governmental agencies throughout the world. Far from being considered dangerous, religious morality is widely considered to be a valuable resource for moral thinking in the modern world. That judgment is more likely to be correct than the diatribes of those who travesty and lampoon what religious moral thinking is really like.

15

By Faith Alone

The Word of God takes personal form in Jesus of Nazareth. Personal relationship with Christ is a form of direct personal knowledge, which transforms the life of the knower, just as any intense personal relationship transforms the participants. By the commitment of faith, human estrangement from God is overcome and the Spirit of God unites us inwardly to the love of Christ. For the Protestant Reformers, the church is the invisible communion of all in whom the Spirit works to enable us to love Christ and to share with him in the love of the Father, the source of all.

The Bible as the Standard of Protestant Faith

In 1440 Johann Gensfleisch invented printing by movable metal type. Some years later he printed a version of the Holy Bible, now known as the Gutenberg Bible. This was a discovery that was to change the face of Christianity. It was not long before a great many people, not just clergy, had access to the text of the Bible. Soon they were able to read it in their own languages, not in the Latin of the official Vulgate version. The church still claimed the sole right to interpret the text. But once the text got into the hands of the general literate public it became much harder to stop individuals interpreting it for themselves. That is the hallmark of Protestant Christianity. The Bible is available to all in a language they can understand, and they are encouraged to read it and interpret it for themselves. Christianity was re-thought as a religion of the book.

The Protestant Reformers did not wish to leave the church; they wished to reform it. Virtually everyone agrees that some reforms were needed to remedy widespread abuses, most famously the abuse of selling indulgences for money. But as Reformers looked to the Bible as the source of true doctrine, it seemed to them that a very different view of the church than that which had become common in Western Europe was to be found there.

The Roman Catholic Church had developed a doctrine of the church as one visible institution, defined by the communion of its members with the Bishop of Rome (except for the awkward case of the Eastern Orthodox churches). The Pope, as successor of Peter, had the divinely appointed role of defining correct doctrine in faith and morals. Membership of the church was by baptism; continuance in it was by confession, penance and communion.

The Reformers failed to find these doctrines in the Bible. Certainly there was a church in the New Testament, but the church seemed to be a fellowship of those who were disciples of Jesus. Paul had founded many churches, and they seemed to be more or less autonomous local fellowships, where prophecy and speaking in tongues were common, and where leaders were appointed in accordance with their particular gifts from among the congregation. There were links with the apostles, just as missionary churches today preserve links with the original missionary organisations. But, partly because of the difficulty of communication, local churches functioned more or less autonomously. They were influenced by, but did not seem to consider themselves under the authority of, the Jerusalem apostles. Indeed James, leader of the church in Jerusalem, who sent out envoys to persuade local churches to obey Torah, was repudiated as troublesome by Paul, and no doubt local churches came to their own decisions about this and other matters of concern. Over the years the churches came to be organised under five patriarchs, but the early patriarchates seem to have constituted a federal organisation rather than a top-down institution.

As the Reformers read it, the New Testament churches were local fellowships that accepted Jesus as Lord and Saviour, as redeemer from evil and giver of eternal life. There was no mention of a class of celibate priests, offering the sacrifice of the Mass for the souls of the living and the dead, and being informed of the truths of faith from a central source.

Faith as Personal Encounter

Classical Protestants seek to base their doctrines and practices on the New Testament. To them, that suggested that the church exists, as both

Luther and Calvin held, wherever the gospel of Jesus as Saviour is preached, and the two sacraments of baptism and the Lord's Supper, both mentioned in the New Testament, are celebrated. There is no magisterium, no teaching office, of the church. There is no hierarchical priesthood. There is no class of celibate priests and no religious elite, whether monks or nuns, who have higher spiritual standing than others. There is no control by any central authority over the content of faith. There is only the preaching of the gospel, and faith in Jesus. As Luther put it, justification (acceptance by God) is by faith alone, by a living trust that Jesus died and rose to redeem humanity. To make the point, Luther inserted the word 'alone' after the word 'faith' into his German translation of the letter to the Romans, chapter 3, verse 28, which actually reads, 'We hold that a person is justified by faith apart from works prescribed by the law.' It is ironic that he had to change the biblical text to make it say what he wanted!

In any case, he was adamant that salvation cannot be accomplished or helped by good works, penances, obedience to the Pope, or attendance at Mass. It is a matter of the relation of the believer to Christ the Lord, not needing any intermediaries, any visible institution or any teaching authority. The Mass remains, for Luther, a rite that makes Christ truly present, and for the person of faith it is a way of expressing and strengthening the personal union of disciple and Lord. But mere attendance at its performance does not save, and it cannot be offered in private to save those who are not present. So the pulpit, as the place where the word of God is read and preached, takes precedence over the altar.

The Reformers tried to make the Mass (or the Lord's Supper, as many call it) a focal event for the believing community, where the presence of Christ is celebrated (or where, for extreme Protestants, Jesus' sacrifice on the cross is devoutly remembered). It is a service of communion for all present, a meal that is a foretaste of the feast of the kingdom of God. So to have a Mass celebrated by priest on his own for the sake of someone who is not present is to miss the meaning of the rite. It is to replace a celebration of a truly personal relationship with what was often referred to as a 'quasi-mechanical' conveyance of merit. And to adore or carry in procession a consecrated and reserved Host is to disconnect the sacrament from the personal act of God in communion.

In this respect, Reformed practice tried to make the sacrament more constitutive of a local community and more communicative of a personal relationship than a rite efficacious simply by its private performance. Whereas the Mass had become, for some, the observation of the elevated Host far away and almost hidden by a choir screen, the Reformers wanted the community to come together and share the life of the risen Lord in fellowship. And they were concerned that people should know what was going on. Preaching assumed a new importance, and the rite was conducted in the local language with the active participation of those present (most of these reforms were to be implemented by the Catholic Church at the Second Vatican Council).

Luther said, 'Christ's kingdom is a hearing-kingdom, not a seeing-kingdom.'[1] It is by hearing the word that one comes to saving belief. Without that, all rituals and all images are empty. Luther did not ban images or rituals entirely. But in Lutheran churches images were often removed, walls whitewashed, and in Reformed (Calvinist) churches the stone altar was replaced by a wooden communion table. The central artistic image of Lutheranism is not a painting of the passion or a statue of the Virgin, but the sound of Bach's musical settings of the words of the Bible.

Protestants and Pluralism

For classical Protestants, it is still right to speak of a catholic – a universal – church. But that church is the company of all who trust in Christ, located in thousands of different fellowships of different sorts. Thus Protestantism is essentially pluralistic, in acknowledging many forms of Christian fellowship, without any one central authority. It is essentially diverse and is logically bound to permit many ways of understanding the gospel and the Bible, since it accepts no authoritative interpreter of the Bible.

It did not work out like that in practice. Since the New Testament is a diverse and unsystematic assembly of Gospels and letters, there are many possible ways of interpreting it, and once Protestants decided to make the Bible the only test of faith, all those ways were tried.

That is not odd or unexpected. The oddity is that each of them tended to declare itself to be the one true interpretation, to the exclusion of the others. Lutherans excluded followers of Calvin. They both excluded Zwinglians. And hundreds of denominations sprang up, most of which excluded everybody else.

---

1 Luther, *Sermon delivered in Merseburg*, 1545, W.A., 51, p. 11, l. 25.

For political reasons, the organising principle of Protestant faith came to be that the ruler of a state or nation would choose a form of belief, and the members of that state would then find themselves obliged to profess it. They could move over the border, where that was feasible, and profess a different form of faith. But acceptance of pluralism was not a marked feature of the classical Protestant world in Europe. That had to wait until the founding of America as a secular state, when religion would truly become a matter of free choice. Even in America, however, there was much local intolerance as various Protestant churches tried to ban others as heretical and dangerous.

It is clearly very difficult for Christians truly to accept full freedom of belief. In the contemporary United States of America, freedom of belief exists. Yet hundreds of churches do not hesitate to exclude those of their members who have the 'wrong' beliefs and to deprive them of teaching positions in their training colleges. It looks as if everyone is free to start their own church, but within it they can be as intolerant as they like.

The irony of all this, within Protestantism, is that the whole Protestant movement exists because it asserted the right of dissent (from the Catholic Church), the importance of free personal decision (a personal decision of faith in Jesus, not simply baptism into a religious group), and the rejection of an authoritative teaching authority (the magisterium of the church).

The problem is that Protestants still believed that salvation is, literally, a matter of life and death – eternal life and eternal death. The way to eternal life is much more rigorous than the traditional Catholic requirement of being a good member of the church, making confession and attending Mass. It is really believing, with the whole heart, that Christ is your personal Saviour.

In order to do that, you must know who Christ is, what salvation is, and be confronted with the necessity of making a personal decision for faith. Preaching, and preaching the truth, becomes vital for salvation – whereas, for most traditional Catholics, it did not matter much whether you never heard a sermon, or whether the Mass was in a language you did not understand. For Protestants, everything had to be made plain, and everyone had to understand it. Protestantism became a didactic faith, and preaching had to be precisely correct.

The source of this correctness, in the absence of the Pope, had to be the Bible itself. The text had to be self-interpreting and clear, and all preachers had to do was expound it correctly – to say what the Bible itself really says. The strange thing was that when they did this they came to many different and conflicting conclusions.

Most classical Protestants did not in fact derive all their doctrines from the Bible alone. They accepted the decisions of the first ecumenical councils of the church. They accepted, for instance, that Jesus was fully God and fully man and that the Trinity was three persons in one substance. They also tended to accept some specifically Western doctrines, as formulated by Augustine – that humans are born with original guilt, that the 'saved' are predestined by God and that human free will is compatible with such predestination. Many of them accepted a theory of atonement that derived from Anselm, as adjusted by Calvin, that we can only be saved because Jesus died 'in our place', to pay the penalty of death that God's justice required for our sins. (Aquinas, it may be recalled, denied the necessity, but not the actuality, of such a payment, and the Orthodox do not make this account central to their understanding of the death of Jesus.)

So Protestants did not in fact rely on Scripture alone for their doctrines, as they sometimes claimed. They relied on a number of traditional interpretations of Scripture, interpretations that got more and more specific and exclusive, until in the end some of them relied on Luther, some on Calvin, some on Zwingli and some on other less famous but equally cantankerous interpreters of the allegedly 'self-interpreting' Scripture.

This is a matter that requires some explanation. How can it be that a faith that insists that even general councils of the church can err may in practice insist on the exclusive correctness of one man (like Luther) as interpreter of the Bible? The Protestant rule must surely be that, if the church has erred, then any interpreter of Scripture can err, including you and your own church. The Protestant rule is that anyone may be mistaken. This does not mean saying, 'I think I am wrong.' But it does mean saying, 'I am not certain I am correct.' You must allow that, while you do not agree with other views, you could be the person who is mistaken. An admission of personal and institutional fallibility is built into Protestantism. But it does not always seem like that.

The rejection of any infallible teaching authority, and the establishment of the right to dissent on grounds of conscience seem to me the distinctive marks of Protestant Christianity. They seem to entail the provisional nature of most doctrinal beliefs, especially very complicated ones – meaning that we admit our interpretation could be mistaken. This in turn entails to their understanding of the death of Jesus; pluralism, in the sense of acceptance of a diversity of interpretations of the faith.

Faith and Intellectual Assent

The fact that many Protestants seem to be absolutely certain of their beliefs, even when they know that a majority of other Christians disagree, and that they find themselves unable to live together with people who have different interpretations of doctrine, is a mystery. It can only be accounted for by thinking they have been so influenced by the Latin tradition that they think three highly questionable things, which their own faith should undermine. They think that people can only be saved by believing correct doctrines, they think that the commitment of faith requires theoretical certainty and they think that there is some set of doctrines that needs to be defined as correct by some authority, which can then exclude and condemn contrary views as heretical. But none of these beliefs is really consistent with the basic character of Protestantism. They are precisely the beliefs of the Catholic Church that Protestants denied, and that traditional Catholics used to condemn and exclude Protestants.

In classical Protestant thought, these three beliefs are put in question by a strong emphasis on the importance of personal commitment to Christ, and on personal experience of the risen Lord or of the Spirit. This arises from Luther's emphasis on justification by faith, that is, by living trust in Christ, and from Calvin's emphasis on faith as giving assurance of final salvation. Whereas faith in Catholicism is primarily an assent of the will to the authoritative teachings of the church, for Luther and Calvin it is a perfect trust in Jesus, and especially in his death as atonement for our sins. Protestants typically speak of 'making a decision' for Christ, whereas Catholics tend to think that, if you are baptised, there is no specific, decisive decision to be made. You just naturally grow in the faith to which you belong.

Although Protestantism, I have suggested, remained largely intellectualist, it gave to personal experience an importance it had not previously had. Of course there were devotional movements in the Catholic Church, and mystics who claimed direct experiences of God. But to profess the faith was to be baptised, probably as an infant, and accept the teachings of the church. Personal experience remained a matter for you and your confessor.

For classical Protestants you must be confronted with the need of personal salvation from sin. You must consciously and explicitly commit yourself to Jesus as Saviour. You must have the experience of 're-birth' in the Spirit, whereby Christ comes to be known to you as an inner personal and renewing presence. This emphasis on personal choice, on commitment and on dramatic and inner experience of the Spirit, with the concomitant downgrading of all external rituals, religious imagery and such things as bodily prostrations and pilgrimages, re-draws the lines of faith in a radical way.

Faith becomes a purely inner encounter with a life-transforming Spirit, for even the act of commitment is possible only when the Spirit evokes it. God encounters you in the preaching of the gospel. God convicts you of sin. God impels you to bow before him in repentance. God brings Christ to birth within you. And God gives the assurance of eternal life.

All this is a drama played out within the soul, and it is hidden from the eyes of the world. Protestant churches, or meeting rooms, need no ornaments or images, for the dramas of the Spirit are played out in the secret places of the heart. The true, holy, universal and apostolic church is not a visible institution with a visible head. It is the invisible communion of those whose hearts have been claimed for God, by God, whose membership is unknown and whose head is invisible to the public gaze.

Luther and Calvin were clear that good works, the attempt of humans to do good things, were irrelevant to this inward drama of the Spirit. They should have been equally clear that the acceptance of correct doctrines, the attempt (as Protestants thought) of humans to formulate correct beliefs, are irrelevant to the drama of salvation. But they were not.

The point is that if God saves you by predestinate grace, God does not have to wait until you believe all the right doctrines before salvation can take effect. You are not saved because you have correct beliefs. You are saved solely by grace, through faith. And that faith is just the inward assent to the work of the Spirit, as it unites you to the divine life, the life of Christ.

Good works may follow from faith, as the Spirit empowers you to goodness. Correct beliefs may follow from faith, but only insofar as those beliefs are immediate entailments of true faith. It is not, for instance, entailed by transforming encounter with the risen Lord that the doctrine of double predestination, of God predestining some to salvation and some to damnation, is correct. The Chalcedonian definition of Christ's person is not entailed either, though it would be necessary that the new life that comes through Christ truly unites you to the divine life. There may, however, be various ways of trying to spell this out more completely, if you were inclined to do so.

Faith, in the Protestant sense, does not require theoretical certainty, especially about widely disputed doctrines, and it does not require acceptance of a set of 'correct' doctrines. Moreover, since God will save whomsoever God will, there is no set of doctrines and no institution that we must defend at all costs, in order that the faith will survive. Heresy need not be suppressed as a danger to human souls. For salvation is purely in the hands of God, and if it is the divine will that the gospel should be preached effectively, then it will be, whatever humans may do. Toleration becomes a Protestant Christian virtue when it is recognised that, for the vast majority of Christians, Protestants are the heretics, and intolerance would wipe them out. More importantly, since salvation is by grace not human works, we do not need to guard the truth by policing the souls of men and women. God will ensure that God's purpose is carried out. And, if Jesus is any model, it is not by violence and repression that it will be carried out. Salvation is by the grace of God, which is neither hampered nor hindered by the plans of men and women. And it is appropriated not by assent to a complex set of doctrines, but by faith, by living trust in Jesus as personal Saviour.

Inspiration and Scripture

Of course to trust in Jesus you must believe that Jesus existed and had a specific personality or character, that he did and taught specific things. So there must exist a trustworthy record of Jesus' life. That argument is strong, though even then, if what is important is personal relationship to a living Lord, the information about the historical character of that Lord does not need to be very detailed. It might be a positive advantage to have different accounts and assessments of Jesus, showing the ways in which he affected very different people.

However, classical Protestants usually went on to say that the Bible can be trustworthy only if it is given by God, and, since God cannot lie, the text must be true in every detail. It is true that God cannot lie, but why should it be thought that the text is actually given by God? Divine dictation has never been part of a Christian view of most of the Bible. What is required is something both vaguer and more subtle. If God wishes us to know and love the divine in and through the person of Jesus, then God must ensure that we know that person in sufficient detail to be able to identify him. So God must ensure that there exists a reliable tradition or traditions about the historical Jesus. But how God ensures this, and in what form, is not entailed by these requirements.

All Christians agree that the New Testament contains records of the life of Jesus from very near apostolic times. All agree that they provide the best evidence we have for the life of Jesus. All Christians agree that the evidence must be reliable or trustworthy. It is reasonable to think that God ensures that such a reliable record exists. The question is: how?

God could dictate it; but that does not seem compatible with the varying styles and authorship of the texts, and the fact that some texts are occasional letters written to churches. It is also in tension with the fact that Jesus did not write or dictate anything himself – which suggests that dictation is not the means of Christian revelation.

God could preserve it from all error, but that is incompatible with the varying accounts of incidents in Jesus' life (see chapter 1).[2] It is also in tension with the results of archaeological and historical study, which throw doubt on many historical accounts in the Old Testament.

An alternative possibility is that God could ensure the general reliability of the New Testament, exercising a guiding influence on the selection of Gospels and letters that go to make up the canon of the New Testament, so that the rather subjective emphases of one account are balanced by complementary emphases of other accounts, and the whole is sufficient to give a clear account of how Jesus can be a channel of the divine life.

This is vague, because it does not say exactly when or how God exerts such influence. It is subtle, because it suggests that 'reliability' is necessary only insofar as it preserves what is necessary for a saving relation to God through Christ – and that, too, is left undefined. Presumably we need to know that Jesus was a man filled with the divine Spirit, and therefore was wise, spiritually powerful, and loving. He was empowered to forgive sin and to inspire his disciples. His vocation to be God's Anointed was genuine. He died voluntarily, for the sake of the redemption of the world, and was raised from death. These are the things we need to know if we

2 See chapter 1, 'Strange Messiah', in *Rethinking Christianity*.

are to relate to God through him as mediator. It would be reasonable to think that God would ensure these things were recorded reliably.

But reliability does not entail that an account is without any error. It entails that the accounts are accurate and full enough to give a correct impression of Jesus' character, and of his death and resurrection. But this suggests that God's influence works through the process of gathering together the documents that were to make up the New Testament, as well as through the writing of them. And that influence must continue to work through subsequent history, to ensure that a saving relation to God remains a living possibility, not just a recorded historical fact.

In other words, it seems reasonable to think that whatever form of inspiration or guidance God exercised in the composition of the Bible will continue in the history of the church. God may not preserve the church from all errors, but God might well guide the church so that it remains a vehicle of saving knowledge of God, a community in which the Spirit acts.

A Reformed and Liberal Church?

There is an evident tension in the frequent Protestant claim that the Bible is inerrant and the sole source of authority whereas the whole Catholic Church seems to have become irredeemably corrupt. The tension is that if God worked through groups of humans over many centuries to write and compile the biblical documents, it is strange to think that God ceased to guide the church at all over the next thousand years.

We can ease that tension by denying the total inerrancy and sole sufficiency of the Bible, and also by denying that the church is irredeemably corrupt. In practice this is what Protestants have largely done. In accepting the theological interpretations of the councils and of Augustine, they accept some tradition of interpretation in addition to bare text. And the Protestant movement is meant to be one of reform, not of denial. When Luther pinned his ninety-five theses to the door of the castle church in Wittenberg in 1517 – an event that many see as the crucial beginning of the Protestant Reformation – he did not intend to found a new church. He hoped for reform within the Catholic Church. He hoped that the church, as the set of many communities that accept the apostolic faith and celebrate new life in the Spirit of Christ, would remain the divinely mandated way of salvation. But the Reformers believed that many errors had crept into the Western church, and some of these were re-affirmed at the

Council of Trent. They included the doctrine of papal supremacy over councils of the church, doctrines of merit and indulgences, the invocation of saints, especially of Mary, and the veneration of relics and images.

When the Reformers rejected these doctrines, they did not reject the church. They claimed to be returning to the original apostolic faith, and often tried to model their churches on New Testament accounts. That faith had never been lost. It had just been overlaid by practices and beliefs that were no part of the apostolic faith.

The apostolic faith was never quite as the Reformers pictured it. For a start, it had no New Testament, and so could hardly be called a 'biblical church'. It also undoubtedly contained many Jewish Christians, who upheld the strict observance of Torah. It was much more closely related to Judaism than were the Protestant churches, which regrettably tended to be anti-Jewish. And it almost certainly had never formulated views like substitutionary atonement, Chalcedonian Christology, predestination, sacramental theology and all the complicated versions of the 'second coming' that many Reformers seemed to be fixated with.

Still, the idea of a return to apostolic faith is a powerful one. It is a traditional Catholic view that the deposit of revelation ended with the death of the last apostle. It might be useful advice to say that no doctrine should be regarded as absolutely necessary to Christian faith unless it was part of the apostolic faith. Our only written evidence for that is the New Testament. So, while the Reformers may have thought that too many of their doctrines were apostolic when they were not, and though some of them may have had an exaggerated view of the inerrancy of Scripture, one may feel a great deal of sympathy with the recommendation that the New Testament is the only source of doctrines that are strictly necessary to Christian belief.

This would not commit us to accepting that everything in the New Testament has to be believed today – I have argued that such a position is insupportable. But it might commit us to saying that no belief is absolutely necessary to being a Christian if it cannot be supported by the New Testament. That, we have seen, leaves a lot of room for disagreement and development, and it would leave even the incarnation and the Trinity open to many diverse interpretations.

If that is so, Protestants should allow much diversity of interpretation of the texts, and should be very careful not to claim certainty in matters that are highly disputed among intelligent readers of the texts. Perhaps the besetting heresy to which Protestants are prone is to claim certainty in matters that do not allow of certainty, and to fail to see the diversity of Scripture, and the necessity of following some interpretation of it which will not be found in Scripture itself and is bound to be less than universally appealing.

Surprising as it may seem to some, Protestantism is thus essentially liberal, in the classical sense of allowing, and even encouraging, diversity of interpretation, the right of dissent, and personal freedom of belief. It calls for liberty of conscience, as a condition of its own existence – even though it sometimes practises intolerance of disagreement within its own fellowships. It calls for the equality of all before God. In rejecting a central teaching authority and in insisting upon an open Bible, which all can interpret for themselves, it undermines any spiritual hierarchy – even though it has reinforced many social hierarchies in its church organisation. It calls for fraternity and brotherly love and fellowship, in rejecting any distinction of clergy and laity, any special class of 'religious', and in stressing the participation of all in the communion service and in the running of the churches – even though some of its tracts are still filled with vitriol against Christians of different persuasions.

V

Inter-faith Dialogue and Disagreement

16

The Study of Truth and Dialogue in Religion

Philosophy and the Religious Traditions

Philosophy is an important part of Religious Studies because it is concerned with questions of meaning and truth. The two main philosophical questions are, 'What does it mean?' and 'How do you know it is true?' Since most religions have beliefs as part of their content, we do need to know what those beliefs mean, and how anyone could set about discovering that they were true, or how anyone can be justified in claiming that they are true. Philosophers do not have to concern themselves with religion; there are many other sorts of belief worth serious critical attention. And there can be hostility between some religious attitudes, which resent critical study or analysis, and the Socratic questioning of grand claims to universal knowledge. Yet truth can only be advanced by clear understanding and the preparedness to justify one's beliefs as far as possible; so the philosophical study of religious beliefs is important both to religion and to philosophy.

The practice of philosophy in this sense has mostly developed within a Christian context. Though there have been major Jewish and Muslim philosophers, the theoretical analysis of beliefs has been of less interest in those traditions than the interpretation of the religious law. Christianity, with its very theoretical and Platonically influenced doctrines of the Trinity and Incarnation, has always had a strong inclination towards philosophical speculation, though it has been less receptive to the sort of critical questioning espoused by Socrates and by most post-Cartesian philosophers. Thus the philosophy of religion has mostly in practice been the philosophy of Christianity.

In the nineteenth century Hegel did write a large work in which he attempted to deal systematically with all the world religions; but the main impetus for this was to show the inherent superiority of Hegel's version of the (Protestant) Christian faith over all other religions. In general, 'other religions' were regarded either as masses of superstition or as inferior precursors of liberal Christianity, and so not worth serious philosophical treatment. In the hey-day of German-influenced Idealism, religion tended to be seen as a mythical or pictorial expression of truths about the ultimate reality of one Absolute Spirit, which could be better expressed in philosophical terms. Because it increasingly saw this, and was prepared to renounce old sacramental superstitions in favour of a more austere ethical monotheism, liberal Christianity was seen as the supreme form of religion.

It is only within the last century that, with a growth in the knowledge of world scriptures in their original languages and a rediscovery of important medieval philosophical works in Islam, Hinduism and Buddhism especially, it has come to be thought that even liberal Christians may have something to learn from other religious traditions. As the techniques of historical and literary scholarship seemed to undermine claims to biblical infallibility, and as philosophical criticism seemed to cast doubt on human ability to prove the existence of God, so it began to seem that historical Christianity was not, after all, on a much stronger rational footing than many other faiths. Indeed, the Hegelian philosophy itself was in many ways nearer to Vedantic Hinduism than it was to traditional Christianity. So the way was open to look again at the great religious traditions of the world, and to extend philosophical questions about meaning and justification to all those traditions, instead of confining them to the Christian.

Problems of Religious Truth

It soon became apparent that in many religious traditions similar claims to spiritual experience are made; similar reverence is given to the moral heroism and asceticism of the saints; and similar appeals to the authority of outstanding religious teachers are made. It began to seem arrogant to claim that one set of religious beliefs was absolutely true while all others were false – a position that has been termed 'exclusivism'. This view has been held by a number of influential Christian theologians, of whom Karl Barth and Emil Brunner are probably the best known. They simply assert that there is no way of knowing God except through Jesus Christ, so that all other religions are in error. But since other religions can say that they have the absolute and sole truth just as bluntly, there does not seem to be much to choose between them, as far as justification goes.

But it seems not much less arrogant to claim in Hegelian fashion that one's own beliefs are superior to all others, though the others might contain lesser approximations to the truth. What was soon called the 'inclusivist' view began to seem like simple prejudice in favour of one's own beliefs. Thus the Roman Catholic theologian Karl Rahner held that sincere believers in other faiths could be called 'anonymous Christians', slightly inferior versions of real, explicit Christians. This seems to be as misguided as calling Catholics 'anonymous Muslims', and this version of inclusivism has not found widespread favour.

However, since the faiths differ from each other on so many points, it hardly seems possible to say that they are all true, as they stand. Thus a serious philosophical problem is created as soon as one acknowledges that there are many diverse religious traditions, none of which has a clearly superior justification. It is not the philosophers' job to defend any particular set of religious truths; but they are concerned with the sorts of justification that can be offered for religious beliefs. Now if many differing beliefs can be justified on equally strong grounds, this creates a problem about the concept of truth in religion, since the concept of truth is closely connected with the idea of having some method of coming to agreement, at least in principle, about what is true. If there is no such method, there is a strong argument for saying that the notion of truth does not apply, that it must be renounced. One could, like many early anthropologists of religion, hold that virtually all religious beliefs are false; that, as Sir James Frazer put it, the religious history of humanity is 'a melancholy record of human error and folly' (*The Golden Bough;* abridged ed., London, 1941, p. 711). But some philosophers have gone even further, and declared that religion is not so much false as irredeemably irrational or even meaningless. The course of English-speaking philosophy of religion in this century was set by A. J. Ayer's provocative dismissal of religious talk as meaningless, in his beautifully lucid book, *Language, Truth and Logic,* of 1936. According to him, believers were literally talking nonsense, since their beliefs could not be verified by appeal to any available sense-experiences.

Of course, Ayer never seriously asked religious believers what they meant. He applied a ruthless test to religious beliefs – could any observations show them to be true? – which he thought they all failed. But his rather high-handed approach stimulated other philosophers to concentrate on the question of whether religious assertions do refer to observable matters of fact or not. It seemed to many that they do not do so in a very straightforward way, if at all.

Non-Cognitivist Accounts of Belief

Three different approaches to this question have existed, and still exist, in English-speaking philosophy; and they suggest rather different answers to the question of how different religions are to regard one another. First, philosophers like R. B. Braithwaite (*An Empiricist's View of the Nature of Religious Belief,* Cambridge, 1955) and Don Cupitt (cf. *Taking Leave of God,* London, 1980) hold that religious beliefs do not refer to observable matters of fact at all. They are stories or myths which recommend commitments to act in a loving way, or which evoke helpful psychological attitudes. Religion is not about the facts; it is about ways of life, attitudes and moral policies. Now if one takes that view, different religions will just be different sets of stories recommending forms of life which may be different in detail, but may be very similar for all that. For most religions try to encourage lives of love and compassion, of self renunciation and inner peace – at least in theory. So this view encourages us to look beyond the boundaries of any one tradition of faith and see all the great traditions as culturally influenced patterns for particular forms of human life. It offers a great degree of tolerance between religions; for we can learn to appreciate them all, much as we can learn to appreciate different styles of music.

However, it must be said that, in another way, it is not a very tolerant view, because it says that all religious beliefs about happenings in history or about supernatural beings (like God) are not true; or at least that their truth is irrelevant to the real business of religion. This does not appeal much to most religious believers, who tend to think their beliefs are true. These philosophers – the non-cognitivists – have to say that such believers (the vast majority, probably) are just wrong; and that is not so tolerant after all! So when Don Cupitt argues that Christianity and Buddhism can come together in a fruitful alliance, what he means is that their stories, which are literally false, outline helpfully complementary ways of life. And that does not please most Christians and Buddhists very much. These views seem very helpful to religious dialogue; but only on their own terms, after all.

Religions as Forms of Life

A second sort of interpretation of religious beliefs is provided by thinkers like Ian Ramsey (cf. *Religious Language,* London, 1957) and D. Z. Phillips, utilising some of the later work of Wittgenstein. On this view, one must not try to make the meaning of religious assertions conform to some *a priori* criterion of meaning like Ayer's verification principle. The meaning of an assertion or class of assertions is to be discovered by seeing how such assertions are actually used, within various forms of human life. Religion can be seen as a specific form of life, including ritual activity, worship and prayer; and religious language has a specific use or function within such forms of life. This function is to be neither straightforwardly fact-stating nor wholly prescriptive. Religious terms are cognitive; they do state facts of a sort; but not empirical facts.

So Ramsey proposes that religious language is rooted in certain sorts of situation, which it tries to express and evoke in others. He calls these 'disclosure-situations', and describes them as situations in which, as well as all the observable features one can apprehend, there is an indescribable 'more', a sense of an inexpressible reality which evokes in us a total commitment to respond by living in a certain way. When we say, 'God is Love', we mean that in situations of human love, we may come to apprehend a depth and significance which is cosmic in scope, and draws from us a commitment to love in response. We are not saying that there is some metaphysical being, God, who has a set of properties including that of being loving. We are saying that a sense of the inexpressible is conveyed to us which evokes love from us, as an appropriate response to the complex reality which we confront in all our experience. Even to try to describe it in these words changes the meaning subtly; and really the only way to see what sort of reality this is, is to use religious language. The language is untranslatable into any other terms; it means what it means; and to know what that is, is to participate in a particular religious form of life.

D. Z. Phillips amplifies this account, stressing that there is no way of justifying religious language in factual, metaphysical or even non-religious moral terms. To understand the meaning, we have to understand the use; and we cannot do that without participating in the appropriate form of life. There is a cognitive dimension here, but it cannot be put in the quasi-scientific terminology of traditional metaphysics. To take a clear example, when Christians speak of 'eternal life', they do not in practice mean that they will exist after they have died – that, he says, would be absurd. They mean that they participate in a form of life which can only be properly understood from within, and which can be characterised as living in the light of eternal values, whatever happens.

It is clearly possible that Buddhists, in speaking of Nirvana, for example, are using language in a similar way, or with a similar function. So on this view, the different great religious traditions become culturally conditioned ways of responding to a reality which is not adequately describable in terms of scientific language, and which makes its own distinctive and irreducible sort of claim upon us. There is no way in which we can call one tradition 'true', and all the others 'false'. Truth is a concept which only operates within the language-games, the concepts and forms of thought which are defined by particular forms of thought. Metaphysical speculation is the great enemy of true religion, on this view, even though it often threatens to hijack faith and turn it into pseudo-science. Believers do not actually use their language to construct large-scale theories about the nature of the universe. They use it to cope effectively with selfishness, despair and loss, and to discern structures of meaning in experience which give their lives depth and coherence.

On this view, it is silly to try to say that one set of religious beliefs is true and all the others false, or to compare religions for truth against some supposed external reality which we can never match against our language. On the other hand, it is doubtful to what extent we can ever really understand a very different religious tradition; since we cannot participate in many very different religious forms of life at the same time. The 'exclusive' view that I am right and everyone else is wrong becomes impossible. But neither can I say that everyone is right. I must simply say that I cannot fully understand many religious beliefs and pictures; I do not use them; they have no significance for me. I can be committed to one tradition if it grasps me by the power of its evocative language, but I am not entitled to denigrate other traditions which do not regulate my life. A gap of understanding opens up between the faiths, and I can no longer say that they are false, precisely because I do not grasp their meaning. Nor can I say, like Ayer, that they are meaningless; for they are successfully used, and there are criteria, internal to them, for proper and improper use. So religious assertions are not purely regulative or practical; they are also disclosive of something that cannot be put in any other way. Holding such a view of religious language, I cannot assert that only my beliefs are true. But I must assert that many others are unintelligible to me, and offer alternative patterns of disclosure and commitment.

The great danger of this view is that religions seem to enter ghettoes of intelligibility, closed to outsiders. And they become divorced to a large extent from other areas of human activity and interest, like science and philosophical speculation. Many religious believers do make factual assertions about the world – that they will live after death; or that there will be a final moral consummation of the universe; or that there is a cosmic law of moral cause and effect which ensures that good and evil will be rewarded or punished. The disclosure view cannot cope with such beliefs, and so it seems to apply only to a radically revised form of religious belief. That would be very ironic, since it began by seeking to ask how religious language is actually used, and it ends by asserting, no less than Ayer, that most believers are misusing their language, or at the very least are grossly mistaken when they come to give a reflective account of it. It seems that religious believers are only to be trusted when they are actually praying or worshipping; one cannot take them seriously when they come to give an account of what they are doing when they pray. This view, too, is not as tolerant as at first it may appear to be.

Realism in Religion

The third main type of response to the verification challenge is to meet it head on and say that religious assertions are fact-stating, even though not establishable as true by presently available techniques of observation. Richard Swinburne and John Hick (cf. *An Interpretation of Religion*, London, 1989) can be taken as major representatives of this view, both defending the necessity of metaphysics for religious faith. The word 'metaphysics' can be very misleading, and it is worth taking a moment to clear away some possible misconceptions. The word itself came into use when the editors of Aristotle's works wanted a title for some lectures that came after his lectures on physics, a subject that he virtually invented. Aristotle seemed to call the notes in question 'theology' – reflections about *theos*, or God. But they simply called them *meta ta physica* – the lectures after the ones on physics. The word stuck; and for many years it was taken to mean part of what Aristotle was talking about in those lectures, the first principles of being, or the ultimate character of the things which exist. P. F. Strawson was therefore right when he called any sort of thinking about the most basic character of the set of concepts we use to talk about the world 'descriptive metaphysics'. If you say that the world consists of material things causally interacting, simple and obvious though it seems, that is a form of descriptive metaphysics. And if you ask whether

'God' is one of the sorts of things which exists (whether there is a God), that is a metaphysical question.

It is in this sense that many religious beliefs depend upon metaphysical beliefs – they depend on saying that there is a God, or that there is an ending of sorrow, or that there is a Self of all. Part of the trouble with the word 'metaphysics' has been that people have thought it refers to some flighty and abstract speculation about realities 'beyond the physical'; so that to do metaphysics is to pretend to know a lot about supernatural realities of one sort or another. That is completely wrong; for any statement about what sorts of things exist – that there is a God; that there is not a God; that humans are free; that they are not; that there is life after death; or that we all die and that's the end of us for ever – all these are metaphysical assertions. We just cannot escape metaphysics, if we think at all. The only question is what sort of metaphysical views we have.

Swinburne and Hick have both defended the necessity of metaphysics to religion; and such questions are factual, even if we cannot decisively settle them now. Any realist view of truth – that some assertions really are true, whether we believe them or not – must accept that there could be factual assertions which humans, with their limited cognitive faculties, cannot settle. Hick has proposed that there will be an 'eschatological verification' of such claims – that after death the experience of being fully conscious of God would verify God's existence and nature. It may seem, therefore, that he must assert one religious tradition to be true, and the others false. Instead he has proposed 'the pluralist hypothesis': that the great religious traditions agree in positing the existence of one transcendent reality, and offering ways of overcoming egoism and relating to this reality in a life-fulfilling way. They thus offer authentic experiences of 'the Real' and valid ways of salvation. Where they differ, they either offer partial and complementary assertions about a reality that transcends all our concepts; or they differ on points irrelevant to the real business of religion, which is salvation by relation to a reality of supreme objective value.

Hick sometimes puts these points too strongly, as it hardly seems possible that all religious beliefs could be *equally* authentic when they differ so much. But he seems entirely right in saying that no tradition can justifiably claim an obvious superiority in truth over all others, and that all traditions fail to state the truth about ultimate reality completely or incorrigibly in all respects. Thus the question of truth in religion becomes closely connected with the existence of dialogue between religions, wherein each can learn from the perspectives of others and help to correct inadequacies in its own presentation of truth by being open to critical and constructive opposition. The great traditions all stress the ineffability of the supremely real, and the primacy of a practical commitment to compassion and selflessness. Where our most basic religious beliefs are bound to be more or less inadequate to the reality they seek to express, there is a necessity for dialogue which may lead to a mutual transformation of belief, as each seeks more adequate forms of expression.

The Need for Dialogue

In this respect, the work of Ninian Smart and Cantwell Smith is of major importance, in bringing us to see each set of religious truth-claims in the context of a wider global vision. Perhaps, as Cantwell Smith (cf. *The Meaning and End of Religion*, London, 1978) argues, the very word 'religion', when used to create opposed totalities of exclusive belief, is fundamentally misleading. We might rather speak of personal faith, as expressed and worked out within a variety of cultural forms and traditions, which are constantly changing and interacting in very fluid ways. A growing-point for the philosophical study of religion in this new context is analysis of the ways in which practical commitment and theoretical belief interact; of the very complex nature of metaphorical and symbolic language in religion; and the deconstruction of 'religions' as exclusive totalities locked in immutable opposition.

The philosophy of religion has come a long way since the terse three pages in which Ayer dispensed with the whole subject in 1936, and even Ayer more recently conceded that religions do propose *prima facie* meaningful explanatory hypotheses (though he still thought that they turned out to be empty on inspection). Meaning, justification and truth remain its central concerns; and I think it has become clear that if truth does not necessitate attainable agreement, it at least requires a self-critical and open dialogue between a multiplicity of differing perspectives which seem to be equally justifiable. In such a dialogue, one must be prepared for much change; and this is made easier by a knowledge of history which shows how much change has already taken place within each tradition of faith. It is also made easier by a practice of philosophy which shows how precarious and fallible our claims to truth are, and how ambiguous and multilayered the meanings of religious assertions are. If this proves worrying for certain forms of dogmatic belief, it is wholly compatible with a firm commitment to the search for truth and goodness, to the demand to renounce self in love and compassion, which comes in response to our discernments of the supreme reality though the filter of our own cultures and systems of belief.

Religious Studies is good for philosophy, since it keeps alive the questions of ultimate meaning and value which are its lifeblood. Philosophy is good for Religious Studies, since it keeps alive the questions of truth and justification which preserve religion from complacent dogmatism. The discipline of Religious Studies now offers to philosophers a much wider and more informed base for the investigation of questions of meaning and truth in religion; and the most fruitful results are to be expected from the increasingly inter-disciplinary approach which is being adopted in British Universities. It may even be that forms of religious faith will change as believers take seriously the question of what it means to believe and of how such beliefs can be justified. Yet to the extent that religious belief is seriously concerned with truth, it has nothing to fear and much to gain in the way of tolerance and understanding from supporting such scholarly study of the whole phenomenon of religion.

17

Truth and the Diversity of Religions

I will be concerned with only one problem about truth which is raised by the diversity of religions which exist in the world. The problem is this: many religions claim to state truths about the nature of the universe and human destiny which are important or even necessary for human salvation and ultimate well-being. Many of these truths seem to be incompatible; yet there is no agreed method for deciding which are to be accepted; and equally intelligent, informed, virtuous and holy people belong to different faiths. It seems, therefore, that a believing member of any one tradition is compelled to regard all other traditions as holding false beliefs and therefore as not leading to salvation. Since each faith forms a minority of the world's population, all religious believers thus seem committed to saying that most intelligent, virtuous and spiritually devoted people cannot know the truth or attain salvation. This is a problem, because it is in tension with the belief, held by many traditions, that the supremely real being is concerned for the salvation of all rational creatures. How can this be so if, through no fault of their own, most creatures cannot come to know the truth and thereby attain salvation?

Among those who have seen this as a problem and have proposed a philosophical defence of one solution to it, John Hick must take a foremost place. His book, *An Interpretation of Religion* (London, 1989), is a statement of the position which has come to be known as religious pluralism. This major work, filled with illuminating discussions of the phenomena of religious belief and with fresh and lucid insights, is meant to be, not the end of the debate, but an opening up of discussion which might clarify the problem and its solutions further, and might establish a coherent framework for developing inter-faith dialogue and for a credible religious faith held in full awareness of and with full respect for the beliefs of others. My aim is to contribute to this discussion; and I shall do it by using the time-honoured philosophical technique of niggling and irritating criticism of various theses Hick presents. My argument will be that Hick's position is philosophically unacceptable as it stands, though it would be unwise simply to reject it wholesale; and I hope that my attack, such as it is, will be taken as a tribute to the force of the issues Hick places before us.

The pluralistic hypothesis is that religions provide different valid but culturally conditioned responses to a transcendent reality, and offer ways of transcending self and achieving a limitlessly better state centered on that reality. Thus no one tradition possesses a set of absolute and exclusive truths, while all others are delusory and ineffective for salvation. All will, or at least can be, saved by adhering to their own traditions, which purvey differing, but authentic, responses to the ultimately real. All can know the truth and attain salvation in their own traditions; so believers no longer have to condemn all others as mistaken, and no longer have to wonder why their God leaves the majority of creatures in mortal error. Here is an elegant and morally attractive solution of the problem of error in religion; and it is one that has great appeal for those who are reluctant to say that they alone are right and everyone else is wrong.

Nevertheless the hypothesis is riddled with difficulties; and the most obvious one can be put very forthrightly. To believe a proposition is to think that it is true. To think that it is true is to affirm that reality is as it is described by that proposition. Insofar as our affirmations are fallible, it is always possible that reality is not as some proposition asserts it to be. Thus an affirmation by its nature excludes some possible state of affairs; namely, one which would render the proposition false. If an assertion excludes nothing, it affirms nothing. In that sense, all truth claims are necessarily exclusive.

It immediately follows that, where any truth-claim is made, it is logically possible to make another truth-claim which the first claim excludes. It is logically impossible for all possible truth-claims to be compatible. So it is possible for religious traditions to contain incompatible truth-claims, claims which exclude one another. Since this is a matter of logical possibility, it is a necessary truth that not all possible religious traditions can be equally true, authentic or valid. One can easily construct traditions which are strictly incompatible and of them, at least, pluralism must be false.

That is, they will not consist of equally valid concepts of ultimate reality. One does not even need to invent such traditions, since, for example, Satanism and Christianity are fundamentally opposed both morally and factually.

But if this version of pluralism, which we might call 'extreme pluralism', is incoherent, it might nevertheless be the case that many religious traditions, and maybe all the major ones that exist on our planet, do not contain mutually exclusive beliefs, but are equally valid paths of salvation and of authentic experience of the Real. This is 'hard pluralism'; and it is a contingent hypothesis; whether or not it is true will be a matter for careful investigation. But it certainly looks as though many claims exclude one another. The Buddhist assertion that there is no creator god excludes the Christian assertion that there is one all-perfect Creator. The Muslim assertion that Allah has no son excludes the Christian assertion that God has an only-begotten Son. What is the pluralist to do about these *prima facie* incompatible claims?

Hick's strategy is to retreat from discussing particular religious beliefs and to talk instead of 'religion'; to retreat from discussing specific truth-claims and to talk instead of 'religious traditions'. This may seem innocuous, but it can be, and turns out to be, very misleading. It is well known that definitions of religion are hard to find; and Hick proposes that we regard 'religion' as a family-resemblance concept, so that there is no essential core definition. Yet he is concerned with only one sort of religion or one feature of religious beliefs. He characterises the central strand of religion with which he is chiefly concerned as 'awareness of and response to a reality that transcends ourselves and our world' (p. 3). Fairly rapidly, he nominalises the verb 'transcends', and speaks of 'belief in the transcendent', saying that 'most forms of religion have affirmed a salvific reality that transcends human beings and the world' (p. 6). What he is doing is to pick out one class of religious beliefs, or one set of religious phenomena which can be defined in terms of belief in a transcendent salvific reality. There is nothing wrong with that; but it should be noted that it picks out one area of agreement in truth-claims by definition. Faiths which lack that central belief are not going to be counted; conversely, faiths which are counted are assured of a minimal degree of agreement to begin with. They will all agree on something, so they will not be incompatible in all respects. But, so far, this is not really pluralism (the acceptance of very different beliefs as equally valid); it is exclusivism at a relatively abstract and general level (those are excluded who do not believe in one transcendent salvific reality). It is also an acceptance of some truth-claim – the claim that there is such a reality which can bring creatures to a limitlessly good state – as 'absolute', or true for everyone, regardless of their point of view or cultural situation.

Hick argues at length in *An Interpretation of Religion,* that we cannot reasonably claim 'that our own form of religious experience ... is veridical whilst the others are not' (p. 235). He allows that virtually every religious tradition has done so; but then proposes the following argument:

(1) By something akin to Swinburne's Principle of Credulity, *A* is justified in thinking that what seems to be the case probably is the case, in the absence of strong countervailing reasons. So if *A* seems to apprehend God's presence, she is justified in thinking that God is in fact present, and therefore that God exists.
(2) By the principle of universalizability, however, *B* is similarly justified in believing that reality is non-dual, on the basis of her experiences of *samadi* or enlightenment.
(3) Since the fact that '*A* is me' is not a relevant reason for giving *A*'s views greater force than *B's,* it seems that *A* and *B* are equally justified in believing contradictory things.
(4) Therefore it is implausible to believe that all religious experience is delusory except one's own.
(5) This suggests the Pluralistic Hypothesis, that different types of religious experience are veridical but partial responses to a reality which cannot be adequately described by any set of beliefs alone.

This argument is plainly invalid. The trouble lies with step (4). A sharp distinction is to be made between justification and truth. I can be justified in believing something false (e.g. that the earth is flat) due to imperfect knowledge. In complex situations, given rather different initial information, people may be justified in believing contradictory things. But contradictory beliefs cannot both be true; so all that follows is that at least one person is justified in believing something false. Hick has already argued that both atheists and theists can be rationally justified in adopting the views of the world they do adopt, given the ambiguous nature of that world. But it does not follow that each must accept the other's view as equally true. The very reverse is the case. If I am rationally justified in believing *X;* and you are rationally justified in believing *not-X;* then we are both justified in believing the other to be deluded, or in some other way mistaken.

Now something *does* follow from this about the character of such beliefs. I must admit other believers may have reasons which seem just as strong to them to accept their views as I have to accept mine. Therefore I cannot claim that they are obviously or detectably mistaken. And I cannot seriously claim that my view is obviously or clearly true. So I must admit the equal right of others to exist and hold the views they do. And I must admit the fallibility and theoretical uncertainty of my view. To accept this might in itself be a great advance in religion, but it does not constitute a reason for accepting hard pluralism. It could be a reason for denying any right to believe any view in this area. However, one can argue, as Hick does, that the matter is so important that I am justified in making some choice. It may even be that I *must* believe something in this area, though it is hard to say how detailed my beliefs must be. In fact Hick vacillates, sometimes saying that, because conflicting views have so little to choose between them, it is not important to hold such views, and one should concentrate simply on the practical matter of salvation. But at other times (e.g. as between realist and non-realist religious views) he says that it is important to choose a realist and cosmically optimistic view, because only that offers good news to all.

Whichever he says, it *is* reasonable to claim that our own experiences are veridical whilst all others are not. It is unreasonable to claim anything else. But the situation does not have to have this all-or-nothing character. Surely we do not wish to say that centuries of prayer, meditation, sanctity and devotion in other traditions are founded on illusion? Surely they must be putting people in touch with the real spiritual reality, whatever it is? Hick himself gives the answer: 'There seems to me to be no difficulty in principle in the thought that a person may be correctly experiencing some aspects of reality whilst falsely experiencing others' (p. 220). That is, there may well be something veridical in what great religious traditions experience; but also (very often) something false. He even tells us how to discriminate: we accept some belief as veridical 'because it evokes a confirming echo within our own experience' (p. 220). We reject others because they clash with our experience. There are many echoes of our experience in the religious experiences of others; and we may take these to be veridical. By parity of reasoning, we may think that our own tradition, even our own present experience within that tradition, is liable to contain many mistakes, though we will not know what they are. Humility is certainly in order; it does sound arrogant to say 'my religious experience is perfectly correct; all others are totally false'. But we can say: 'My religious experience is correct in important respects, though it may contain many errors. The experiences of others may contain many veridical elements; but there are important misinterpretations, too'. The veridical elements will be those which seem to echo my own, the errors those which clash with my own; nor will I be able to identify the errors in my own. I can be on the lookout for such errors, and look to other traditions to help me identify them. And I can look for elements other traditions have which may complement, rather than contradict, my own. Thus my beliefs are always revisable; and others may always be capable of disclosing new insights. Yet those beliefs which lie near the core of my belief-system must be given preference over competing beliefs.

Hick does precisely this, of course. He identifies many errors in the Christian tradition – belief in Hell and literal belief in incarnation are just two which he takes to be morally undesirable and rationally insupportable. His core-beliefs are that one should turn from selfish egoism to attain a limitlessly good end-state by some sort of relation to a reality of supreme value; and he is only prepared to accept beliefs which are compatible with these. The suggestion is that any set of beliefs which result in such an end-state is likely to be true; others are not. The trouble is that this criterion is quite unusable, as Hick's discussion makes very clear. Some of the most obviously deluded, restrictive and exclusive belief-systems produce astonishing commitment, assurance, love and self-sacrifice. On the other hand, as Hick points out, the great scriptural traditions have histories replete with hatred, intolerance and violence; so that none of them emerges as much better than any others, in the long sad history of human fanaticism. It seems, then, that either the suggested criteria of adequacy do not enable us to choose between many different beliefs; or that they are in tension with the criterion of consistency with other well-established knowledge. Hick tends to dismiss metaphysical speculations, together with particular historical claims, as unsettlable and unnecessary to salvation. But of course his whole book is a metaphysical exploration of what can be intelligibly said about the object of religious faith; and the fact that his version of pluralistic religious realism is unsettlable and highly disputable does not stop him from asserting both its truth and its importance for a correct (non-exclusive) understanding of salvation.

This brings us to the question of whether unsettlable beliefs can be necessary for salvation. Hick finds this 'implausible' (p. 369); but it is rendered immediately more plausible by the consideration that the very concept of what salvation is involves beliefs which are theoretically unsettlable in practice. If one asks what is necessary for salvation, one might be asking whether any beliefs are requisite for the final attainment of wholly fulfilled human life. Atheists, of course, will deny that there is any such final attainment, or even any such possible notion as that of a wholly fulfilled life; 'do your own thing' might better be their motto. So the mere acceptance of the concept of a wholly fulfilled life presupposes the very contestable belief that there is a proper goal of human activity. If there is such a consciously attained goal, then one cannot achieve it without having the correct belief about what it is, and how one has come to achieve it. In this sense the possession of some particular beliefs is necessary to salvation. People without those beliefs will not attain salvation, for the simple reason that salvation consists in attaining a state which entails possessing such beliefs; i.e. it entails that one knows what salvation is and that one has attained it. At such a point, of course, one may suppose that religious disputes will finally be settled. As Hick says, 'To participate knowingly in fulfillment would confirm the reality of God beyond the possibility of rational doubt' (p. 179). In other words, at least some important metaphysical claims about the existence and nature of God are settlable by experience in principle.

But one might also ask whether any beliefs are requisite *now* if one is to have a reasonable hope of attaining salvation later, or if one is to be on the right path towards salvation. Different views exist on this question; but Hick seems to me correct in thinking that if there is a God of universal love, he will not make our loss of eternal life dependent merely upon making an honest mistake. So one might suppose that a positive response to whatever seems to be good and true, by a conscience as informed as one can reasonably expect, and a commitment to seek truth and realise goodness, is sufficient to dispose one rightly to salvation. Some beliefs are requisite; but they will depend on particular circumstances, since what one is justified in believing at one time may well be different from what one is justified in believing at another. Nevertheless, if one believes in such a God of love, one will also think that he will eventually bring rational creatures to know whathe truly is, so that the search for truth will issue in a specific set of true beliefs sometime. Thus it is misleading, though in one sense true, to saythat no metaphysical beliefs are essential to salvation. It may not be essential to your eventual salvation that you hold them now; but it is essential to your actual salvation that you come to hold them. Metaphysics, however difficult and disputable, is important to faith (I don't mean anything very grand by this; just beliefs about the nature of what is ultimately real).

In a recent paper, Hick refers to the 'novel', 'astonishing' and 'bizarre' doctrine that 'the salvific power of the dharma taught five hundred years earlier by the Buddha is a consequence of the death of Jesus'. But one need not deny that the dharma is an effective way of overcoming egoism and attaining inner peace and compassion, when one asserts that it does not bring one into a conscious loving relationship with a personal God. Nor is it bizarre to hold that one can be brought into such a relationship only by the saving activity of God uniting human nature to himself in the life and death of Jesus, and subsequently in those who come to accept Jesus as Lord and Saviour, It is not that Buddhists attain salvation by the Middle Way, though somehow the efficacy of this way depends on something that had not yet happened. Buddhists do not attain Christian salvation, since their Way does not lead to that personal relationship with God which is salvation. They attain a high degree of compassion and inner peace; and their unselfish devotion to the truth as they see it will surely fit them to receive salvation from a personal God when his saving activity becomes clear to them. There is a salutary reminder here that metaphysics is not what saves us; for Christians, the act of God, establishing creatures in knowledge andlove of him, does that. But metaphysics is needed to set out the coherence of the concept of a God who can so act in a world like this.

It may help at this point if we distinguish what we may call soft pluralism from hard pluralism. Soft pluralism is the view that the Real can manifest in many traditions, and humans can respond to it appropriately in them. I think this view is defensible and important, and it is certainly different from the view, held by many, that there is only one God, who only reveals himself in one tradition and only saves those who belong to that tradition – the restrictive interpretation of the decree of the Council of Florence, 'Outside the Church there is no salvation'. It is coherent to hold that there is a God who is infinite and beyond human comprehension in his essential nature, who discloses something of that nature, as it stands in relation to us, in many religious traditions. It is coherent to hold that in many (though not all) religious traditions, believers aim to overcome selfish desire in relation to a supreme objective value which promises bliss, knowledge and freedom; and that this does constitute a positive and appropriate response to God, as disclosed to them. It is also coherent to hold that no tradition has the completeness of truth about God; that all contain many revisable and corrigible beliefs, and that we should look to other traditions to complement, correct or reshape our own. This is certainly part of Hick's thesis.

But another form of the thesis is also at work; a thesis both more intolerant of virtually all actual religious traditions and sliding at times into incoherence. The intolerance surfaces in many stringent remarks about the bizarre, primitive and astonishing beliefs held by orthodox believers. The incoherence appears in the claim of hard pluralism that all (or at least all 'great') traditions are equally valid paths to salvation and equally authentic modes of experience of a Real which is a completely unknowable postulate of the religious life. It is the stress on equal validity, equal authenticity and complete unknowability which is incoherent. These three claims constitute an inconsistent triad of propositions, since one cannot assert all of: (1) There is something wholly unknowable; (2) all experiences of it are equally authentic; and (3) all paths to fuller experience of it are equally valid. If (1) is true, (2) and (3) cannot be asserted. Not only is there no way of knowing if they are true; they cannot be true, if they entail (as they do) experiential knowledge of the wholly unknowable. If there are any criteria of authenticity at all, it must be possible to distinguish more and less authentic experiences. But this can only be done by means of some concept of the Real which can be described more or less adequately. Once one has such a concept, there may indeed be experiences which give equally authentic knowledge of it; but that can only be so if those experiences are complementary, not contradictory. That means (as is the case with the often quoted wave-particle duality of light) that competent observers must agree that both of two descriptions of an object can be true, in different conditions of observation. Unfortunately, most Buddhists will not agree that it is true that there is an omnipotent personal agent who brings about changes in history; and most Christians will not agree that the idea of God is an imaginative projection which needs to be overcome in the recognition of one non-dual reality. Hard pluralism is as strongly falsified as any contingent hypothesis is ever likely to be.

Yet it might be insisted that this situation must be changed. There is another version of pluralism, which might be termed 'revisionist pluralism', which asserts that all the scriptural traditions need to be radically revised, in consequence of the rise of the natural sciences, of biblical scholarship and of post-Enlightenment critical thinking in general. The idea of an infallible scriptural revelation will need to be discarded, and many particular beliefs revised in the light of new knowledge of the world and of human psychology. Now if this is done in all the great scriptural traditions, one will be much less clear about which beliefs are essential or even central to each tradition; and the revised beliefs may well turn out to be compatible with similarly revised beliefs in other traditions.

If a Buddhist is prepared to regard belief in re-incarnation as a myth, a Christian thinks of the incarnation as a mistaken fourth-century doctrine, and a Muslim agrees that the Qur'an is a fallible and morally imperfect document, they might well be able to agree much more than they used to. One can see the scriptural faiths, defined by their acceptance of infallible revelation (and even the Buddhist scriptures are regarded in that way by many orthodox believers), as belonging to past history just as surely as their tribal predecessors do. Religion can move to a more universal phase, in which insights are selected from many traditions, while most of their differences are relegated to the museum of dead beliefs. I suspect that Hick wishes to commend revisionist pluralism, too. There is much to be said for it; but it cannot be said that it sees all existing traditions as equally valid perceptions of truth. On the contrary, most existing traditions have to be radically purged of error, in the light of the more adequate views of a post-Critical age. It is ironic that this view, which sees the great traditions as 'earlier stages in an evolution of which it is the culmination' is precisely of the type which Hick earlier characterises as unacceptably arrogant (p. 2). Revisionist pluralism makes it own absolute and exclusive claim – it is just true that there is one Reality of supreme value which will bring all creatures to good; and anything which denies this or tries to restrict the ways in which this may happen is false.

Revisionist pluralism is incompatible with hard pluralism, since it denies that unrevised traditions are equally adequate forms of religious truth. It is compatible with soft pluralism, but not entailed by it, since it is possible that one existing tradition characterises the Real most adequately; that is, that its central truth-claims are more adequately descriptive of the Real than competing alternatives. To the extent that the Real is a personal and active self-disclosing agent, one might think that an existing tradition which claims to have witnessed the self-disclosing acts of this agent is more likely to be adequate than the conclusions of a highly abstract and speculative philosophical hypothesis. But that is a question of the acceptability and coherence of particular conceptions of ultimate reality, which needs to be argued out in detail. One thing is certain, that revisionist pluralism is not in a position to assert moral superiority, greater tolerance or greater impartiality over any particular tradition as such, when traditions are taken as not excluding ultimate salvation for others; since the claims each must make for itself are logically on a par.

Religious believers do not have to suppose that the majority of the human race are excluded from salvation, as long as they have a view which allows for a development of knowledge after death. They are, however, committed to thinking that most people are mistaken in their beliefs about the ultimate nature of reality. That is, after all, not a very surprising thought, though it is a sad one. It should lead to a keen sense of one's own fallibility, a deeper appreciation of the attempts of others to understand human nature and destiny, and a firm stress on the primacy of moral and spiritual practice in religion. These are the leading themes of John Hick's recent work, which he formulates in the pluralist hypothesis. I have suggested that in at least one sense (soft pluralism) his case is persuasive. There are other senses however which, if I am right, are not sustainable. On this, at least, truth is exclusive, and one of us must be wrong.

18

Theology as a Comparative Discipline

Confessional and Comparative Theology

The proposal that the theologian should begin by studying the religious phenomena of the world before moving on to say what the characteristics of revelation are and what sort of certainty is obtainable in religion may seem to be both impossible and undesirable. It seems impossible, for it takes a lifetime to understand even one religious tradition properly. How can one begin by trying to study the huge number of religious traditions that exist throughout the world? Would one ever finish this preamble to faith? And if one did, would it not be bound to remain superficial?

I understand this objection, and have no wish to turn the systematic theologian into an amateur collector of religious curiosities. Nevertheless, I think the time has come when it is positively misleading to consider religious traditions in isolation. Theologians have in fact always taken their interpretative clues from philosophical or cultural factors not confined to Christianity. Aquinas, for example, took Aristotelian philosophy, well seasoned with Platonism, and used it to rethink Christian doctrine in the thirteenth century. For a short time, his works were even banned from the University of Paris as dangerously subversive; but it was not long before they became definitive for the Roman Catholic Church. Does it make sense to treat the content of a religion as a self-contained corpus, as though it at least was immune from external influence, and as though light could not be thrown upon it by a consideration of claims made by other faiths?

One cannot understand the person of Jesus unless one knows something about the Judaism of his time. That in turn requires some knowledge of earlier Judaism; and then one needs to know about Canaanite religion and other Middle Eastern cults. So one is already involved in the study of religious traditions in general. Such a study is essential if one is to set the development of Judaism and Christianity in its historical context. It is reasonable to think that a wider study of other traditions will also throw light on the way in which Christian faith has developed as a vehicle of Divine revelation.

I am inclined to say that one cannot properly understand the mode of Divine revelation within Christianity unless one can set it in the context of human religious activity in general, for only in its widest context can one discern the true meaning of such revelation. It may be that this is too difficult a task to be performed properly by one person. Yet we now have much greater access to a mass of scholarly work on various religions, and it would be myopic simply to ignore it. One must, therefore, use such scholarly results in trying to obtain a general view of the nature of religion, within which one can set one's own understanding. Scholars must continue to work on painstaking details. But the systematic theologian must make some attempt to understand the broad sweep of religious life, before being ready to make an informed judgment about the sources and methods of Christian theology. Christian revelation is not a self-contained whole, uninfluenced by other contexts and perspectives. Further, the wider one's perspective, the more reliable one's religious judgments might be.

Even if starting from as general a view as possible of claims to religious revelation is possible, is it desirable? It may be seen as an attempt to study religion neutrally, as if from some superior standpoint; whereas, it may be said, theology must be rooted in a particular faith. The view I have so far outlined moves away from seeing theology as an exclusively Christian discipline, founded on an inerrant and exclusive scriptural revelation. But it still sees theology as a confessional discipline, existing in diverse traditions and seeking to articulate their tacit culture of faith from within those traditions. I have noted that this already requires attention to and conversation with other traditions. Perhaps a bolder move can be made, to disconnect the practice of theology, at least in part, from a necessary internal relation to a particular tradition. This view is strongly opposed by Aidan Nichols. 'Theology,' he says, 'presupposes the truth of the Christian faith.'[1] 'To be a theologian, one must share the common *fides quae*, the faith of the people of God.'[2] Its source is Divinely given faith in the revelation of God, and supposes, at least for him, that the Catholic revelation is authentic.

---

1 Aidan Nichols, *The Shape of Catholic Theology* (Edinburgh: T. and T. Clark, 1991), 32.
2 Ibid. 16.

For such a view, theology is essentially a confessional discipline, a working-out of the faith of a particular community, of which the theologian is the servant. Of course, the Roman Catholic Church has the right to appoint a certain class of people to do this. The implication is, however, that other Christian Churches should have their own theologians, all exploring the faiths of their own communities. Even Louth, with whose account I am generally in sympathy, concludes by saying that 'theology is the apprehension of the believing mind combined with a right state of the heart'.[3] Theology becomes very much an activity from within the believing community. One cannot be a theologian who happens to be a Roman Catholic, or a Presbyterian, or nothing at all; one must be a Catholic theologian or a Presbyterian theologian, appointed by the Church to explore its own understanding of revelation. One finds what almost amounts to a *reductio ad absurdum* of this view in Schleiermacher, who holds that 'Dogmatic theology is the science which systematises the doctrine prevalent in a Christian Church at a given time.'[4] Not only are theologians confined to one Christian sect; they are confined to a particular time and cultural group. It seems that on such a view there would be as many theology faculties as there are religious buildings and societies.

This seems to me an unduly restrictive understanding of theology. There is a proper intellectual study which tries to explore religious beliefs and practices, enquiring as to their truth and rationality, which is not *as such* committed to the views of one faith-community. Nichols offers a working definition of theology as 'the disciplined exploration of what is contained in revelation'.[5] But revelation is taken as a given, as something settled, definitive, and complete. Moreover, as a Roman Catholic, he takes revelation to be authoritatively interpreted by the magisterium of that Church, so that certain questions can be closed to critical enquiry by the magisterium. A Roman Catholic cannot query the Chalcedonian definition of the incarnation or the dogma of the Immaculate conception of Mary, though a theologian might explore their meaning further.

Nichols does not, however, accept the view that the theologian comments on the pronouncements of bishops and popes. New questions can be raised and explored, so that the theologian can make it possible for the

3 Andrew Louth, *Discerning the Mystery* (Oxford: Clarendon Press, 1989), 147.
4 F. E. D. Schleiermacher, *The Christian Faith* (Edinburgh: T. and T. Clark, 1989), para. 19.
5 Nichols, *Catholic Theology, 32.*

magisterium to see what the sources revelation contain,[6] on many matters which have not been defined or which may not interest the present group of bishops. But if, as he says, theology is something wider than a commentary what popes and bishops have said, may one not suspect that it issomething wider than a commentary on what some settled revelation contains?

What is this wider thing? It is the whole range of Divine manifestations in the world, the whole phenomenon of religion in human life in its many varied forms, the whole array of human speculations about and alleged experiences of the Divine. If theology is an intellectual enquiry into God, it cannot be confined to reflection on just one tradition of revelation, regarded from the first as being complete and final. For that understanding of revelation is itself one of the matters set before one for critical reflection. When the theologian considers the question of what revelation is, this is not a mere preamble to faith, setting out a defence of what has already been decided in advance (that this revelation, and this understanding of it, is the best and truest there can ever be). It is a part of religious enquiry itself, which must affect in the most fundamental way everything that follows.

One can therefore distinguish two types of theology. One is confessional theology; the exploration of a given revelation by one who wholly accepts that revelation and lives by it. The other may be termed 'comparative theology' – theology not as a form of apologetics for a particular faith but as an intellectual discipline which enquires into ideas of the ultimate value and goal of human life, as they have been perceived and expressed in a variety of religious traditions. It is therefore naturally, though not exclusively, concerned with the concept of 'God' as it arises within many such traditions. Comparative theology differs from what is often called 'religious studies', in being primarily concerned with the meaning, truth, and rationality of religious beliefs, rather than with the psychological, sociological, or historical elements of religious life and institutions.

There are those who hold that the only true theology is confessional. Aidan Nichols says that any study of religion which is not rooted in Catholic faith is bound to be 'epistemologically defective'.[7] John Mac-

6 Ibid. 30.
7 Nichols, 15.

quarrie, an Anglican, begins his *Principles of Christian Theology* by saying, 'Theology may be defined as the study which, through participation in and reflection upon a religious faith, seeks to express the content of this faith.'[8] This entails that theologians must be participants in a religious community and should aim to express the faith of their own community. But at this point one may begin to perceive a danger that the theologian will become merely a propagandist on behalf of one religious organisation, bound to defend its views in public whatever his or her own personal opinions may be, bound to submit to the authority of that community even if critical enquiry begins to question its assertions.

Many great theologians have taken exactly this view. Calvin certainly thought that Protestant Christians should submit unreservedly to Scripture, and Karl Barth has held that any attempt to subject the Word of God to human judgment is a form of sinful pride. One immediate problem is that Roman Catholic theologians would have to submit to a different authority – for Scripture must be interpreted by a magisterium which disagrees with Calvin at many points. Each theologian will have a set of protected propositions – different in detail in different confessions – which are exempt from questioning. So how does one decide which set of propositions is to be so exempt? Presumably by seeing that this is the set authoritatively defined by a specific community. But that pushes the question a stage farther back: why should one accept this community's authority? And to what extent should one accept it? If this is not merely to be decided by something like an accident of birth, it seems that there must be a proper reflective discipline which investigates precisely the doctrine of proper religious authority, its sources and limits.

The traditional discipline of natural theology belongs here, as the attempt to show that there is a God and that God has been truly revealed in a specific tradition. The project of traditional natural theology is to demonstrate by appeal to reason alone that God exists then to show that the evidence of miracles and fulfilled prophecies demonstrates that the Church has been founded by Christ as God's authorised teacher of dogmatic truths. Once the Church has been shown to be the properly authorised teacher, in this way, it only remains for the theologian to articulate the truths authoritatively taught by that institution. Even on this model, if natural theology is a proper subject, then the definition of theology *per se*

8 John Macquarrie, *Principles of Christian Theology* (London: SCM Press, 1966), 1.

as disciplined exploration of what is contained in revelation is too restricted. Theology must also explore what revelation is and what the criteria are for accepting one revelation. Theology cannot simply presuppose the truth of a particular faith, for it must investigate the grounds for supposing that faith is true. But for traditional natural theology, this could be accomplished successfully by reason alone.

There are very few competent theologians who would now be able to accept this model. Philosophers and historians are now more critical and skeptical than they used to be. Philosophers would have to agree that purely rational arguments will leave many people far from convinced of the existence of God. Historians would accept that the evidence for the sort of miracles recorded in the Bible is too poor to be acceptable for establishing any particular belief beyond reasonable doubt. And theologians would doubt whether the New Testament documents license one in supposing that Jesus actually founded anything like any present Church at all. The point is not that these traditional beliefs are false; on the contrary, they may all be true. The point is that none of them can be accepted on purely rational grounds of argument and evidence. So the traditional model of natural theology can no longer serve as the foundation for the acceptance of a particular ecclesiastical authority.

One now seems to be impaled on the horns of a dilemma. On the one hand, one cannot presuppose the truth of a specific alleged revelation, since its claims must be investigated; and where competing claims are made, some judgment must be made between them. On the other hand, there is no neutral vantage-point, without any beliefs at all, from which a dispassionate judgment might be made on this subject. So it might be more honest, after all, to accept that one just stands within a given tradition and admit that all one's judgments will be made from that standpoint; a rational investigation of such basic claims is impossible. If the confessional theologian can be seen as a prejudiced propagandist for one view among many, the comparative theologian can be seen as a self-deceiving claimant to perfectly neutral rationality, who is bound to be divorced from any specific religious commitment. Neither position is acceptable; but is there any alternative?

Criticism and Commitment

It is clear that we do not start with a *tabula rasa* and choose all our beliefs with impartial rationality. We learn our basic interpretative concepts from others and as we begin to reflect we do so from a specific cultural and historical position. It would be quite false, however, to say that because of this one can find no universal and certain truths at all. That chairs and tables exist, that the world has existed for many years before we were born, that we were born and will die – these things are unequivocally true. Many truths of this sort are very hard to discover or be sure about; and that includes truths about the existence, acts, and words of Jesus or Buddha. There are many truths of which we will remain in various degrees uncertain. Other truths are such that they involve large-scale matters of interpretation which are unlikely to be resolved by any process of empirical investigation. These would include matters like the existence of God, or life after death, or of the law of karma. It is likely that we will have initial beliefs about these matters, which we receive in the first place from our culture.

Whether it can be said that this makes us members of 'a tradition' is not clear. Beliefs may be picked up in many ways from many different sources; and the set of beliefs we have may neither be coherent nor match with any one set of beliefs which is identifiable with a specific social institution. People speak rather loosely about a 'spirit of the age', or about our 'cultural inheritance'; but such things are very difficult to specify and probably consist of a large collection of beliefs from different sources which we have formed as a result of many different social interactions. Only a few people consciously align themselves with political, religious, or social interest groups, whose aims may be explicitly stated or whose attitudes are pretty clear in practice. Thus if I am a Jew living in Britain in the twentieth century, I may (or may not) feel some need to support the state of Israel; I may (or may not) attend synagogue; and my 'Jewishness' may be defined more by what other people ascribe to me than by what I am myself inclined to believe. In fact, it is not uncommon for a tradition to be defined by those who wish to identify something they are opposed to rather than by those who wish to belong to an identifiable group. To be Jewish may be to conform to an image other people have of me rather than being anything like an explicit choice. Much the same sort of thing could be said of large numbers of Catholic and Protestant Christians, and of members of most religious traditions.

It is not at all clear, then, that the beliefs of a given person will conform to a set of beliefs taken to characterise a particular institution, even if – by birth or by some ceremony undergone in youth – one is taken to be a member of that institution. Typically, some people will find security in identifying with a social institution and being loyal to its declared aims and beliefs. Others, however, may well find many of the declared beliefs to be badly evidenced or results of intellectual lethargy, even though membership of the institution offers sufficient benefits to make it attractive. So it is a distortion to think that everyone belongs to some tradition, if this is thought to involve sincere and complete adherence to some declared set of beliefs in a particular institution. Especially in the case of religious institutions, the reality of social membership is so complex and the reasons for membership so diverse that it would be quite false to think it was a matter of intellectual assent to all the declarations of the institution.

Seen against this background, the confessional theologian might be seen as a sort of systematiser who tries to establish or defend an official set of beliefs which includes elements which are widely disregarded by many members of the institution. Such a person will conscientiously have come to accept that the institution has a formal teaching authority which can be rationally defended. But many other options are possible. If a given institution cannot be established as authoritative by some universally convincing rational argument, then those who reflect on the nature of revelation may conscientiously dispute its authority; or they may feel able to be members of the institution, while disputing many elements of its self-interpretation. One may feel, for example, that a Christian Church truly mediates the mystery of Christ and sustains faith and hope in God, while it is yet mistaken in some of the claims it makes, including some of the claims it makes authoritatively about itself. I take it that all non-Roman Catholics, as well as many Roman Catholics, believe this to be true of the Roman Church. There is, after all, no entailment between a Church being a true mediator of the Divine Life and its being correct in all its official beliefs. To get to that position one needs a strong argument that one cannot be a true mediator without being correct in all one's official beliefs; and it is hard to see any such argument succeeding, since the Gospels themselves contain errors, however unimportant, while mediating the Divine Life pre-eminently.

If Churches can err, it may be important for theologians to be free to challenge the official statements of those Churches, while yet remaining members of those Churches as long as conscience allows. On the other hand, the most piercing criticisms of a Church may come from those who are not its members; and such people may even articulate the logically basic beliefs of such a Church more clearly than members of it who are unable to discern their own hidden presuppositions.[9] I therefore see no reason why theologians should necessarily be participants in a religious community; and I see good reason why theologians who are such participants should not be taken to be official spokespersons for that community. Their office may often be that of critic rather than of advocate, and it is in that function that they may best serve a Church in the long run.

One may properly be described as concerned with questions of the meaning and justification of the concepts of God and revelation, even though one concludes, whether gladly or regretfully, that no justification can be found. Scholars of any religious persuasion or none may engage in questions of comparative theology, the analysis of the concepts of God and of revelation. I doubt, despite what Fr. Nichols says, if their adherence to a particular faith or their devotion to prayer will give them greater epistemological adequacy; though naturally believers will tend to follow theologians of their own persuasion wherever possible.

Pluralism in Theology

I am not suggesting that theologians should have no personal beliefs; that is scarcely possible. I am suggesting that *theology* is *a pluralistic discipline*. In it, people of differing beliefs can co-operate, discuss, argue, and converse. Even within one Church, discussion and argument is an obvious feature of a lively religious practice. Understanding grows by debate, by hearing others and by hearing how others hear one's own views; by opposition as well as by consensus. Different religious groups will have different ways of seeing their own authority in such matters. But one cannot fail to note how in the last 150 years those theologians who have said things quite unpalatable to Church authorities have made lasting advances in theological understanding. One can think of Strauss, of Schweitzer, of Kung; and there are many others. There is a real danger in seeking to prevent radical theological thinking and enforce assent to received opinion. While religious groups are entitled to employ their own apologists, truth is best served by the advocacy of free intellectual enquiry. So it is important even for such groups that they should be in

9 Alisdair MacIntyre has argued that some cultures may be better understood, in a certain sense, by others than by themselves: 'Rationality and the Explanation of Action', in *Against the Self-Images of the Age* (London: Duckworth, 1971), 244–59.

active conversation with apologists of other groups. Unless one characterises others as irredeemably sinful, ignorant or stupid, there may always be something to learn from them. Unless one is sure that one's own view is irrevisably correct, there is always a possibility of error or at least of restricted vision. There is a danger in unrestrictedly free thinking; but it is a preferable danger to that of compulsory intellectual conformity.

To try to avoid misunderstanding here, I am not saying it is a bad thing for believers to do theology; on the contrary, all theologians believe something. Nor am I saying that it is not intellectually respectable to advocate the beliefs of one's own group; on the contrary, it is better to do that openly than to pretend that one is wholly neutral in matters of belief. I am suggesting that it is wrong to limit theology proper to one's own group and make it simply an exploration of what is officially believed by that group or even of what is contained in the Scripture and tradition of that group. I would go further and suggest that to advocate a 'Catholic theology' or an 'Anglican theology' or even a 'Christian theology' is unduly restrictive. For it suggests that there is a specific intellectual discipline which can only be undertaken by Catholics or Anglicans or Christians. It seems preferable to say that theology is the discipline of reflection upon ideas of the ultimate reality and goal of human life, of God, and of revelation. It can be undertaken by people of many diverse beliefs. It is better undertaken in knowledge of and in conversation with those of beliefs other than one's own. In it one may well find oneself defending a particular view of God and of revelation, which may involve one in obedience to the authority of some religious group, but one can pursue the discipline without advocating the views of such a group. One may even wish to ally oneself with a group while actively disputing some of its beliefs, even those which some members of the group hold to be essential.

I am not arguing that everyone should be like that; only that people who do this are full and proper theologians. And in fact most of the creative theologians in Europe since the seventeenth century have been in such a partly revisionist position within their own faiths. There is revisionist theology as well as confessional theology, and if the strength of the latter lies in its loyalty to a body of doctrine believed to give true insight into the nature of God, the strength of the former is its refusal to bow to the pressures of conformity and authority as an answer to real intellectual problems.

To put a view at the opposite pole from that which I have called confessional theology, we can turn to none better than Schleiermacher, who says,

> Belief ... usually so called, which is to accept what another has said or done, or to wish to think and feel as another has thought and felt, is a hard and base service ... it must be rejected by all who would force their way into the sanctuary of religion. To wish to have and hold a faith that is 'an echo, proves that a man is incapable of religion.[10]

Schleiermacher's protest is against accepting a belief simply because another believes it; and in that protest one can hear the voice of the Enlightenment crying out for autonomy, for personal choice and freedom of individual belief against the authorities, religious and political, which had restricted free scientific and historical enquiry. Such a protest will hardly be effective against a considered and free submission to some authority that is taken to be in the best position to know certain things. But deep underlying questions are raised here about the proper extent of authority and autonomy in belief, and about the nature of belief itself. Is it primarily a matter of assent to a set of doctrines, or commitment to a range of images and symbols or to a way of life? These themes precisely belong to comparative theology.

The picture I am presenting is not one of some tradition-neutral investigator, free from all prejudice, able to judge with supreme rationality between an array of differing beliefs, a rationalist theologian of straw indeed. If I have any picture in mind, it is of someone whose mind has been formed by overlapping traditions of thought which are themselves in a state of rather confusing change. That person is aware of other traditions which the modern world has made present and living options for belief, and of the way in which changes in scientific and moral understanding have placed all traditions in a rather different light. To be a theologian at such a time is not to pretend to some a historical rationality, but to accept one's place in a continuum of historical change and to accept one's role as a vehicle of continuing change, as all traditions interweave in complex and novel ways. One is not trying to sit loose to all traditions, but one cannot be satisfied with seeing a tradition as an unchanging, fixed set of irreformable

10 Schleiermacher, *The Christian Faith, 90.*

beliefs. Rather, one seeks to extend one's tradition as it encounters new understandings and situations, both continually going back to its resources and looking forward to its applications in very different contexts. Pluralism (in the sense of a conversation of differing viewpoints) and revision (in the sense of imaginative rethinking in new contexts) become part of the intellectual framework of such a theologian; and this must be in tension with acceptance of one final truth, contained in one religious group. One may come to the conclusion that there is such a final truth, maintained in its wholeness by just one group; one may have that view both as one's starting-point and as one's final conclusion. But one must accept that theology, as the disciplined enquiry into God, contains other possibilities – and has a place for serious enquirers with rather different starting-points. And if the intellectual enquiry is to be extensive in its range and thorough in its discipline, it will need to meet in conversation with them and not be closed to any increase in understanding which may result.

In seeking to characterise what theology is, it is much too restrictive to limit it to the exposition and defence of one settled body of truths about God. The world of theology is, for many, a world in which everything is put in question, not one in which doubts can be comfortably resolved. It should offer resources for coming to informed decisions about religious belief; but it should also expose the difficulty and profundity of ultimate questions, and therefore perhaps cause one to be more uncertain about some previously unconsidered matters. I have no wish to expel the confessional theologian from the academic community; but such a person must accept that a more pluralist and revisionist form of theology also exists; and should, I think, accept that it is a positively good thing to engage in this wider theological enterprise, even for those whose own commitment is settled.

Seen from this perspective, comparative theology must be *a self-critical discipline,* aware of the historical roots of its own beliefs; *a pluralistic discipline,* prepared to engage in conversation with a number of living traditions; and *an open-ended discipline,* prepared to revise beliefs if and when it comes to seem necessary. There is nothing to prevent a comparative theologian from being committed to one religious tradition, even a very authoritarian one, unless that authority prohibits such a study. Then the area of revisability may be restricted to some extent, though even then new forms of understanding ancient formulations may be possible and desirable. For some, it will be possible to assert that commitment to the unrevisable authority itself is in principle revisable, even if one cannot foresee any real possibility of revising it without loss of faith. One must – as one does, anyway – live alongside others who see revision as a continual necessity in a changing world. But one is not at all constrained to be always looking for revisions; a comparative theologian may properly feel that a self-critical, pluralistic, and open-ended discipline is likely to corroborate the beliefs of one group. Thus apologists and revisionists can converse together in the wider community of theological discourse.

I have noted that the project of traditional natural theology seems unacceptable. So the basic problem remains of how one can construct a rational account of revelation, in a context of many diverse authoritative traditions which stress diverse primal disclosures of reality and value. One natural place for such construction to begin with is a study of the phenomena of religion in history and with the places in human experience where religious beliefs arise. In this way theologians can test the adequacy of their own initial view of religion against a wider range of human experiences and perhaps come to form new views in the light of perspectives they had not considered. Comparative theology can thereby help to form a view of the sources, nature, and limits of authoritative claims to revelation, a view which will naturally determine subsequent theological reflection on particular religious traditions.

I am writing from within one (Anglican) strand of the Christian tradition. What I say is an attempt to articulate that tradition in a global context; so it is in a sense a confessional theology. But it is a contribution to a comparative theology of revelation from a particular perspective. It tries to take many traditions, and the history of human religious thought, seriously; and explore what can be said of them in the light of central Christian beliefs, and what light they in turn shed on those beliefs. Confessional and comparative theology need not, in all their forms, exclude each other.

If no one person can hope to provide an adequate account of such matters, one can at least begin the attempt to enter into discussion with others and invite them to respond. One may then begin to attain a wider perspective in which initial views commitments may be better understood. As one of the great pioneers in this field, Wilfred Cantwell Smith, has put it: 'To oneself as in principle heir to the whole religious history of race thus far, and the community of which one is a member as in principle the human community ... is not to dissolve the question of religious truth but for our day to bring it into focus.'[11]

11 W.C. Smith, *Towards a World Theology* (New York: Orbis Books, 1981), 188.

19

Religion and the Possibility of a Global Ethics

Is there such a thing as a global ethics, a universal system of ethics or a set of moral principles which all humans could agree to live by? For many years, especially at the beginning of the twentieth century, some anthropologists argued that human moral systems were so diverse that there was no point in speaking of any universally accepted moral principles. Inuit were alleged to eat their grandparents, South Sea Islanders to have sex with anybody, and National Socialists to think that genocide was morally right. In such a world, searching for moral agreements on even the most basic issues seemed a hopeless quest. In less spectacular ways, there seems no way of resolving moral disagreements on such matters as capital punishment, abortion, and the treatment of animals. Human moral views were said just to be fundamentally diverse. There is no point in seeking anything like a global ethics.

On the other hand, it is clear that human beings all have certain things in common. They all have forty-six chromosomes. They all belong to a species that is, on earth, uniquely capable of abstract intellectual thought and responsible moral action. They all have basic biological needs like eating, reproducing, and obtaining shelter from the elements. Is there not a possibility that some moral principles, however general and vague, may be based on these common qualities, and thus be universal among humans?

Moral Principles and Basic Human Needs

Such a thought underlies an approach to ethics which has been well established in Christian tradition for centuries, an approach that seeks to found basic moral principles on the basic needs and inclinations of human beings. Humans may claim to have many different needs and inclinations, but a basic need is one that is necessary to surviving as a human being, and to obtaining any of the diverse things that humans might desire. In some countries owning a television set might be classified as a need, but it is clearly not necessary to surviving as a human being. Although it might be necessary to obtaining many specific desires, like watching quiz programs, it is not necessary as a condition of obtaining the satisfaction of human desires in general, of obtaining anything at all that humans might find desirable.

An example of a basic need is the need for food and drink. If these are not forthcoming, humans cannot survive, and in that sense food and drink are necessary to obtaining anything at all that humans might call desirable. As basic needs, food and drink are basically desirable. All humans (indeed, all animals) have good reason to desire them. Something that all humans have good reason to desire is a basic good, on the simple supposition that what is desirable is as such good, as long as it carries no overwhelming harm in its train. Thus in a very simple way one can see that there is at least one basic and universal human good, the good of having food and drink. Whatever the Inuit or the Trobriand Islanders are alleged to do, they have in common the belief that nourishment is a basic human good. It is good, not just for me or my family, but for all humans.

That may not seem like very much, but it does mean that every thinking person really knows that the provision of food to the hungry is a basic human good, and that withholding food when it could be provided and when it is needed is a basic evil. We do know some simple truths about good and evil, without any need of revelation and without being inclined at all to think that it is just a matter of personal preference. There are at least some universal moral truths.

The provision of food is a basic good for all animals, not just for humans. It is also very largely an instrumental good. Eating and drinking are not primarily good for their own sake, but because they are necessary to health and to survival. They in turn are necessary conditions of doing anything that one believes to be worthwhile. Of course, they may also produce pleasure, and one may well think that the pursuit of pleasure and the avoidance of pain are not only instrumental but intrinsic goods. They can be considered worthwhile objects of the pursuit of a rational being simply in themselves.

The Principle of Benevolence

Bentham and Mill were surely right in thinking that every rational sentient being has a good reason to wish to avoid pain and to experience pleasure. When this personal desire is generalised by the application of the simple logical rule that what is a good reason for one sentient being is, other things being equal, a good reason for any being of the same general sort, one obtains the moral rule that it is bad to cause pain to any sentient being – or, in the positive version, that it is good to sustain or increase the pleasure of any sentient being. Thus, from these simple considerations, one obtains a basic and universal moral principle which could be called the principle of 'benevolence' or 'compassion.' It is morally good to decrease the pain of all beings and to increase their pleasure.

Of course, there are many different ways of understanding what pleasure is. Someone who thinks that eating, drinking, and sensual pleasures are the greatest pleasures thinks very differently from someone who thinks that the love of music or the worship of God is the greatest pleasure. John Stuart Mill, in particular, agonised about this problem of distinguishing different sorts of pleasure. It does not seem unreasonable to say that all pleasure is, as such, good. But many sorts of pleasure may carry with them other consequences that are evil – as the pleasure of sex with another person's partner will be far outweighed by the harm done to the personal relationships involved. Pleasures may be outweighed by other goods, and many pleasures are quite low-level goods. In saying that pleasure is a good, one is not committed to saying that it is the only good, or that all pleasures are alike.

Yet one must not overlook the fact that some of the very highest goods of religion, like the attainment of human liberation or the beatific vision of God, involve supreme pleasure. *Nirvana* is spoken of as a state of bliss, and the beatific vision is obviously one of supreme happiness. Some may think that 'pleasure' is a very inadequate term for such states, and so it is. Yet they lie on the same continuum as the pleasures of eating and drinking, even if at the opposite end of it. Some religious views recommend self-denial and the setting aside of sensual pleasure. But that is for the sake of a deeper and longer-lasting happiness, untainted with suffering, if not for oneself then for other beings. The most self-denying Christians consider it right to work for the happiness of others, and the most selfless Buddhists work for the liberation of all beings from suffering. It is true, then, that there are a number of different conceptions of what true pleasure is, ranging from the view that anything goes ('pushpin is as good as poetry,' as Jeremy Bentham said) to the view that only a life free of sensual desire can achieve freedom from suffering and supreme bliss (as the Buddha taught). In this respect, as in others, religious views typically recommend the subordination of sensual pleasures to intellectual and spiritual goods. They recommend the subordination of personal pleasure to the good of others. All those goods, however, involve pleasure, and it would be absurd to say that it is not good to take pleasure in loving God or in attaining final freedom from suffering.

So although one can arrive at the principle of benevolence simply by reflection on basic human desires and the respects in which human beings resemble one another, there are different views of what exactly benevolence implies, and religious faiths give distinctive interpretations of benevolence. I will consider only two main traditions of religious thought, rather broadly conceived as the Indian and the Semitic. Indian traditions, at least in their non-theistic forms, often tend to concentrate on the fact that existence inevitably involves suffering, from which liberation is to be sought as the main spiritual goal. They tend to see happiness in an overcoming of the distinctive sort of individuality a person possesses in this lifetime, aiming at the overcoming of a sense of distinct individual personality. For instance, the Jain principle of *ahimsa* enjoins that no harm must be done to any sentient being. The goal of liberation is the attainment of pure consciousness, free of all trappings of this-worldly identity. There is an extreme of renunciation among Jain saints, and it may seem that sensual pleasure is completely denied. Nevertheless, lay people and householders are usually counselled to enjoy life without attachment, and to take pleasure in simple things, acknowledging their transience. Even the Jain saint will seek to attain supreme pleasure in being free from desires and in possessing unlimited knowledge.

In the Semitic traditions happiness is usually found in some sort of conscious relationship to God, and it is usually seen as a fulfillment of the individual personality. Judaism and Islam have divinely revealed laws that outline the will of God and which cannot be overturned. Pleasure is certainly not denied, and paradise is seen as a place of enduring pleasure. But it must conform to divine law. In these traditions and in Christianity, as well as in Indian theistic traditions, however, there exists a more personalist view which would see all earthly pleasures as good, as long as they can be set in the context of a loving relationship with God. So the rule of benevolence is interpreted primarily as doing good to other human beings. It is not considered wrong to seek pleasure for oneself. Indeed, one rabbinic saying states that all humans will be judged on the good things they might have enjoyed, but did not. One should certainly cause minimal harm, and seek the happiness of others and oneself. This happiness will come primarily from loving and obeying God, so it springs from a certain sort of personal relationship. One cares for created things because God creates them, and they are to be treated as God commands. Happiness lies in accepting the relationship of love that God offers to created persons, not in some state of liberation from all earthly desires.

That seems very different from the Jain view. Both the extent of compassion for other beings and the nature of the goal that brings true happiness differ. Nevertheless, no observant theist would deny that one should have compassion for God's creatures wherever they suffer, and no pious Jain would deny that the worship of a divine being involves the renunciation of purely selfish desires and an insistence that the sensual must be always ordered to higher spiritual goods of worship and love. No religious view permits the pursuit of personal or sensual pleasure where it is not subordinated to the pursuit of a supreme spiritual good for its own sake. Jains and Buddhists think that the nature of the supreme good (the liberation of the soul from the material realm) rules out sensual pleasure and requires the avoidance of all harm to living beings. Jews, Muslims, and Christians think that the nature of the supreme good (knowing and loving God fully) allows or even enjoins the enjoyment of many sensual pleasures, though it subordinates them to more distinctively human pleasures. And they think that benevolence is more a matter of helping other persons to enjoy life than of avoiding any harm whatsoever. The differences in ethical assessment are due to differences in the conception of the supreme good and the conditions of its attainability by human beings. The basic moral principle is the same, for them and for non-religious views too. But how it is interpreted depends upon whether one believes there is one supreme good, what its nature is, and how humans can attain it.

The Principle of Liberty

Religious faiths are most unlikely to think that pleasure is the only or even the main goal of human activity. The mixture of so many pleasures with so many evils and the nature of the human condition, in which pleasure is only one factor in human endeavour and self-knowledge, make pleasure a very improbable candidate to be a supreme human good, even though without pleasure there would perhaps be no supreme human good. It is partly for that reason that religious believers feel wary of the utilitarian philosophy of seeking the greatest happiness of the greatest number. The greatest number, believers are likely to say, do not fully realise what true happiness is or how to attain it. And there are more distinctively human goods that are more important, and which are required to make human striving after greater self-understanding and self-control intelligible.

What are these distinctively human goods? They are again to be found in a consideration of what any rational sentient being has good reason to desire, if they desire anything at all. Humans are distinguished from the vast majority of other animals by possessing the ability to think conceptually and intelligently, to understand truth and to appreciate beauty, and also by having the capacity to act responsibly and freely. These two capacities, of rational thought and responsible freedom, are distinctive to humans, on this planet at least. They have a good claim to be the essential capacities that constitute a truly personal life, and in human beings the exercise of these capacities becomes a condition of achieving most of the things that humans might want. If a person wants anything, it is good, and often necessary, that they should have knowledge and understanding of what it is and of how to get it. And it is necessary that they should be free to get it, without being prevented by conditions beyond their control. Two basic moral principles follow from these facts, and I will consider each in turn.

The first is based on the fact that every rational responsible agent has a good reason to wish to avoid restriction and constraint, and to extend the range of free action as much as possible. By the principle of generalization, it can be seen that it is bad to constrict the freedom of any responsible agent, or, more positively, it is good to preserve or extend the range of free actions of any responsible agent. This gives rise to a principle that could be called the principle of liberty, the principle that it is wrong to infringe the freedom of others without good reason, and that it is right to extend the freedom of others as long as all have roughly equal possibilities of freedom of action.

The formulation of this principle already contains the possibility of a tension between alternative interpretations. Some would stress the negative interpretation of not interfering with the freedom of others, even to bring about greater equality. Others would stress that freedom should be extended only by not allowing vast inequalities which will inevitably limit the freedom of some in comparison to that of others. So commitment to the moral principle of liberty is not going to prevent moral disagreements about whether adherence to the principle of liberty lies in the preservation of absolute personal freedom or in the provision of more or less equal freedom for all. Commitment to a basic moral principle does not bring reflective thinking to a stop. It provides the firm basis from which reflective thinking can begin. So to say that liberty is a basic moral principle is not to say that all will agree on what liberty is. It is to say, however, that freedom is a good for each and every responsible agent and that the moral good lies in seeking the best way to ensure that this good is preserved and extended. Any view that entails that one need not care about the freedom of all, or that one should impede freedom even when it is not harming others, is ruled out.

Religious traditions are concerned about freedom, even though they may sometimes seem to be indifferent to considerations of political freedom and they often oppose unrestricted liberty. Even a human in a prison cell, it may be said, can be spiritually free, and one main monastic virtue in Christianity is obedience, which is a voluntary restriction of freedom. So it may seem at first as though freedom is not a major religious virtue. On closer inspection, however, it is clear that believers are very concerned about 'true' freedom. In the Indian traditions, the concern is with freedom from attachment, and most of those traditions describe the liberated state as one in which there is complete freedom and power over all the states of one's own being. In the Semitic traditions, one seeks freedom from sin, and God is of course a being of supreme power and creative freedom, with whom one seeks relationship. There is a supreme state of freedom which the believer can hope to achieve, and which is rather different in kind from the sorts of freedom most people may desire. Once again the consideration of typical Jain and Semitic views may give a good idea of the range of interpretations that can be taken.

For a Jain, true freedom lies in not being bound to matter and the suffering that matter entails. Each liberated soul is free in being self-determining, content in its own state of supreme knowledge, in need of nothing and desiring nothing. This idea has something in common with the secular notion that freedom consists in being able to do whatever one wants. The liberated soul wants nothing, for it sees the vanity of all sensual desires. So Jains have little interest in extending the sort of freedom that will result in bondage to desire. Such a renouncing tradition in its full severity is for the few. Most householders will have an interest in the freedom to practise their faith, and thus in the construction of a society in which freedom of conscience is secured. There is a social dimension to freedom even in the most extreme renouncing traditions, for renouncers cannot exist without householders to support their practice. Nevertheless in general the ideal of freedom is determined by the ideal of the supreme good as one of freedom from suffering.

For a theist in the Semitic tradition, by contrast, true freedom lies in the ability to enjoy the good things of life without being oppressed and enslaved. Freedom has a political or social dimension, and to be free is to be creative in making and enjoying the many good and beautiful things God gives. Some would stress the primacy of divine law, which lays down the limits of permissible human freedom. But such law typically has many possible interpretations, and it is believed to be given by God for human good. So a law-based religion need not be as inflexible as it sometimes is, and there may well be an inner impetus in such traditions to see the law as a living tradition of divine teaching (which is what 'Torah' properly means), rather than as an immutable set of literal rules. Other theists prefer to emphasise the creative freedom of growing into the sort of self-expressive agent that truly mirrors the creative agency of God. In either case, the idea of freedom is again determined by the ideal of the supreme good as God, a being of supreme creative power who creates the universe for the sake of its goodness.

The interpretation of freedom thus presupposes a certain sort of insight into the way the world is, into its deepest possibilities and the proper goal of human beings within it. Yet that insight is itself highly evaluative. Renouncing traditions see the sensory world as filled with suffering. Theistic traditions see it as essentially the product of a good creator. Is such evaluative insight itself a moral matter? One may hesitate to call it moral, on the grounds that morality is concerned with the principles that guide human relationships. But it is not neutrally descriptive and unaffected by the perspective of the perceiver. It is a mixture of what one finds worthwhile and of how one describes the world one experiences. To know what is really worthwhile requires both experience and insight, and such knowledge claims to be of what is objectively the case (whether or not particular individuals think it is the case). It is knowledge that is possessed in differing degrees, and those who are accepted as great religious teachers are said to possess it pre-eminently. The *tirthankaras* of the Jains discern the vanity of sensual desires in their own experience, and see that the true description of the universe involves knowledge of higher realms than the material. The prophets of Judaism see the corruption of the human heart by egoism and discern the existence of God as the real ground of all existence.

There is a sort of knowledge here, not accessible to all, which is closely bound up with an appropriate evaluation of the elements of human experience. Knowledge and evaluation are here bound inextricably together. The sage sees what is truly of intrinsic and supreme worth, which may be known only by few, and the sage sees how that supreme value is instantiated in a realm beyond the material. Perhaps that is the foundational claim of religion, that there is a supreme value, known by few, and that it exists and is realizable or knowable by human beings. It is because it is known by few that such a claim is a matter of revelation or of authoritative teaching. It would seem that it must therefore far transcend any common knowledge of universal moral principles. In the prophetic or enlightened experience, perception of a supreme spiritual reality and insight into what the highest values are go together.

Renouncers, servants of divine law, and personalist theists all accept the value of liberty. None will interpret liberty as freedom to pursue any of life one likes, and in that respect they all stand distinct from many views. Such liberty would be, in their view, bondage to desire or to self-will. True liberty is liberation from such bondage, and on that agreed. For the renouncer, true liberty is freedom from all attachment, whereas for the theist, liberty lies in realizing the creative possibilities God has given, in a society in which such possibilities can be expanded by co-operative action. These are different ideals but for each the idea is supremely instantiated in one supreme case, the liberated soul or the being of God, and it is the experience of existent ideal which governs the interpretation of human freedom.

How is this relevant to the question of global ethics? It means that all are agreed that liberty is a basic moral value, and that it is, other things being equal, good to preserve liberty and bad to impede it. This is the 'natural' or non-revealed basis of ethics in this respect. Its implementation in particular principles and social codes requires much discussion and reflection, but at least it should be clear what one is trying to implement. For religious believers, there is also a 'revealed' aspect of ethics. It gives to concepts such as liberty an interpretation that may be surprising to many, but which follows from the alleged perception of an existent ideal that instantiates liberty in a supreme degree (the liberated soul or the being of God). Even if it is surprising, the religious view does not undermine or contradict the natural basis of morality. It seems clear that a global ethics cannot be based on some religious view, if only because religions are many and diverse and based on different revelatory experiences and traditions. Perhaps in some sense religious beliefs need to be shaped by natural moral perceptions, if they are not to be harmful and destructive. From a moral point of view, for example, religions ought not to impede liberty of conscience by refusing to allow people conscientiously to adopt or leave a particular faith. The fact that such a statement is highly contentious in some parts of the world shows that religions could yet profitably reflect on the natural basis of a global ethic. Yet religious views certainly modify natural moral perceptions in distinctive ways. That modification may turn out to have very important implications for the implementation of a global ethic, which I shall seek to spell out a little later.

The Principle of Truthfulness

For the moment, however, I will turn to the other distinctive human value that grounds a universal moral principle, the value of conceptual thought, reasoning, knowledge, and understanding. There is always good reason to have knowledge of what is possible and of how to make it actual. So at the most instrumental level, knowledge is a universal human good, the lack of which decreases possibilities of free action and enjoyment. Every conscious and intelligent being has good reason to avoid ignorance, misinformation, and deceit and to be able to accumulate knowledge or understanding, which is both useful to the success of one's endeavours in general and also of intrinsic value and interest. By the generalization principle, it is bad to restrict or frustrate the cognitive capacities and achievements of any intelligent agent. Positively, it is good to encourage and extend the knowledge and understanding of any intelligent agent. This might be called the moral principle of truthfulness, ranging from the minimal condemnation of lying to the idealistic injunction to seek complete understanding and appreciation of the world.

Human cognitive capacities include both the ability to formulate and understand general principles in science and philosophy, and the ability to appreciate the intrinsic beauty of works of art. To understand the nature of things and to appreciate the beauty of particulars are values of intrinsic worth which engage the most distinctive conceptual powers of the human mind. Religions are concerned with an understanding of the ultimate nature of things, the truth that underlies all other truths. Theistic faiths often describe God as absolute truth and beauty. The glory of the divine being is its beauty and magnificence, and the ultimate disclosure of the divine being is the truth that sets one free from all illusions and partial perceptions.

Non-theistic religions do not find final truth in the beauty of a personal Lord. But they are concerned with the discovery of the ultimate truth of things – perhaps the truth of conditioned co-origination, as in Buddhism, or of the ultimate unreality of dual consciousness, as in Advaita Vedanta. They often characterise the liberated state as one of omniscience, or of discernment of the real character of being. Truth is thus a fundamental value for religious thought, though typically knowledge of the truth requires great wisdom and is hidden from many.

Religions sometimes ignore the sorts of truth that are discovered in the sciences and the sorts of beauty that are expressed in the arts, finding them irrelevant to the spiritual quest or even distractions in the search for ultimate truth. The war depicted in Plato's *Dialogues* between the philosophers and the poets is legendary, and many religious believers have turned aside from works of art and drama and from the investigation of the natural world. Such attitudes spring from a feeling that the material world is itself a realm of illusion or deceit, which needs to be escaped to find ultimate truth. There is no despising of the value of truth in such views. But there is a belief that spiritual truth is very different from the truths known through sense experience.

There can be no doubt that some religious traditions present within every world faith are in this sense world-denying. They turn aside from engagement with the material world, in all its manifestations, in order to explore a spiritual reality that is above and beyond it, or which is its negation in many ways. It cannot be said that religion as such enjoins such attitudes, however. For most theists, the fact that God has created this world for the sake of its goodness implies that the good things of the material world are to be understood and appreciated as fully as possible.

For most religious non-theists, too, insight into the transience of all things does not deprive them of value, but rather intensifies one's experience of the present moment, to be enjoyed without clinging or attachment.

There is a tension, however, between religious attitudes that think of the material world as illusory or corrupted, and secular attitudes that seek truth only in the material world if only because there is nowhere else to find it. This reflects a more general tension between valuing the things of the material world as intrinsically good and finding them to be corrupted to such an extent that one must seek true intrinsic values beyond that world, either in complete renunciation or in obedience to God's will alone.

The variety of religious attitudes means that there is no simple relationship between the basic value of truth and the principles of truth seeking which religions recommend. It is precisely in this area that great disputes between secular and religious attitudes arise, some secularists arguing that truth can be found only by scientific methods of observation and experiment and some believers holding that truth comes only from revelation, which must be obeyed unquestioningly. Both, however, need not try to prevent the others from seeking truth in the way they desire. Recollection that truth seeking is a basic value should remind religious believers that such a search should be respected, whatever form it takes, as long as it does no harm. And for some believers, at least, the search for scientific truth is part of respect for the world that God has created.

What I have attempted so far is to bring out some basic principles that are rooted in human nature and to show how they form the basis for universal or global ethical principles. It is apparent that elucidating such a basis does not eliminate moral disagreement, though it helps to locate the points at which such disagreement arises, and the reasons for which it exists among morally serious people. Religious views take these global principles as fundamental parts of the objective moral ideal that they uphold, but again interpretations of them vary, as revelatory insights into that ideal vary from one tradition to another and as ideas of liberation, of divine law, or of devotional theism predominate.

The Principle of Justice

There is one other basic value, implicit in the generalisation of benevolence, liberty, and truth, that it is worth making explicit. It is based on the fact that humans are social animals and can realise their potentialities only by co-operation with others in society. So there is always good reason for humans to desire co-operation with others. It is bad to destroy the basis of such co-operation and good to build on it. This may be called the principle of justice, interpreted in a positive way to include the virtues of friendship and family. There are many particular principles of justice, but they all focus on sustaining a society where people shall be encouraged to do co-operative and useful actions and dissuaded from harming social institutions, where all can see that things are ordered fairly and where friendship and family are supported by social sanctions, both positive and negative (rewards and punishments).

Religions are social phenomena, and they usually have authoritative rules of justice by which their societies are ordered. Some religions, notably Judaism and Islam, believe that the revealed laws of justice operate over the whole of society, so that all activities can be ordered according to the love and fear of God. They hold that God is above all a God of justice, who rules justly and commands justice for the good of creatures. So justice is given an objective instantiation to a maximal degree by being associated with the one and only creator God.

Divine laws need to be interpreted and applied, and there exist various traditions of interpretation. At the limit of such interpretations lies the reading of the law in terms of a few basic principles of justice and mercy, such as 'love God, and your neighbor as yourself' in Christianity. Here personal relationship largely replaces law, but considerations of justice are not overlooked. In Christianity, divine forgiveness and healing are stressed to an overwhelming extent, but God is still the judge of all the earth and requires just dealing of the human race.

In the Indian traditions the idea of divine law and judgment is not primarily stressed. The constant background to Indian reflection on these matters is the law of *karma*, by which the deeds one does, good and bad, all determine one's future destiny. In Hinduism, this belief has been associated with the caste system, but it can easily be dissociated from that system, as it often is in the renouncing traditions. In any case, laws of caste do not excuse social injustice, since there is a cosmic law of justice, if an impersonal one, which inexorably repays all injustice with suffering. It may seem that monks and nuns do not contribute much to social justice, since they renounce all activity in society. However, there exist many movements of socially engaged Buddhism and Vedanta in the modern world, which maintain that the principles of compassion and selflessness that inform the monastic community should be applied appropriately in the world of householders, who can and should exercise active service of others.

Religious traditions do have a primary concern with justice as a basic value, and they do objectify justice either in the person of a just creator and judge or in the cosmic law of *karma*. Nevertheless, there is often conflict between secular ideas of democratic justice and religious views. This seems most obvious today in conflicts over the imposition of the religious law of *shari'a,* and in the question of whether either Islam or the Roman Catholic Church can or should ever be truly democratic. What religious traditions object to in the idea of democracy is what Plato called the 'rule of the mob,' the idea that a simple majority (or even a dominant minority in most democracies) can make moral and social decisions of great importance. Religions may have an authoritative teaching or a revealed law of what makes for true human good, and they may hold that a democratic vote can never have power to countermand it.

The ideas of social equality and the democratic participation of all the people only truly saw the light of day with the French and American Revolutions of the eighteenth century. Before that, social hierarchy was regarded as natural and was usually supported by religious authorities. Religious institutions have not usually been in the forefront of movements to extend democratic participation, even though there have been notable individuals motivated by their faith to espouse causes thought revolutionary in their day, like Lord Wilberforce in the case of slavery, and there have always been radical religious movements in favour of democratic ideas. However, there is a natural tendency in religious groups to form hierarchies protective of the revelatory tradition and to regard spiritual insight as more important than democratic agreement. Religious societies also tend to require obedience and self-negation of their adherents and to limit their lives in various ways for their own ultimate good. It may be thought, then, that religion is not by nature democratic.

This does not mean that religions tend to be unjust. It means that their idea of justice is liable to conflict with an egalitarian and fully democratic idea. It will tend to favour proper order in society, the rule of the wise (or of those committed to safeguarding revelation), and sometimes the suppression of those whose acts or words undermine the faith. It must be appreciated that the revolutionary doctrines of equality and democracy arose in large part as a protest against the perceived oppressiveness of social and religious authorities in Europe, resulting either in the deposition of the old regime or in the establishment of a new country in America. Proper order had become social oppression. The rule of the wise had become the rule of the hereditarily stupid. The suppression of heresy had become the extermination of all dissent. The European Enlightenment was a protest against the corruptions of religiously backed views of justice.

It cannot have gone unnoticed that the Enlightenment has had its corruptions too. The 'inalienable right to the pursuit of happiness,' in Jefferson's memorable phrase, all too easily becomes a license for unmoderated self-indulgence. Liberty becomes the freedom of the rich to leave the poor in some unnoticed backwater of the world. Critical inquiry turns easily into skepticism about reason itself. And the defense of democracy, as Plato feared, turns into populist appeals to the mob to be able to give them a better time than one's political opponents. There is some point in religious criticisms of secular humanism, even though that humanism was a revolt against religiously sanctioned oppression.

There is not, it is clear, just one vision of justice. There are many, and all are corruptible. The religious visions – which include the ones I have described, of justice as the cosmic law of retribution, of justice as the divinely given commands of God, and of justice as the means to the universal flourishing of created persons – stand in tension with the vision of the secular Enlightenment. Yet this tension is not necessarily opposition. Although religious traditions can deny many secular values, they can also accept them, while subordinating them to religious considerations, or they can even positively affirm them, seeking only to transform their character by relation to ultimate religious values. These three attitudes of denial, subordination, and transformation can and do exist in each of the three religious traditions here outlined.

Three Religious Attitudes to Basic Human Values

The renouncing tradition may seem most obviously to deny the values of the material world. Yet the religious elite are concerned with the life of the vast majority, who are not monks and nuns but householders with families and social responsibilities. They may attempt to imbue the ordinary social virtues with a temperament of compassion for all beings and non-possessiveness and to encourage social action for justice and benevolence. In a paradoxical way, they may come to embrace the material world as an object of delight, when seen with right mindfulness. Thus what one may think of as the Enlightenment values of the search for individual happiness, of realizing the creative potential of the individual, of free critical inquiry, and of social democracy can find their proper place within the renouncing traditions of religion.

The divine law tradition may seem most likely to subordinate secular social issues to the revealed law, and the rhetoric of the ultra-orthodox in those traditions is sometimes strident in its demand that the law alone must govern society. This attitude is very unrealistic, since the orthodox do not even agree with one another about how the law should be implemented and a vast number of issues in modern government are not covered by the law without a great deal of supplementary interpretation. So, while one can find those who proclaim that only the *shari'a* or Torah should govern society, it is more usual to find the religious authorities requiring only that secular laws should conform to *shari'a* where that is a relevant consideration, not that *shari'a* should actually be the source of all such laws. Moreover, there are strong movements in Islam, for instance, to claim that democracy IS implicit in *shari'a* and that respect for other traditions and for freedom of conscience and inquiry is an integral part of the qur'anic faith. Since the divine law is, after all, given to promote true human well-being, it is quite consistent with a divine law tradition to insist on freedom and democracy, as long as the divine law is not violated. Though exponents of divine law traditions are often insistent that secular foundations for social morality are dangerous and unstable, they may nevertheless appropriate the insights of Enlightenment humanism so as to interpret the divine law in ways that fully respect individual rights to freedom and participation, while appealing to revealed law to guard against the libertarian corruptions of humanism.

Devotional traditions can be rather introverted and self-satisfied, not seeking to deny or subordinate secular concerns but simply being indifferent to them. What, after all, they may ask, has Jerusalem, the holy city, to do with Athens, the capital of humanistic thought? The answer to that question, historically speaking, is that Athens has mediated the faith of Jerusalem to the gentile world and, in the course of doing so, has sanctified that world as a place in which God can be experienced as present and active. So art and music become sacraments of a transcendent presence and value. As God became incarnate in matter, Christians would say, so he made the material a vehicle of the divine. Still, this attitude can be rather restrictive about the sorts of material existence which can properly express the divine. The religious may still seek to control the artistic and scientific spirit, and confine it within bounds that impede free inquiry into beauty and truth. It took the revolutionary impact of the Enlightenment to allow the devotional tradition to break out of its self-imposed limits on propriety and find in the secular worlds of art and science a true celebration of finite forms of goodness which reflect in their own way the creativity and sensitivity of the creator.

What general conclusions might one draw from this discussion? The first would be that there are indeed basic global values and among the most important and obvious are the values of benevolence, liberty, truthfulness, and justice. The second would be that there is not a simple relationship between religious belief and these values. There is a range of religious traditions, and I have discussed three major sorts of attitude which are found to varying degrees within most traditions: renunciation, obedience to divine law, and devotional theism. The third is that even then one cannot simply relate these traditions to the global values in a direct way. All religious traditions have a distinctive interpretation of basic human values, which is determined by some revelatory experience of a reality of supreme value, which sets the goal of spiritual striving. But how that religious vision relates to basic human values depends on many other factors and can range from denial through subordination to mutual transformation. The fourth is that, despite the existence of universal moral principles, moral disagreement seems set to be a permanent feature of the human condition, which no appeal to religion or revelation will resolve. Even among Christians, some find artificial methods of contraception to be morally forbidden whereas others find them to be obligatory in certain circumstances. And seemingly irresolvable disputes about pacifism and justified violence, socialism and capitalism, and the right to take innocent lives in some circumstances are not alleviated by appeals to revelation.

This need not, and I think should not, be taken as an acceptance of some form of moral relativism – that different moral principles are acceptable by different social groups, without any further reason being called for. But it might be taken as an indication of the great difficulty of coming to know the truth in matters of morality, even among serious and morally concerned people. Religions will not alleviate this situation, for however much they may claim certainty for their beliefs, other faiths will claim equal certainty for different and often conflicting beliefs. It may seem, then, that religions only make a complex situation of moral diversity even worse. Despite the existence of a global basis for ethics, which does enable moral conversations to take place, there will never be universal agreement on all moral principles. Religions often seem to intensify moral disagreements by opposing ordinary secular moral views and adopting positions based on revelation that others find hard to accept.

Religion and Supreme Objective Value

Religions, however, can have a much more positive role than this. It is extremely difficult to find a general characterization of religion which will prove acceptable to most scholars. But I think there is one thing that can be said about most religions in the contemporary world, even if one hesitates thereby to claim to have successfully defined what religion is. What most religions do is to promulgate ways of overcoming egoism and attachment and achieving knowledge of, or union with, a being or state that embodies the highest possible degree of reality and value. This seems to be true of the major traditions of both Semitic and Indian origin. There is no religion in those traditions which holds that it is right to be selfish and to pursue material prosperity as the ultimate goal in life. The overcoming of egoism, whether phrased in terms of losing a sense of self, of realizing one's unity with one all-embracing self, or of obeying or loving a higher self, is basic to religious practice. So religions ally themselves with those who seek to decrease egoism, and in that way they support the most basic moral motivation, the pursuit of what is right, whether or not it is conducive to one's own good in this world.

However, religions are not merely societies for overcoming egoism. Their more important function is to relate human moral striving toward a goal that is considered to be of supreme intrinsic value. Theists aim at knowledge and love of a God who is supremely blissful, compassionate, creatively free, faithful, and just. The goal is knowledge of a being who embodies to a maximal degree those values that are basic to all personal life. Such knowledge will bring an appropriate sharing in those values, but the being of God itself defines what those values are in a distinctive way and gives them objective reality.

Non-theistic traditions aim at the attainment of *nirvana* or release. In that state, which may be conceived of as the liberation of the eternal soul, the cessation of duality, or simply the attainment of enlightenment, there is a supreme realisation of bliss, compassion, freedom from suffering, knowledge of truth, and complete impartiality. These are the same basic values as in the theistic case but given an interpretation in terms of a realizable human state instead of in terms of relation to a supreme deity.

In both these major religious traditions, the basic values become not just values that humans may decide to adopt or that are somehow 'right' in a rather obscurely self-evident way. They are embodied objectively in reality and to a maximal extent either in an existent God to whom humans can relate or in an existent state beyond direct description into which humans can enter.

What difference does this make? A religious view may make a difference to the way in which one interprets the basic human values. The ideas of freedom and truthfulness will be given a distinctive interpretation if one sees them as supremely embodied in God or in a state of the liberated soul. They will certainly not be interpreted merely as freedom from political oppression, as freedom to do whatever one wants, or as the duty to avoid telling lies or breaking promises. They will be seen much more positively in terms of creative power to do what is worthwhile, and complete knowledge of all that is possible and actual.

Insofar as one wishes to imitate God or to achieve the liberated state, one will strive for such positive values, both for oneself and for others so far as that is possible. Morality will not be merely a limit or constraint on desire. It will define the supreme objects of well-ordered desire. The most satisfying object of desire, for a theist, is God and the relationship to God which obedience makes possible. For a religious non-theist, the most desirable state is the state of freedom from suffering which only liberation can completely give. The religious believer has a reason that the unbeliever cannot have for striving to realise moral values. This is because the unbeliever has little reason to suppose that the supreme values are actually realised anywhere at all and little reason to suppose that they can be realised by human effort, whereas the believer thinks that supreme values are realised and can thus be an object of desire and striving for their own sake. Moreover, such values can be realised in one's own life, not by sheer effort perhaps but by divine or supernatural help.

So one difference religious belief can make to natural morality is that it makes moral values objects of desire and striving, as existent states to which one can be consciously related. The morally motivated secularist cannot do this but must simply aim at acting out of respect for moral principles for their own sake, simply because it is right to do so. That is wholly commendable. But to do something simply because it is right is very different from revering a supreme value as part of an existent reality that is the highest object of rightly ordered human desire. To that extent a religious morality is rather different in character from a secular morality not necessarily better or worse but decidedly different. The moral life, for the religious person, is primarily a matter of responding to the lure of an objectively existing supreme value, of seeking to understand it more fully and to desire it more undividedly. A life of response to a perceived supreme value (whether in God or in the example of liberated souls) is very different in character from a life of heroic obedience to self-legislated moral principles.

Naturalistic and Religious Morality

This means that religious morality will have a motivating power that non-religious moralities lack. Both may possess the motivation of doing right for its own sake. And it may be held that this is the only motivation that matters. Yet it may come to seem rather odd if one gives, for example, a wholly naturalistic account, from evolutionary psychology perhaps, of morality as a set of genetically embedded beliefs that have been implanted because they had survival value at some earlier stage of evolution. Once one recognises that the sense of obligation is a possibly obsolete survival mechanism, it may come to seem reasonable to weaken or obliterate it if one can think of more effective ways of surviving and flourishing. For example, one may choose to eliminate the genetically 'defective' in order to increase the health of the species, subduing one's moral urges to keep them alive as outmoded survival mechanisms that are no longer efficient.

The point I am making here is not that naturalistic moralists will tend to do immoral things or to be morally worse than religious moralists. It is rather that naturalistic moralists will have no particular reason to prefer a traditional sense of obligation to new and rationally formulated policies of action. If those policies are oriented to the survival of the species, as they think the traditional obligations once were, then accepted moral beliefs may be overturned with impunity, if it is possible to do so. Thus the sheer sense that one ought to do certain things will not be enough to form a moral obligation that should not be overridden. Rationality can take over from the sense of 'ought,' and it will rightly pursue whatever goals and purposes humans decide to adopt. Such goals may not be in line with those of religious moral ideals. But there is no particular reason why they should be. Indeed, to the extent that all religious views are regarded as false by naturalistic thinkers, there is some reason why they should not be. The policies of the religious and of the non-religious may therefore well diverge.

But what of the universal ethical principles that I have defended? Will ethical naturalists not be bound to adopt them? My argument has been that they are rationally bound to agree that happiness, freedom, truth, and justice are basic goods for all humans whatsoever. But on this account to say that something is a good is just to say that it is rationally desirable by all responsible agents. The question is, why should I do what is rationally desirable by all? Why should I even care what all such agents think? Logic compels me to say that what is good for me is equally good for any being who is just like me. But logic cannot compel me to aim equally at the good of all. It may be as good for you to have a new car as it is for me to have a new car. But I will still buy the car for myself, not for you, because it is my good I care about.

If moral principles state that I should aim impartially at the good of all, or at least of a group of beings, why should I adopt them? For the naturalist, my sense of obligation, my sense that it is simply right to do so, is genetically programmed and may be reprogrammed with the right technology or even willpower. I need another reason for acting on moral principles. But what could that be? Of course the naturalist can think of some reasons – other people will like you better, and perhaps morality pays in the long run. But these are rather pragmatic considerations, which may well be overridden in particular cases. The naturalist has reasons of a pragmatic and defeasible sort for acting in accordance with moral principles. And herein precisely lies the difference from religious morality.

The religious believer has non-pragmatic reasons for acting morally. The theist will do what is right because it is commanded by a God who has the good of the whole universe at heart and who is supremely perfect. The theist who cares to know anything of God will do what is right out of love of the supremely perfect God, and love is a non-pragmatic reason. Similarly, the renouncer will do what is right because it is the only means to the ending of suffering for all beings. It must be noted that this attitude expresses universal compassion, compassion for all beings and not simply desire to escape suffering oneself. That would be a selfish motivation and would be self-defeating according to the renouncer's viewpoint. Compassion is the appropriate attitude because there is a way of liberation from suffering for all, not because I can escape suffering myself.

So religious morality can appeal to different sorts of motives than non-religious morality. This is not always, one may think, a commendable thing. Some religious believers may appeal to God in defense of the extermination of their enemies in a holy war. They may set aside basic moral rules in the belief that God has commanded them to do so, whereas secularists may be appalled at the suffering such strange beliefs seem to cause. On the other hand, religious believers may also appeal to their love of God, and God's love for them, in defense of their policy of self-sacrificial service. And secularists may decide that there is good reason to abandon the commonly agreed rules of morality if they can get away with it, and if it accomplishes non-morally justifiable ends they decide to follow, like those of racial purity or ethnic superiority. Moral ends, they may say, are not so important after all.

So there is no simple equation of religion with superior moral observance. Nevertheless, there is little doubt that the sort of religious belief that asserts the objective existence of a supreme value offers a sort of motivation for moral obedience that naturalistic thinkers would find it very hard to match.

I have stressed that this motivation is not prudential. It is not a matter of saying that it will pay if I am moral and that is why I am moral. Such a motivation would, I have suggested, be self-defeating. Yet there is another element of religious morality that does hold out the hope of a sort of success that naturalism cannot guarantee, or even render very likely. The purposes of God will eventually be realised. *Nirvana* can be attained. So even if present moral effort seems to be futile, to produce no discernible results, the believer may believe that there will be results of a very definite sort. Things will be objectively better in future because of my moral striving.

Although this is not a prudential consideration, since I am not primarily concerned about my own future good, it is a consideration about the objectively good consequences of moral endeavour. The believer has a hope, grounded in belief in a moral order in the universe, that can sustain effort even in the face of apparent futility. That is an element that a totally secular view might find hard to sustain, since there is no power, for the secularist, that can ensure future moral success and so there may be no attainable goal of human moral striving. This is no doubt one of the factors Immanuel Kant had in mind when he argued that moral commitment requires one to believe that a moral goal – of happiness in accordance with morality – will be achieved. Although this argument has not generally found favour with subsequent critics, it does seem to be true that belief in the realizability of the moral goal provides a very strong additional reason for moral commitment.

Finally, for many religious believers God, or a compassionate *bodhisattva,* will help moral endeavour by empowering one's life in a positive way. Morality will be empowered by an objective being of supreme compassion and wisdom and so is a co-operative enterprise rather than a matter of heroic self-determination.

In all these ways religious belief makes a great difference to one's conception of morality and to the way in which one lives a good life. Although all may agree on basic universal goods, whatever their world-views, religious believers will have a distinctive attitude to such goods and a distinctive way of interpreting them. This may have good or bad consequences, depending on one's point of view. But it is something that must be taken into account in any attempt to formulate a global ethics.

Moral Principles and the Religious Ideal

My conclusion is that the real driving motivation of morality will not come from some sort of agreed global ethic, the foundations for which can seem rather abstract and hypothetical. Religion needs the proper autonomy of humanist ethics, the recourse to thinking about the foundations of ethics in natural human desires, to prevent it from interpreting religious rules in ways that are dismissive of those who differ from oneself or repressive of basic human goods. But humanist ethics needs religion to give its moral principles a strongly motivating moral goal and a real hope of its realisation. People's hearts will not be moved by considerations of a rather abstract universal rationality alone. They will be moved by a vision of goodness which is empowering and realizable.

This is what that great humanist Immanuel Kant wanted to provide, in adding his postulates of God and immortality to his analysis of the moral life, though he never found a satisfactory way of putting it. This is largely, I think, because he missed what is for most believers the most important part of religion, the experience of God (or of liberation) as a life-transforming encounter. It is such experience which grounds the claim that morality is encountered as an inexorable moral command or as a way to a supremely desirable goal, which provides a ground for hope that such a goal can be realised, even if only by divine help.

In the Semitic traditions, it is very clear that the prophets encounter God as a morally demanding power, who wills justice and mercy and who promises that a society of justice and peace can be realised, whether in this world or in the world to come. In the Indian traditions, the emphasis is rather on the renunciation of desire for the sake of realizing one's true nature. There may not be a moral command here, but there is a sense of the true self beyond desire or of a liberated state that is beyond change and suffering. It is out of the sense that such a realisation or liberation has been experienced and is open in principle to all that the motivation comes to pursue liberation as the greatest goal. The vision of liberation attracts by transforming one's vision of sensory and desire-led experience and by promising the eventual attainment of a goal of complete freedom and peace.

If the sense of axiological transcendence found in these religious traditions is combined with the focus on human flourishing which autonomous ethical reflection stimulates, then forms of religious faith could develop which might help to shape a convergent global vision of the sort of human life which is truly worth living. In the enormously diverse cultural pattern of the contemporary world, that may only be one vision among others. But it is one that has been shaped in the light of the new global vision of one fragile earth for the whole human race, and which perhaps holds out our best hope for a continuing and truly human future.

Selected Bibliography of Keith Ward's Publications

I. Books

Fifty Key Words in Philosophy (London: Lutterworth Press, 1968).

Ethics and Christianity (London: Allen and Unwin, 1970).

The Development of Kant's View of Ethics (Oxford: Basil Blackwell, 1972).

The Christian Way (London: SPCK, 1976).

The Divine Image: The Foundations of Christian Morality (London: SPCK, 1976).

The Concept of God (Oxford: Basil Blackwell, 1974).

The Promise (London: SPCK, 1980, revised 2010).

Holding Fast to God: A Reply to Don Cupitt (London: SPCK, 1982).

Rational Theology and the Creativity of God (Oxford: Blackwell, 1982).

The Living God (London: SPCK, 1984).

The Battle for the Soul: An Affirmation of Human Dignity and Value (London: Hodder and Stoughton, 1985); reissued as *Defending the Soul* (Oxford: Oneworld, 1992) and *In Defence of the Soul* (Oxford: Oneworld, 1998).

The Turn of the Tide: Christian Belief in Britain Today (London: BBC Books, 1986).

Images of Eternity: Concepts of God in Five Religious Traditions (London: Darton, Longman & Todd, 1987); reissued as *Concepts of God: Images of the Divine in Five Religious Traditions* (Oxford: Oneworld, 1998).

The Rule of Love: Reflections on the Sermon on the Mount (London: Darton, Longman & Todd, 1989).

Divine Action (London: Collins, 1990); reissued (West Conshohocken, PA: Templeton Foundation Press, 2008).

A Vision to Pursue: Beyond the Crisis in Christianity (London: SCM Press, 1991).

Religion and Revelation: A Theology of Revelation in the World's Religions (Oxford: Clarendon Press, 1994).

God, Chance and Necessity (Oxford: Oneworld, 1996).

Religion and Creation (Oxford: Clarendon Press, 1996).

God, Faith and the New Millennium: Christian Belief in an Age of Science (Oxford: Oneworld, 1998).

Religion and Human Nature (Oxford: Clarendon Press, 1998).

Christianity: A Short Introduction (Oxford: Oneworld Publications, 2000); reissued *Christianity: a Beginner's Guide* (2008).

Religion and Community (Oxford: Clarendon Press, 2000).

God: a Guide for the Perplexed (Oxford: Oneworld, 2002).

The Case for Religion (Oxford: Oneworld, 2004).

What the Bible Really Teaches: a Challenge to Fundamentalists (London: SPCK, 2004).
Pascal's Fire: Scientific Faith and Religious Understanding (Oxford: Oneworld, 2006).
Is Religion Dangerous? (Oxford: Lion, 2007; new edition with additional chapter on evolutionary psychology, 2010; in the USA, Grand Rapids, MI: Eerdmans, 2007).
Re-Thinking Christianity (Oxford: Oneworld, 2007).
Christianity: a Guide for the Perplexed (London: SPCK, 2007).
The Big Questions in Science and Religion (West Conshohocken, PA: Templeton Foundation Press, 2008).
Why There Almost Certainly Is a God (Oxford: Lion, 2008).
Religion and Human Fulfillment (London: SCM Press, 2008)
The God Conclusion (London: Darton, Longman, & Todd, 2009); in the USA *God and the Philosophers* (Minneapolis: Fortress Press).
The Word of God? The Bible after Modern Scholarship (London: SPCK, 2010).
More than Matter (Oxford: Lion Hudson, 2010).
Is Religion Irrational (Oxford: Lion Hudson, 2011).
The Philosopher and the Gospels (Oxford: Lion, 2011).

II. Articles

'Moral Seriousness' in *Philosophy* 45 (1970).
'Kant's Teleological Ethics' in *Philosophical Quarterly* 21 (1971).
'The Law of Christ', John Coffin Memorial Lecture, 1981.
'Is Autonomy an Educational Ideal?' in *Personal, Social and Moral Education* ed. Richard Pring (Falmer, 1983).
'The Just War and Nuclear Arms' in *The Cross and the Bomb* ed. Francis Bridger (Mowbrays, 1983).
'Reinhold Niebuhr and the Christian Hope' in *Reinhold Niebuhr and the issues of our time* ed. Richard Harries (London: Mowbray, 1986).
'The Step of Faith', in *In Search of Christianity*, ed. Tony Moss (British Television Series, Firethorn Press, 1986).
'Christian Ethics' in *Keeping the Faith* ed. Geoffrey Wainwright (Minneapolis: Fortress, 1988).
'God as Creator' in *The Philosophy in Christianity* ed. Godfrey Vesey (Cambridge: Cambridge University Press, 1989).
'The Study of Truth and Dialogue in Religion', in *Turning Points in Religious Studies* ed. Ursula King (Edinburgh: T. and T. Clark, 1990).
'Embryo research: an irresolvable dispute?' in *Experiments on Embryos* ed. Tony Dyson and John Harris (London: Routledge, 1990).
'Imperialism and Co-existence in Religious Ideology' in *Religious Pluralism and Unbelief* ed. Ian Hamnett (London: Routledge, 1990).
'The Study of Truth and Dialogue in Religion', in *Turning Points in Religious Studies* ed. Ursula King (Edinburgh: T. and T. Clark, 1990).
'Religion and the Objectivity of Value' in *What Does it mean to be human?* (Yoko Civilisation Research Institute, Japan, 1991).
'Is Christianity a Historical Religion?', Dr Williams Trust, 1992.
'Is a Christian State a Contradiction?' in *Religion in public life* ed. Dan Cohn-Sherbok and David McLellan (Basingstoke: Macmillan, 1992).

'Is God a Person?' in *Christian Faith and Philosophical Theology*, ed. van den Brink, van den Brok and Sarot (Kok Pharos, 1992).
'Pursuing Global Awareness' in *World Faiths Encounter* (March 1992).
'Religion after the Enlightenment' in *Many Mansions*, ed. Dan Cohn-Sherbok (Bellew, 1992).
'God as a Principle of Cosmological Explanation' in *Quantum Cosmology and the Laws of Nature* ed. Robert Russell (Illinois: Notre Dame Press, 1993).
'Miracles' in *Different Gospels* ed. Andrew Walker (London: SPCK, 1993).
'A Defence of Metaphysical Theism' in *Theism and its modern alternatives* ed. Svend Andersen (Aarhus: Aarhus University Press, 1994).
'The Question of Truth in Religion' in *Dharma*, vol. 19, July 1994.
'The Concept of God', in *Companion Encyclopedia of Theology* ed. Peter Byrne and Leslie Houlden (London: Routledge, 1995).
'Truth and the Diversity of Religions' in *Readings in Modern Theology* ed. Robin Gill (London: SPCK, 1995).
'The decline and fall of reason' in *Faith and Praxis in a Postmodern Age* ed. Ursula King (London: Cassell, 1998).
'Christianity and Evolution' in *Identity and Change in the Christian Tradition* ed. Marcel Sarot (Bern: Peter Lang, 1999).
'The God of the Philosophers and the God of Abraham, Isaac, and Jacob' in *Journal of Jewish Thought and Philosophy*, vol. 8, 1999.
'Christian Vedanta' in *the Myriad Christ* ed. T. Merrigan and J. Haers (Leuven University Press, 2000).
'Comparative Theology: the Heritage of Schleiermacher' in *Theological Liberalism*, ed. Jobling and Markham (London: SPCK, 2000).
'Convergent Spirituality' in *Christianity in the 21st Century* ed. Deborah Brown (New York: Crossroad, 2000).
'Divine Action' in *Zygon*, Dec., 2000.
'Religion and the Question of Meaning' in *The Meaning of Life in the world religions*, ed. Runzo and Martin (Oxford: Oneworld, 2000).
'Cosmos and Kenosis', in *The Work of Love*, ed. John Polkinghorne (Grand Rapids, MI: Eerdmans, 2001).
'Religion and the Possibility of a Global Ethics', in *Ethics in the World Religions* ed. J. Runzo (Oxford: Oneworld, 2001).
'The Temporality of God', in *Studies in Philosophy and Religion 23*, ed. Eugene Long (Netherlands: Kluwer, 2001).
(autobiographical) 'A constructive contemporary theology' in *Shaping a Theological Mind* ed. Darren Marks (Aldershot: Ashgate, 2002).
'Believing in Miracles' in *Zygon*, September, 2002.
'Cosmology and Religious Ideas about the End of the World', in *The Far-Future Universe*, ed. George Ellis (Philadelphia: Templeton Press, 2002).
'The Importance of Liberal Theology', in *The Future of Liberal Theology*, ed. Mark Chapman (Aldershot: Ashgate, 2002).
'The Study of Religions', in *A Century of Theological and Religious Studies in Britain*, ed. Ernest Nicholson (OUP, for the British Academy, 2003).
'Two Forms of Explanation', in *Is Nature ever Evil?* ed. Willem Drees (London: Routledge, London 2003).

'Human Nature and the Soul' in *Science, Consciousness, and Ultimate Reality* ed. David Lorimer (Imprint Academic, 2004).
'Theistic Evolution', in *Debating Design*, ed. M. Ruse and W. Dembski (Cambridge: Cambridge University Press, 2004).
'The World as the Body of God', in *In Whom We Live and Move and Have our Being*, ed. Philip Clayton (Grand Rapids, MI: Eerdmans, 2004).
'Ecclesial Authority and Morality', in *Gays and the Future of Anglicanism*, ed. Andrew Linzey (Winchester: John Hunt, 2005).
'Muhammad' and'Pluralism' in *Abraham's Children* ed. Solomon, Harries and Winter (Sheffield: T. and T. Clark, 2005).
'Contemporary Spirituality and Christian Doctrine' in *Public Life and the Place of the Church,* ed. Michael Brierley (Aldershot: Ashgate, 2006).
'Contemporary Spirituality and Christian Doctrine', in *Public Life and the Place of the Church*, ed. M. Brierley (Aldershot: Ashgate, 2006).
'Human Nature and the Soul' in *Human Nature,* ed. Malcolm Jeeves (Royal Society of Edinburgh, 2006).
'Reason and the Enlightenment' in *The Evolution of Rationality* ed. Leron Shults, (Grand Rapids, MI: Eerdmans, 2006).
'Secular Views of Religion' in *Religions View Religions,* ed. Gort, Jansen and Vroom (Amsterdam: Rodopi, 2006).
'The Triune God', in *In Search of Humanity and Deity*, ed. Robert Morgan (London: SCM, 2006).
'Personhood, Spirit and the Supernatural' in *All That Is: A Naturalistic Faith for the Twenty-First Century,* Arthur Peacocke, ed. Philip Clayton (Minneapolis: Fortress Press, 2007).
'The Idea of God in Global Theology' in *Naming and Thinking God in Europe Today,* ed. Norbert Hintersteiner (Amsterdam: Rodopi, 2007).
'Liberal Theology and the God of Love' in *The God of Love and Human Dignity,* ed. Paul Middleton (Sheffield: T. and T. Clark, 2007).
'Creation and the Abrahamic Faiths' in *Creation and the Abrahamic Faiths* ed. Neil Spurway (Cambridge Scholars 2008).
Biographical Memoir of John Macquarrie, in *Proceedings of the British Academy,* biographical memoirs 8 (2009).
'Darwinism and God', in *Darwin: for the love of science'* ed. Andrew Kelly and Melanie Kelly (Bristol Cultural Development Partnership, 2009).
'Immanuel Kant and the Unknowable Real' in *Knowing the Unknowable,* ed. John Bowker (London: I. B. Tauris, 2009).
'Innovation in Material and Spiritual Culture', in *Becoming Human,* ed. Colin Renfrew and Iain Morley (Cambridge: Cambridge University Press, 2009).
'God as the Ultimate Informational Principle' in *Information and the Nature of Reality: from Physics to Metaphysics,* ed. Paul Davies and Niels Gregersen (Cambridge: Cambridge University Press, 2010).
'Religion and Revelation' in *The Oxford Handbook of Religious Diversity*, ed. Chad V. Meister (Oxford: Oxford University Press, 2010).
'The Role of Faith in Science and in Religion', in *Crossroad Discourses between Christianity and Culture,* ed. J. Gort, H. Jansen, and W. Stoker (Amsterdam: Rodopi, 2010).
'Why Theology should be taught at Secular Universities', *Discourse* vol. 4 no. 1.

Index

Index of Biblical References